THE TROUBLE WITH

Anthropology, Culture and Society

Series Editors:
Professor Thomas Hylland Eriksen, University of Oslo
Dr Katy Gardner, University of Sussex
Dr Jon P. Mitchell, University of Sussex

THE TROUBLE WITH COMMUNITY

Anthropological Reflections on Movement, Identity and Collectivity

VERED AMIT AND NIGEL RAPPORT

Pluto Press
LONDON • STERLING, VIRGINIA

First published 2002
by PLUTO PRESS
345 Archway Road, London N6 5AA
and 22883 Quicksilver Drive,
Sterling, VA 20166–2012, USA

www.plutobooks.com

A catalogue record for this book is available from
the British Library

A catalogue record for this book is available from
the Library of Congress

ISBN 0 7453 1747 2 hardback
ISBN 0 7453 1746 4 paperback

10   9   8   7   6   5   4   3   2   1

Designed and produced for Pluto Press by
Chase Publishing Services, Fortescue, Sidmouth EX10 9QG
Typeset from disk by Stanford DTP Services, Towcester
Printed in the European Union by Antony Rowe, Chippenham, England

CONTENTS

to Aiden and to Callum, our nascent migrants of identity

PROLOGUE: THE BOOK'S QUESTIONS

Nigel Rapport and Vered Amit

This book is a dialogue between two anthropologists; it concerns *the conceptualization, the ideology and the practice of community in the contemporary world*. All three of these dimensions of community involve a tension between efforts to fix social and political relations in communal frames and the considerable pressures toward individuation and fragmentation which regularly undo these efforts, but may also be constrained by them. The book offers a review and a reassessment of community as a political, legal, theoretical and ethnographic concept within anthropology.

As the new century begins, politico-economic restructuring continues further to embed local economies, economic networks and polities within global systems of production and labour and within transnational systems of law and political identity. The relation between work, place and family is reconfigured, new forms of mobility within and across state borders are precipitated, and new discourses concerning international relations – 'subsidiarity', 'asylum seekers', 'human rights' – are construed. These processes have frequently dislocated the conventional connections between individuals and taken-for-granted institutions and collectivities. Yet we also see in many parts of the world, popular and intellectual discourses of identity that insist on the political and ontological primacy of various forms of community. While capital moves with ever greater speed and freedom across state borders, while international law expands its translocal remit, migrants frequently face renewed barriers to their own movements. While the 'postmodern turn' in anthropology has rejected the fixity of expertise, place and boundaries, this does not appear to have dislodged a conventional expectation that the construction of community and culture – of 'cultural community' – will continue to situate both the ethnographic enterprise and its ethnographic subjects, perhaps all the more so when these are no longer fixed conveniently in singular places.

Our efforts as co-authors, as two anthropologists of modernity, is to grapple with these complexities in this book; in the process we bring to bear a range of ethnographic expertise and a variety of theoretical

1

perspectives. We do not expect to provide a single answer or one way of properly looking at the issues involved. Rather, we propose *an authorial dialogue* that engages multiple vantage-points and brings into juxtaposition the different ways in which we have sought to situate and adjust our anthropological fieldwork, analyses and broader moral gaze to the unstable contrivances of community in a world of movement.

The dialogue is organized around a set of questions which, in their separate sections of the book and in their different ways, both authors set out to address:

1. How do people conceive of community and work towards effecting its continued existence – to the extent that they do – in a world of movement?

2. Given that 'fieldwork' and 'the field' have been traditionally conceived of in anthropology as pertaining to places fixed in time and/or space, how should anthropology reconceptualize its data, reconceptualize the conditions of being of its informants, in a world of migrant identities?

3. Given the history of 'community' as an analytical construct, and the political valency it currently enjoys under the aegis of 'communitarianism' (of 'identity politics'), how should anthropology employ the term in future?

4. Inasmuch as 'society' and 'culture' and the processes, practices, institutions, forces and structures which they have been seen to embody, were traditionally conceived of as fixing individuals, their behaviours and cognitions, within certain systems of signification, classification and identity, how is anthropology theoretically to approach a world characterized by plurality, transgression and irony concerning socio-cultural identities?

5. Inasmuch as a world of movement brings together a plurality and diversity of identities – and, more precisely, their individual proponents – what has anthropology to say, pragmatically, politically and morally, concerning the way in which a civil society might hope to accommodate, and constitute a secure environment for, the ongoing construction and the rightful expression of such identities?

6. In the wake of a postmodern critique of objective knowledge – a calling into question of rationality, of technical expertise, of disinterested language, of knowledge with any claims to singular authority and transcendence – how should anthropology now situate and conceive of its project: as merely one kind of narrative, evolving discourse or rhetoric, situated among a host of contesting kinds in the world, or still as a something more – a science of the human condition?

In fine, this book provides an investigation into the ways in which anthropology might engage, theoretically, ethnographically, politically, morally, with what might be described as its perennial theme – individuals vis-à-vis communities – in a world of movement which calls into question the erstwhile seeming fixities of its disciplinary identity: 'culture' and 'society'.

ACCORDING TO VERED AMIT

Part I of the book is entitled 'An Anthropology without Community?'. In recent years, Amit observes, anthropologists have been increasingly willing to accept the 'loss of place as a dominant metaphor for culture' (Olwig and Hastrup, 1996: 7). But would they prove as willing to give up the anchorage of collectivity or community? Even more than place, she argues, the notion of collectivity or community has served a fundamental purpose in the anthropological *Zeitgeist* as the medium for cultural process, mediating between the individual and larger political and economic systems while also framing ethnographies. One should not assume, then, that a reorientation of the anthropological gaze away from localized social relations and practices has necessarily involved an equivalent relocation away from community. To the contrary, there appear to be some indications that the conception of collectivity, or at the very least of collective identity, has become an even more crucial anchor for the efforts of anthropologists attempting to locate transnational or multi-sited ethnographic fields. Collective identities, in short, whether defined in terms of nation, ethnicity, occupation or political movement, are all too often invoked to fill the vacuum of location once filled (literally) by place.

The result, Amit argues, is that so much of the 'new' literature on mobile transnationals seems very familiar to readers of an earlier more localized ethnographic literature: labour migrations (now labelled transnational or transmigrant) or ethnic enclaves (albeit now attributed diasporic consciousness). And these foci, far from signalling a new capacity for and interest by anthropologists in dealing with fragmentation, dislocation, destabilization or flux, more often seem to concern integrated and bounded fields of social interaction demarcated by well-entrenched institutions, predictable events and criteria of membership. In anthropology's dogged search for new delocalized 'peoples' the discipline seems in danger of reproducing the fictitiously integrated fields that were once derived from an association between place and culture.

The search for collectivities is propelled by two quite distinct but nonetheless mutually reinforcing impetuses, Amit explains, which provide an epistemological and political context for anthropological research. On the one hand, the small-scale social groups which have traditionally provided the locus for anthropological fieldwork are being incorporated into ever expanding systems of political, economic and cultural connections. These processes of incorporation have thrown question marks around the viability, structure, the very ontology of these social groups.

Anthropologists have had to work harder to account not only for the context in which the group operates but also for its very rationale. On the other hand, anthropology's reliance on participant observation, its status as a social science and its focus on 'culture' all contrive to encourage a continuing bias towards collectivities as the proper locus and subject matter of anthropological investigation. So anthropologists have often continued to seek out collectivities even as many of the processes they were analysing seemed to throw the possibility of community into doubt.

At the same time, in many locales, the politics of multiculturalism and nationalism have increasingly featured claims couched in terms of insistent and essential cultural and communal differences. There is much in identity politics that resonates with anthropological tradition and it can be very tempting to converge a quest for familiar anthropological 'fields' with the essentialist categories appearing in public discourses and to justify this as attentiveness to the 'voices' of subordinated 'others'. Both developments – incorporation and the politicization of 'identity' – have encouraged a retention of community but increasingly as an idea, a categorical referent rather than an actually mobilized social group. Anthropologists whose fieldwork methods have privileged face-to-face relations now rely on an idea of community increasingly devoid of social content as a means of locating their own practices and gaze.

But there are other kinds of social discourses in which even the 'idea' of community cannot act as an ontological anchor. There are many categories of social actors (migrants, students, contract workers, tourist-workers) who are trying to bridge the dislocating and contradictory outcomes of economic restructuring in similar ways but may not be aware of each other; or, if they are, have either not come to think of themselves as sharing a collective identity or else actively resist the possibility. There are individuals who experience repeated cross-border movement without either participating in emergent transnational collectivities or attributing a new social identity to the experience of mobility. Indeed for many, the very premise of social and geographic movement is constituted by a very different paradigm of movement: one of disjunction, compartmentalization and escape.

On the other hand, many other people fashion a sense of more collective fellowship through mundane daily opportunities for consociation, circumstances variously of work, leisure, being neighbours, education and more. In the course of these opportunities, people may come to attach names to familiar faces, share experiences and so establish a sense of contextual fellowship. In short, they may come to feel that, at least for a time, they have something in common. These forms of consociation are often partial, ephemeral, specific to and dependent on particular contexts and activities. And, in many cases, they will not be marked with strong symbolic markers of categorical identity. They are therefore not forms of collectivity that can be accounted for in the oppositional terms of ethnicized identity.

To the extent that anthropologists have recently relied on imagined, oppositional categories of community to locate mobile subjects, they may well be glossing over forms of movement framed in different paradigms of identity as well as forms of social engagement that provide fellowship without necessarily giving rise to highly charged collective categories. Using examples drawn from her previous ethnographic work in Quebec (among youth groups), in Britain (among London Armenians), in the Cayman Islands (among contract expatriate professionals) and also from ongoing research among itinerant professionals based in Canada, Amit's section of the book is devoted to an investigation of both epistemological and social disaggregation. Here is an elaboration of situations in which she has had to posit 'fields of investigation' that do not necessarily conform to fields of social relations but instead involve diffuse fields of personal links and ephemeral groupings; and had to seek out individuals who are conceptually but not personally connected, or, conversely, who do not imagine their personal commonalities in ongoing collective identities.

ACCORDING TO NIGEL RAPPORT

In Part II of the book, entitled 'The Truth of Movement, the Truth as Movement: "Post-Cultural Anthropology" and Narrational Identity', Nigel Rapport draws on his past ethnographic experience (of social interaction in an English village, in a Canadian city, in an Israeli new-town and in a Scottish hospital) so as to prescribe a contemporary anthropological practice at once methodological, theoretical and political. He offers an account of 'democratic individuality' and its possible legal underpinnings, of human rights as a discourse of international law whereby to deal with a world in movement, and of an existential anthropology which might do justice to the inherent capacity for creativity, revaluation and irony of the individual subject. If Amit's section of the book centres on a critique of the assumptions that *anthropologists* make regarding notions of the 'collective' and the 'cultural' in connection with their work on 'community', then Rapport's section also encompasses *practitioners* of community.

In a sympathetic review (2001) Steven Lukes reminds us of Robert Frost's ironic appreciation of a 'liberal' as being someone who could not take his or her own side in an argument. Recent years, however, have seen a shift in sensibility, and an increasing realization among liberal writers of the need to reassert liberalism as a 'fighting creed' (Charles Taylor, in Lukes, 2001). This has come about, Lukes explains, in the context of a growing legitimation of communitarian views which posit the basis of identity as being cultural and the basis of agency as being collective. So-called 'identity politics' has spawned a doctrine of cultural sovereignty whereby cultural collectives should possess the right to organize their own affairs, since 'all cultures should be presumed to be of equal value', and (however contradictorily) 'there is no common standard by which to evaluate different cultures and the practices they embody'. In the face of this, the 'fighting liberals' set out to reclaim a theoretical and a practical universalism. 'A liberal' becomes 'someone who holds that there are certain rights against oppression, exploitation and injury to which every single human being is entitled to lay claim', and that 'appeals to "cultural diversity" and pluralism under no circumstances trump the value of [these basic] rights' (Barry, 2000). The liberal sets about enshrining these rights in a legal-constitutional framework of citizenship wherein individuals might ideally make free choices amid just institutions. To be sure, one of these choices might be to community membership – even to communities internally organized in terms of illiberal relations of dominance and submission, and in terms of all manner of notions of the good life. The citizenship framework guarantees, however, that these 'cultures' do not become empires, and do not become ghettos; the legal framework protects both the rights and interests of those outside the community and also the rights and interests of community members to leave and to choose again. In short, the liberal might not be able (or wish) to ensure a coming together of cultural values and belief-systems but the liberal constitution does ensure that (apologists for) these do not achieve hegemony over individual lives; the latter are protected by universal norms of equality and dignity and by legal judgment. The aim of Rapport's essay is to translate such 'fighting liberalism' into an anthropological world-view.

Rapport begins by depicting cultural relativism as a discourse from which anthropology has yet fully to cut loose; the discipline has continued to reproach itself for practices in the past which furthered the aims of imperialism, colonialism and essentialism. An unfortunate consequence of this self-reproach is that anthropology has continued to seek expiation by way of a cultural relativism which denies, in turn, the contemporary possibility of a critical or aesthetic evolutionism, and decries the espousing of an universalistic morality. Rogue voices have been heard, nevertheless, chief among which, until recently, was probably that of Ernest Gellner (e.g. 1995). For Gellner, to adopt a relativistic stance wherein a ranking or evolution in kinds and ways of knowing was regarded as wicked, was a travesty of cultural reality and a dereliction of social responsibility. Formulating a morality beyond culture, as part of a move towards legitimate, global social relations, was, Gellner felt, of overriding importance (however difficult), while inscribing a knowledge beyond culture was not only possible but already lived as probably the most basic 'fact of our lives' (1993: 54). Relativistic anthropology held that the world contained a mosaic of cultures, each with its own version of the universe and its own rights to that version; the reality, however, was that neither such cultural equality nor such cultural autonomy, fixity or coherency existed. The lived reality was that one form of knowledge – scientific – possessed universal and global pertinence. Science represented a cognition which reached beyond any one culture. It entailed an understanding of nature whose propositions and claims could be translated without loss of efficacy into any milieu, and a technology whose application provided a means of transforming the human condition globally. Instead of pretending that science did not exist, or denying its effects in some attempt at expiation or absolution, Gellner concluded, anthropologists should seek an answer as to how such scientific knowledge and order might be amalgamated within social and cultural multiplicity on a global stage: how sociocultural practices (of ritual and religion, of belonging and opposition, of tradition and community) could be retained as a necessary 'theatre' even as civil and political process globally ran than along technical and profane lines (1993: 91).

Borrowing Gellner's distinction between the 'theatre' of cultural expression and the procedure of scientific knowledge, Nigel Rapport argues that, while effecting such a distinction cannot be easy or painless, it is a mistake for anthropology to deny its reality. His essay seeks to develop the distinction and explore its ramifications, an exercise in what he terms 'post-cultural anthropology'. The key to a 'post-cultural turn', Rapport contends, concerns a full anthropological appreciation of the individual actor: as conscious, intentioning, creative and ironic. Here individuals are regarded as more than their membership of and participation in cultural communities; for the latter amount less to objectivities than the subjective realizations of those who symbolically articulate and animate them at particular times and places. Cultural communities do not exist in themselves, do not possess their own energies, momentum or agency, and it is less than truthful and more than dangerous for anthropologists to maintain that they do. Rhetorically, communities may represent themselves to themselves, as well as to others, as homogeneous and monolithic, as a priori, but this is an idiom only, a gesture in the direction of solidarity, boundedness and continuity. The reality is of heterogeneity, process and change: of cultural communities as diverse symbolizations which exist by virtue of individuals' ongoing interpretations and interactions.

It is a mistake, then, for anthropology to take cultural ideologies of collectivity at face value, and further to translate this into so-called rights of cultural difference. Rather than advocating and supporting the supposed collective rights of communities, anthropologists could work towards an accommodation between such 'theatre' and the underlying legal rights of individuals. Attachment to a cultural community should be seen to be a matter of individual choice, not necessity or duty (an achievement not an ascription), and the existence of communities be deemed an expression of free negotiation between individuals. Far from allowing a cultural community to bespeak a collective organism inculcating (and otherwise coercing) its individual member parts, anthropologists should work towards elucidating those contemporary, viable 'social options' which Gellner foresaw. What are the lineaments of post-cultural, and post-national, social milieux to which individuals in movement through space and through their lives might contingently attach themselves?

What is entailed is anthropologists prescribing an 'ironic' understanding of cultural ideologies and collectivities. To the extent that communities claim absolute legitimacy and revelational knowledge, absolute discreteness and difference from others, and to the extent that communities lay absolute claim to individual members' loyalty, thoughts, feelings and lives, these claims can only be respected and regarded ironically. Idioms and ideologies of cultural absoluteness may serve as convenient flags and badges of community belonging, and may be instrumental as currencies of internal exchange, but anthropologists ought not to describe or prescribe them as anything more real, nor as having any ontological or contractual primacy. If the 'theatre of culture' is to be accorded its proper place vis-à-vis a science of individual consciousness and a legalization of individual human rights, then individuals are to be seen as coming first, both ontologically and morally, and communities and all they contain ought to depend, for their continuation and their value, on those individuals' voluntary and contractual adherence.

In short, the ramifications of differentiating between the theatre of culture and the scientific knowledge of the world are, for Rapport, at once ethnographic, methodological, theoretical and political. It is a matter of apprehending movement in the world, being cognizant of the relationship between movement and individual identity, and imaging political procedures wherein such movement is accorded a key moral value.

Finally, Part II of the book draws to a close with an analysis of the 'Salman Rushdie affair', of the recently constituted International Parliament of Writers and its instituted Network of Refuge Cities, through which Rapport looks forward to the possibility of a post-national world. Here, collective identity-politics is replaced by a global archipelago of voluntary communities where citizens are legally sanctioned to contract fluid membership on the basis of a 'narrated individuality'.

IN DIALOGUE

Having set out their individual responses to the book's questions, the authors come together in the book's final section to compare and contrast their views. While Nigel Rapport, for example, would caution against anthropologists taking political claims of cultural communities too literally, Vered Amit recognizes that such claims ring increasingly hollow for many people who find themselves in situations of repeated dislocation, but also wonders what other vehicles for viable self-location and collective identity make take community's place. For Rapport, the point is to secure for the individual legal rights to a personal preserve, free from cultural communities' closures, conventions and coercions; for Amit, the point is to investigate policies whereby the individual, without forgoing the right to a migrant identity, might yet accede to a community belonging.

In this way, debate between Rapport and Amit focuses attention upon the question of the continuing importance and propriety of the concept of 'community' in ethnographic reportage and anthropological analysis. In the face of globalization and other 'postmodern' and transnational processes of identity formation, what kind of 'community' might offer a conceptual meeting-ground between culture, collectivity and individual selfhood? What kind of community might offer a locale, physical and cognitive, for the emerging forms of polity and morality, of citizenship and human rights, that we might hope to find beyond fixed or bounded locales, beyond traditional society and beyond the nation-state?

References

Barry, B. (2000) *Culture and Equality: An Egalitarian Critique of Multiculturalism.* Cambridge: Polity.

Gellner, E. (1993) *Postmodernism, Reason and Religion.* London: Routledge.

—— (1995) *Anthropology and Politics: Revolutions in the Sacred Grove.* Oxford: Blackwell.

Lukes, S. (2001) 'Liberals on the Warpath', *Times Literary Supplement* 5137: 10.

Olwig, K.F. and K. Hastrup (eds) (1996) *Siting Culture.* London: Routledge.

Part I

AN ANTHROPOLOGY WITHOUT COMMUNITY?
Vered Amit

CONTENTS

1   ANTHROPOLOGY AND COMMUNITY: SOME OPENING NOTES

Like their counterparts in sister disciplines, many anthropologists have noted the 'slipperiness' of the notion of community, arguing that it is too vague, too variable in its applications and definitions to be of much utility as an analytical tool (Bauman, 1996: 14; Cohen, 2002: 165). But the very features that tend to produce this ambiguity also help to ensure the persistence of a notion of community both within scholarly literature as well as in popular vernaculars. Like symbols (Cohen, 1985), key lexical terms such as *community, nation, culture* persist in usage because they evoke a thick assortment of meanings, presumptions and images. This kind of thickness doesn't make for precise definitions but it does ensure that the invocation of 'community' is likely to have far more emotional resonance than a more utilitarian term like 'group'. This very resonance is, however, likely to encourage cynical employment of such key concepts as well as more heartfelt references.

Thus, as Gerd Bauman aptly observed, in public rhetoric, 'community' is often opportunistically stretched to accommodate a wide variety of categories:

In Northern Ireland, the 'Catholic community' and the 'Protestant community' are exhorted to make peace for the sake of the 'community'; the BBC speaks of stockbrokers as 'Britain's financial community'; and a British government, during my fieldwork [in the Southall district of London], labelled a poll- or head-tax as a 'community charge'. (Bauman, 1996: 14)

Yet even while this proliferation of hollow calls for community appears, on the one hand, to empty the concept, it also draws on and thereby reaffirms the continuing importance of its antithesis: the appeal of a collective connection that is not merely or even primarily instrumental. As Phil Cohen (1996: 69) and Anthony Cohen (1996) have noted, an indexical term like *nation* is most persuasive politically when it can be refracted through the symbolic intimacies of hearth and home, personal and local experiences. Similarly the resonance of a term like *community* makes it a useful rhetorical adjunct to a wide variety of public appeals seeking to exploit the term's generally positive connotations of 'inter-personal warmth, shared interests and loyalty' (Bauman, 1996: 15). There is a catch-22 here. If the ubiquity of hollow calls for community ever succeeded in entirely emptying out the concept, then its rhetorical usefulness would be fundamentally undermined. Community, one would have to assume, must still 'mean' something, that is to say it must still have substantive referents for a sufficient number of people or it wouldn't continue to be enlisted for so many causes. Yet this very multiplicity of applications is also constantly threatening to reduce the concept to banality. Invocations of community thus pivot on a constant tension between impulses towards or experiences of sociality and platitudes of classificatory fellowship. As such, these entreaties do not present analysts with clear-cut groupings so much as signal fields of complex processes through which sociality is sought, rejected, argued over, realized, interpreted, exploited or enforced. Expressions of community (whether announcing its presence or bemoaning its absence) thus require sceptical investigation, rather than providing a ready-made social unit upon which to hang analysis.

COMMUNITY BAGGAGE

Anthropologists, however, embark on this terrain encumbered with the baggage of a disciplinary tradition that has privileged collectivities as the primary locales and agents of sociality. This orientation was entrenched by a general institutional division of intellectual labour which, over much of the twentieth century, tended to separate the investigation of the personal from the social as the subjects of distinct domains of investigation. The investigation of the experiential, personal and subjective dimensions of human existence was relegated to humanities such as literary studies or philosophy. The social sciences, on the other hand, were to provide objective accounts of and to generalize from observable patterns and structures of aggregate social behaviour. More particular, but similarly encouraging of a focus on collectivities, has been the association of sociocultural anthropology with participant observation, not only as its principal methodology but also as the linchpin of its academic distinctiveness (Amit, 2000; Gupta and Ferguson, 1997a). This form of fieldwork, given its reliance on direct observation of and participation in face-to-face social interaction, has been most amenable to situations involving relatively small social groupings whose members 'recurrently interact in an interconnected set of roles' (Keesing, 1975: 10). For much of the ethnographic record developed by anthropologists, this reliance on participant observation combined with an insistence on holism to treat the identity of such groupings, the places they occupied, the cultural frames employed by their members, as well as their social relations with each other as mutually constitutive elements of the ethnographic field. In other words, the ambit and mandate of sociocultural anthropology were one and the same. The field was the community and the study of communities, read as a convergence of place, people, identity and culture, was construed as the proper subject matter of anthropology.

REORIENTATIONS

But the appeal of this reading as a convenient location for anthropological enquiry has had to wrestle with its implausibility in addressing the complex contexts of modernity. Further developments of anthropological theory and methodology have therefore often involved an uneasy and unresolved oscillation of emphasis between individual choices, consciousness or action on the one hand, and, on the other, the ever present fallback of community. Thus one kind of reorientation has centred on difficulties in abstracting units of analysis as shifts in fieldwork context have thrown into sharper relief questions of boundaries and context. As anthropologists moved with greater frequency into urban locales during the 1960s and 1970s, it became harder to assume a 'natural' circumscription of a small, localized grouping which could accordingly provide convenient limits for fieldwork. In response to this difficulty came an emphasis on personal social networks rather than the enduring groups and institutions which had been the locus of a structural functionalist view of society (Hannerz, 1980: 172–3). Network analysis tended to take the individual, rather than the social group, as its point of departure and so with it came a focus on individual strategic action, on the cumulative construction of ephemeral webs of social relationships which were not likely to outlast their chief protagonists:

network notions seem particularly useful as we concern ourselves with individuals using roles rather than with roles using individuals, and with the crossing and manipulation rather than the acceptance of institutional boundaries. It is in this light we see the connection of network analysis both to what may be termed anthropological action theory and to the study of urban and other complex societies. (Hannerz, 1980: 175)

But the initial burst of interest in and analytical elaboration of the notion of networks eventually became bogged down as efforts to systematize the mapping of individual links resulted in a sterile quest for methodological precision. And even in cities, there was always the temptation to seek out encapsulated groupings, 'urban villages' in which the anthropologist could shut out the impossible complexity of the wider metropolis and pretend that s/he was back in the discrete, localized folk societies of traditional ethnographic fieldwork sites (Hannerz, 1980). The circumscription of the local community might be a fiction but it was still a more comfortable vehicle for defining the limits of participant observation than the indeterminacy of infinitely overlapping tangles of personal relationships.

Ironically, however, given this retreat to urban ethnic groups as approximations of rural collectivities, it was a seminal work on ethnic boundaries which during this same period made a crucial contribution to unpacking the conflation of place, people, identity and culture which had been the linchpin of structural functionalist paradigms. Fredrik Barth's work on ethnic boundaries dislocated the axiomatic identification of categorical or collective identity with shared culture by arguing that ethnic boundaries can persist and be claimed by and/or ascribed to a population of people even in the face of substantial cultural changes and uneven distribution over space and time. As such, Barth's work also contributed to a more contingent relationship between collective identity and place, a contingency which has gained particular currency more recently in the literature on transnational processes (Barth, 1969). Barth's problematization of the relationship between culture, identity and collectivity was not unique within this period, however. He was one of a number of anthropologists, including Ward Goodenough(1971, 1976) and Ulf Hannerz (1969), who, already in the 1960s and 1970s, were questioning the presumption that culture is necessarily shared by its designated or presumed stakeholders. Instead, they focused on the uneven and unequal distribution of cultural ideas, information and production across social situations and actors (Hannerz, 1992). If culture was not necessarily shared but distributed, then how people used or what they made of cultural paradigms was not self evident from their location within particular social groupings. Hand in hand with a distributive view of culture, therefore, came a greater emphasis on individual agency, on individuals attempting to make the best of complex situations, jostling for position and denotation. And with this emphasis came an almost inevitable problematization of community which could no longer be seen as an obvious outcome of aggregation, but rather as the cumulative outcome of a set of choices and strategies employed by individual agents.

The emphasis on agency was further strengthened by the interpretive turn within anthropology, and with it works such as Anthony Cohen's book on the symbolic construction of community (1985). While Cohen reinvested community in the local, in the immediacy and intimacy of face-to-face relations, he strongly rejected any presumption that the mutual recognition of membership in a community carried with it homogeneity of views or interest. Cohen cautioned against conflating the shared forms of communality and cultural expression with the multiplicity of meanings that could be invested in these forms. There was therefore considerable groundwork for a processual view of culture long before the 1980s enthusiasm for postmodernism focused attention on the fragmented, contested nature of cultural production (Clifford and Marcus, 1986; Rosaldo, 1989) and the 1990s preoccupation with transnational links encouraged a more critical reappraisal of place in siting culture (Olwig and Hastrup, 1997).

THE CATEGORIZATION OF COMMUNITY

It is perhaps not surprising that, notwithstanding the frequent broadcasting of profound disciplinary revision, the recent efforts of some anthropologists to shift their fieldwork to multi-sited transnational subjects have featured an element of *déjà vu*. Once again, we find ethnographic depictions less often of coherent and clearly bounded groupings than of personal networks: links formed by particular actors through affinities of family, friendship or occupation (Basch et al., 1994). And once again, we often find notions of community offering a convenient conceptual haven, a location from which to safely circumscribe potentially infinite webs of connection. Yet there is a crucial distinction between this and previous incarnations of community within anthropology.

As I have noted above, whether sought out in the enclaves of urban milieux or in small-scale non-industrial settings, the communities in earlier anthropological expositions were usually actual interacting groupings of people. However, in more contemporary versions, following on from Benedict Anderson's notion of 'imagined community' (1991/1983), anthropologists often appear to have in mind an emotionally charged *category* of social relations. Anderson argued that the rise of print capitalism in the sixteenth century eventually provided the vehicle for a sense of commonality and mutual identification to develop among large dispersed populations. As books became more available and newsheets proliferated, people dispersed across vast spans could come to see themselves as sharing identities and lifestyles. In consequence, the development of nationalism relied on the capacity of a multitude of people who would never meet each other face to face or even know of each other personally, nonetheless to imagine themselves through the mediation of mass printing as part of the same community. Thus Anderson's work deliberately decoupled the idea of community from an actual base of interaction. As Arjun Appadurai makes clear in the quote below, it is this idea of community rather than the earlier anthropological focus on actual interaction which appears to have been enthusiastically incorporated into recent anthropological work on globalization and transnational connections:

It is important to stress here that I am speaking of the imagination now as the property of collectives, and not merely as a faculty of the gifted individual (its tacit sense since the flowering of European Romanticism). Part of what the mass media make possible, because of the conditions of collective reading, criticism, and pleasure, is what I have elsewhere called a 'community of sentiment' (Appadurai 1990), a group that begins to imagine and feel things together. As Benedict Anderson (1983) has shown so well, print capitalism can be one important way in which groups who have never been in face-to-face contact can begin to think of themselves as Indonesian or Indian or Malaysian. But other forms of electronic capitalism can have similar, and even more powerful effects, for they do not work only at the level of the nation-state. (Appadurai, 1996: 8)

At first glance, it might not appear surprising that a field of anthropological research that has reached beyond locality to transnational dispersal would be attracted to conceptions of sociality that do not require actual personal contact. Yet Appadurai's approach is, in certain respects, much less adventurous than the efforts, decades earlier, of urban anthropologists to conceptualize and trace networks of social relations as a means to investigate new forms of interconnections. Although ultimately stalemated, network analysis was at least an effort to develop new paradigms and avenues for anthropological inquiry, whereas Appadurai appears to be trying to stretch an old idea to accommodate new circumstances. And the stretch incorporates some serious conceptual dangers.

First, one has to note the slippage in Appadurai's analysis between group and category, the risks of positing that the new imagined sodalities 'are communities in themselves but always potentially communities for themselves capable, of moving from shared imagination to collective action' (Appadurai, 1996: 8). Over 25 years ago, in a review of kinship theory, Roger Keesing emphasized the importance of starting with a

careful idea of what groups are. Perhaps more theorists of kinship over the years have come to grief or caused confusion by losing track of the difference between social groups and cultural categories than by any other conceptual flaw. (1975: 9)

The distinction between group and category is crucial because, as Keesing noted, any single entity can belong to many different cultural categories (1975: 10). Whether self- or other-ascribed, the assignation of membership in a particular cultural category does not tell us, in itself, which categories will actually be drawn on for the mobilization of social relations. The analytic dangers of assuming a simple relationship between imagined categorical identity and social groups is well illustrated by the long-standing debate in Britain over the category of 'Black'. Of course the imagination and reinterpretation of Blackness was hardly specific or original to Britain, having emerged earlier in the wake of the American Civil Rights Movement as well as de-colonization and national struggles in the Caribbean (Hall, 2000: 149). In Britain, the category of Black became extremely important as part of an effort to mobilize political coalitions against racism. According to Stuart Hall:

> The notion was extremely important in the anti-racist struggles of the 1970s: the notion that people of diverse societies and cultures would all come to Britain in the fifties and sixties as part of that huge wave of migration from the Caribbean, East Africa, the Asian subcontinent, Pakistan, Bangladesh, from different parts of India, and all identified themselves politically as Black. (2000: 150)

Hall goes on to explain, however, that the imposition of this category as a singular identity was itself resented by people to whom it was attributed but who felt that it silenced their own particular experiences and other forms of categorical identifications (2000: 151). In particular, Asian intellectuals rejected the label of 'Black' as a coercive imposition (Werbner, 1997: 243–4). However as Pnina Werbner points out, positioning the debate as an opposition between 'Black' and 'Asian' replaced one reification with another, in the process eliding critical oppositions among other religious, nationalist and linguistic groups: Muslims, Hindus and Sikhs, Indians, Pakistanis and Bangladeshis, Punjabis, Gujeratis and Sindhis (1997: 244). So are the categories of 'Black' and 'Asian' vacuous, devoid of any but the most instrumental of political meanings? Of course not, but the ambiguity and multiplicity of these meanings place the analytic onus even more squarely on investigating the circumstances in which these categories are likely to be invoked, by whom, and how these invocations articulate, collide or are bypassed by particular forms of social relations.

Werbner argues that Benedict Anderson's notion of imagining 'liberated' the concept of community from its previously restricted sociological association with Tönnies' ideal 'as a traditional face-to-face collectivity of consociates, bound in amity' (Werbner, 1997: 246). If, however, the notion of imagining community is seen as absolving scholars from the responsibility to probe carefully the social ramifications and locations of these constructs, then the result can be some conceptual slipperiness from even the most thoughtful commentators. The imagined can all too easily become the reified, category, group, individual subject merging into the possibilities offered by the text of attributed identities. The notion of 'imagination' has become particularly popular within the rubric of cultural studies and, given the literary orientations of this theoretical framework, it is perhaps not surprising that it has often featured a reading of the social imagination as a text on to its own. Yet if anthropologists do the same, they would be skipping over all the truly important and difficult questions that they would normally investigate empirically: the far from self-evident consequences of the frequently tense dialectic between cultural categories, social institutions, practices and relationships. If we hold that the effort to construct communities is fundamentally an effort, whether successful, partial or failed, to mobilize social relations, then, as Fredrik Barth has noted, communities cannot be created simply through the 'mere act of imagining' (1994: 13) or, one could add, the act of attributing.

THE PRESUMPTION OF ETHNICITY

There is a curiously regressive aspect to this contemporary conflation of cultural category with social group, a retreat from the efforts of anthropologists over the last four decades to unpack the homology of collective identity, group, culture and place that formed the foundation of an earlier version of anthropology as the study of cultural communities. It is perhaps not surprising, therefore, to find in Appadurai's work another return to an older version of culture as the production of difference. Thus, Appadurai deliberately conflates ethnicity with culture.

But is this not a way of equating ethnicity and culture? Yes and no. Yes because in this usage culture would not stress simply the possession of certain attributes (material, linguistic or territorial) but the consciousness of these attributes and their naturalization as essential to group identity. That is, rather than falling prey to the assumption, at least as old as Weber, that ethnicity rests on some sort of extension of the primordial idea of kinship (which is in turn biological and genealogical), the idea of ethnicity I propose takes the conscious and imaginative construction and mobilization of differences as its core. (Appadurai, 1996: 13–14)

And with this conflation, we seem to have come full circle, back to the 1970s and an earlier effort at recontextualizing the groups we study. As I argue later in this section, during the 1960s and 1970s, the work of such pioneers as Fredrik Barth (1969), A.L. Epstein (1978), J. Clyde Mitchell (1970), Abner Cohen (1969, 1974) and Glazer and Moynihan (1963, 1975) placed an emphasis on the selective, conscious and creative construction of ethnic boundaries that became a virtual axiom of the study of ethnicity in anthropology and related disciplines. And during this period, anthropologists seemed bent on redefining virtually every group they were studying within the rubric of ethnicity. In so doing, they gradually exhausted the analytical rigour of the concept, leaving it looking 'increasingly tired and threadbare' (Banks, 1996: 182). Thus anthropologists ended up pronouncing or calling for the demise of the concept just as it appeared to be gaining in importance outside the academy (1996: 188). Meanwhile, other anthropologists criticized the emphasis on and reification of difference, which, they argued, had been vested in the anthropological concept of culture (Abu-Lughod, 1991; Keesing, 1994).

But in Appadurai's rendering of modernity and the 'global now', we find ourselves again revisiting a triumvirate of culture = ethnicity = difference. Culture, once that complex web of multiple meanings and significances (Geertz, 1975: 5) is now reduced to the production of only one kind of meaning, that attached to the production and valuation of group identities and differences. There is by now a significant body of literature that has been critical of certain trends in transnational studies, particularly versus the cultural studies approach to globalization with which Appadurai's analysis tends to be identified. This approach has been criticized for exaggerating the ease with which individuals can move across transnational borders, for underestimating the boundedness of transnational movements and the continued salience of the nation-state (Amit-Talai, 1998; Guarnizo and Smith, 1998; Louie, 2000; Ong, 1999; Wilson and Donnan, 1998). And there has been trenchant criticism of a more general tendency, running across a broader cross-spectrum of sociological and anthropological work to 'conceive of transnationalism as something to celebrate, as an expression of a subversive popular resistance: "from below"' (Guarnizo and Smith, 1998: 5; see also Amit-Talai, 1998: 56; Ong, 1999: 15). Guarnizo and Smith also note the analytical fuzziness common in transnational studies, a tendency to conflate social networks, communities and social fields (1998: 27). But there is a presumption which is commonly shared between many of these critics and their targets, namely that transnational processes and practices first and foremost involve the production of ethnic collectivities that straddle state borders. Presented under various appellations: diaspora, transmigration, refugee or ethnic group, the presumption appears to be that what is being structured and perpetuated through contemporary patterns of movement are self-conscious communities organized collectively to accommodate this kind of mobility. Even Guarnizo and Smith, in cogently cautioning against conceptual muddling, argue that transnational social networks or circuits are the 'how' of transnational social relations, but the social organization emerging from these social practices are transnational communities or bi-national societies (1998: 27). And they like other scholars of transnationalism before them (for example, Basch et al., 1994) argue that the history of older migration streams makes it likely that contemporary transnational relations and the diaspora consciousness they give rise to will most likely be reproduced across generations. But haven't we been here before?

One of the major criticisms levelled against the 1970s enthusiasm for ethnic studies involved the presumption that white immigrant groups in the United States continued to maintain their cohesion and values across generations (Alba, 1981; Sanjek, 1994; Steinberg, 1981). This insistence, Sanjek argues, ended up serving a neoconservative agenda. It ignored the rate of intermarriage between 'white ethnics' from generation to generation, or the fact that 'the masses of European immigrants over the nineteenth and twentieth centuries had paid the price of linguistic extinction and cultural loss ... for the privilege of white racial status' (Sanjek, 1994: 9). '[W]hite ethnic persistence was a hoax', Sanjek declared, himself a grandson of Irish and Croatian grandparents, with little consciousness of any European cultural 'roots' (1994: 9). Ironically, it is precisely these kind of European immigrant groups which Guarnizo and Smith now argue provide a precedent for the likely persistence of transnational linkages among more recent immigrants to the United States.

The perpetuation of transnational linkages is a matter for the future historical record to determine but the expectation of this kind of continuity may provide more insight into the persistence of certain conceptual orientations than about the quality of our data. It may not yet be clear whether ethnic communities are being reproduced across time and space but it is clear that what is persisting are the expectations of anthropologists (and their colleagues in sister disciplines) that they will find them.

When, during the 1980s, I directed a study of graduating students at a Montreal high school, we found that the students, many of whose parents had emigrated from south European countries, associated ethnicity with close family relationships, that is, with their parents or close kin, including those still residing in southern Europe, whom their parents sometimes sent them to visit over summer holidays. They seemed puzzled when pressed to consider what ethnic community might mean to them, in spite of the proliferation of Greek, Portuguese and Italian voluntary associations in the city. As the 'community', one student referred us to a festival he had heard about but had never attended. Since we didn't follow them on from high school, I don't know whether this stance shifted as they grew older but it seems likely that, at least for some of them, ethnicity may have remained an aspect of a very personal family history and relations, rather than a more extended social group.

NETWORKS AND GROUPS

Personal social networks are not simply the means for the creation of organized communities. Such networks operate in their own right and on distinctive terms. They are ego-based, that is to say they arise through particular individuals' efforts, experiences and history. As such, and especially so in complex metropolitan environments, they are likely to extend across many different categories and situations. Nor is it necessary or even probable that all the people a particular individual knows will interact with each other independently of this shared link, or even necessarily have knowledge of each other. Because this form of social connection is not institutionalized, it is highly sensitive to the vagaries and life cycles of interpersonal relationships. This, then, is a framework of social linkage that requires perhaps the most intensive, self-conscious and constant efforts from its key protagonists, but which is also the most structurally ephemeral.

This is a very different form of organization than more enduring social groups whose basis for mobilization is institutional or communal. Such groups do not rely for their rationale or configuration on any one individual. They can thus survive, to a greater or lesser degree, shifts in personnel. The members of these groups may not all be personally acquainted with each other but they are at least interconnected organizationally through the performance of commensurate roles, for example, as members of a political association, employees of the same organization, players in the same league, participants in circuits of performance or exchange, etc. The reproduction of these groups thus relies on sustaining, at any one time, a core of individuals capable of and 'willing' to operate in these roles.

While these are inherently very different arrangements for organizing social relationships, they can overlap to a degree that renders them difficult to distinguish. Some personal networks, particularly in small-scale societies, may be largely drawn from one or a few social groups. While institutional groupings have a structure that transcends any one individual, they are nonetheless fundamentally shaped through the relationships and interactions of their members, contacts which themselves have a network dimension. Even the most formal and bureaucratic organizations would not be viable as hollow structures, independent of interpersonal encounters and links. Finally, both personal networks and social groups can call into play cultural imaginings: categorical identities, notions of home, belonging or community.

It is easy to see, therefore, why these arrangements could be conflated, particularly when we are trying to track the contexts in which sociality is imagined and to work through the consequences of such imaginings. I feel 'at home' in Montreal, the city in which I reside because I associate it with intimate relationships and familiar faces. Yet the people who provide me with this framework of familiarity and belonging, do not interact with each other as members of or form one social group. They practise different occupations, live in different urban quarters and their backgrounds are diverse in term of ethnicity, language and religion. But what if this network featured a greater uniformity in terms of one or the other of these ascribed dimensions? What if, for example, a substantial number of my consociates shared a common ethnic background? And what if this dimension contributed significantly to the way I conceptualize my own ethnic identity? Would my network now constitute an ethnic community? And would it still be an ethnic community if, apart from this shared categorical identity, my network of consociates otherwise had no more contact or relationship with each other than in my current situation? If we answer yes to this last question, then we can see why it can be so easy to move just a little further down this continuum to assume, as do Appadurai and Anderson, that if people imagine themselves, even when they do not know each other, to share a distinctive collective identity, then they can mobilize themselves as a community, and to move on from there to presume that to imagine community is already to constitute a community.

To indulge, however, in this kind of slippage between personal network and social group, between category and collectivity, is to minimize the considerable difficulties of structure, logistics, persuasion, ideology and opportunity involved in constructing actual as opposed to imagined communities. It is to presuppose, rather than carefully to investigate the particular circumstances in which personal networks can sometimes become the basis for the mobilization of social groups or the complexities implicit in the tendency for personal networks to cross institutional boundaries even as they draw from the social groupings mobilized within them. Equally important, these conceptual slippages can encourage a critical underestimation of the fragility of the personal networks and consociations most of us draw on for our quotidian senses of belonging, home and social location. Such networks are not easy to develop but they can be even harder to maintain. How many of us can enumerate lists of people we once regularly associated with, perhaps even considered intimates, with whom we no longer have contact? However much we may have intended otherwise, how often have we lost touch with friends, family, acquaintances when we married, moved house, changed jobs, when our children graduated from school, when we stopped attending a club, abandoned a leisure pastime or just stopped calling. Personal relationships cannot rest on the laurels of categorical identifications. If all they needed to remain feasible was a sense of ascribed connection, then surely there wouldn't be so many lonely people everywhere. Personal as opposed to categorical relationships require contact, some measure of reciprocity, opportunity and effort, 'a constant need to recreate the mutuality of the relationship' (Miller and Slater, 2000: 81). Such relationships are thus highly sensitive to changes in context and, as such, are likely to be very vulnerable to geographic distance. Even before the advent of electronic communication, it was sometimes possible to maintain a long-distance relationship but it was and is surely, even today, not easy.

Most of the recent anthropological literature on transnational processes includes at at least a line or two in which the author acknowledges the losses which can be entailed in spatial mobility, 'the personal, emotional cost for the individuals involved, who must live daily with the pain and strain of separation' (Basch et al., 1994: 242). But, having made this acknowledgement, the authors then quickly move on to insist that families are being reconfigured transnationally and reproduced between generations (Basch et al., 1994); 'translocalities' created and reproduced (Guarnizo and Smith, 1998: 7) and that borderlands have become the '"normal" locale of the postmodern subject' (Gupta and Ferguson, 1997a: 48). In the conceptual slippage between category, community and network, the challenges of maintaining simple social connections can be minimized. The result can be not only a distortion of how people actually experience and engage with mobility and social fragmentation; in treating the construction of transnational communities as an inevitable element of contemporary forms of movement, we can also end up inadvertently supporting a neoliberal tendency to treat human beings as if they can and should be infinitely portable, unencumbered economic agents. For, after all, if people can easily form or sustain collective affiliations across space and time, then why shouldn't they be encouraged, even required by their employers or their governments to move? It would be ironic if, having spent a fair number of years criticizing and distancing ourselves from our anthropological forebears' penchant for conflating place, culture and collective identity amongst highly localized groupings, we ended up adopting the same analytical nonchalance for more mobile social relationships. The $64,000 question for anthropology concerns the complexities and enigmas of social mobilization whether local or transnational. The construction of communities should never be treated as simply probable.

2   EMBRACING DISJUNCTION

At an anthropology conference not too long ago, I presented a paper presenting some material from an ongoing research project that focuses on the lives of travelling consultants.[1] The people I had interviewed were part of a growing global army of professionals whose work involves frequent travel across large distances to a succession of distant clients. A number of these people had explicitly structured their career paths to allow for regular travel, this even when other less ambulant work opportunities were available. Thus for Margaret,[2] a consultant specializing in urban development and economics, a career involving travel had been a goal from the outset, but, in the late 1980s, in partnership with two other women, she had been able to establish a small independent consulting firm which specialized in 'international work'. She did this even while her daughter was very young and even though her husband, a managing partner with a large consulting corporation was similarly engaged in frequent travel. She and her husband took turns remaining in Canada to care for their daughter. 'It's the modern career', pronounced Margaret. She was shocked that more people weren't taking up these kind of opportunities for movement. 'When you get paid in US dollars and you get flown around the world, I don't understand why you'd want to do a project in Chilliwack', she said, referring to a somewhat non-urbane and peripheral suburb in the Lower Mainland of British Columbia where she resided.

Yet for Margaret, as for the other willing travellers I interviewed, this openness to movement did not appear to be based on a reading of transnational consulting as a seamless field of professional engagements which had eradicated the importance of place. To the contrary, their vision of this field was insistently, even determinedly disjunctive: limited intimacies, successive sets of workmates, temporary connections, competition, professionalism interpreted as social distance.

John had spent most of his working life travelling. At various times, he had migrated from Britain, his country of origin, to Germany, Switzerland and finally Canada, the country in which he currently resides. And throughout all these moves, he travelled. He changed occupations from computer technician to computer salesman, from employee to the co-owner of first one, then a second company selling communications technology. And throughout these moves he travelled. He travelled throughout western Canada as an employee for one company, then around the world four times and back for his own company which sold products in 52 different countries. The development of a second company he had initially established to conduct business only in western Canada and the United States led instead to travel to Korea, Japan, Hong Kong, Singapore, Australia, New Zealand, France, Italy, England. In 1992, when he was working hard to establish this company, he was away from his wife and children for frequent periods of two to four weeks at a time. The year I interviewed him, 1998, had been a quiet year in terms of travel: ten months into the year, he had only been away between three and four months.

The travel had taken its toll. His wife had never got used to his frequent absences which had, he felt, caused 'irreparable damage to our relationship'. 'I don't think it was like it could have been had I maybe stayed at home.' He had had to 'mend a lot of bridges' with his now adult children because 'really I didn't know them'. But 'on the other hand, if I'd stayed at home, we maybe would have been divorced because I wouldn't have been doing what I wanted to do. And yeah, as a traveller doing what I'm doing, you tend to be a very selfish person I think.' With a few exceptions, his family had not accompanied him on his travels because 'when I travel for business, I really do travel for business and I don't take an extra week here and an extra few days there'. But it would be difficult to argue that these absences and the consequent attenuation of some of his most intimate relationships had been significantly sublimated through the development of close relationships in the course of travel. He was busy these days representing his company at international trade shows and these took place in different countries with different people. A few of his distributors he now counted as friends but 'It's not a very nice thing to say but you can't let your friendship interfere with how you're doing business.'

Margaret was even more dubious than John about the capacity of this lifestyle to generate alternative, de-localized personal attachments. Relationships with other consultants had been kept deliberately 'casual'. She and her partners had intentionally kept some distance from the large consulting firms in order to maintain their independence and had carefully avoided nurturing too strong a friendship with clients:

I think you often find that when you're exposing a lot of difficulties that your client has on delivering on policies, it's often difficult if you've got too close of a relationship with a client. I think you've got to keep a professional role. You can be charming but you still have to be professional.

Among the reactions by members of the anthropological audience to this presentation was a view that there was something quite peculiar, even aberrant, about this voluntary investment in a life of absences and fragments. However, this may say rather more about the relevance of certain persisting anthropological paradigms than about the professionals I interviewed. Far from being exceptional, these business travellers' acceptance, even embrace of disjunction as an emblem of *au courant* professionalism is part of a much broader construction of modernity. Many more of us expect that our lives will feature some disjunction of intimate relationships as our career and educational paths move us from place to place or institution to institution.

ECONOMIC DISEMBEDDING

Some ten years ago, Arjun Appadurai noted that the relationship between the global flow of people, technology and money was 'deeply disjunctive and profoundly unpredictable', even as each acted 'as a constraint and a parameter for movements in the other' (1990: 298). This disjunction is itself part of a process which James Carrier has referred to as economic abstraction:

The core of economic abstraction is the process that Karl Polanyi (1957a) described as 'dis-embedding'; that is, the removal of economic activities from the social and other relationships in which they had occurred, and carrying them out in a context in which the only important relationships are those defined by the economic activity itself. In essence, economic activity becomes abstracted from social relations. (Carrier, 1998: 2)

This orientation, Carrier argues, occurs at both a practical level, that is, the ways in which people organize themselves to carry out economic activities, and at a conceptual level, that is, the ways in which people envision their economic lives (1998: 2). The lifestyles of the travelling professionals that I have described are extreme examples of this process of disembedding. Their work is spatially and socially separated from most of their usual routines and relationships. They leave their family, friends, neighbours and work colleagues, their homes, cities, countries and offices, in order to carry out their work in sites and organizations in which they are only temporarily present. In other words, a significant portion of their work activities stand apart from all their other activities and sites; and, in their occupational roles, they also often stand apart from the places and firms they are serving. They act upon these firms, but they do not become a part of them, they visit places to work in, but they do not live in them.

On a more general level, the expansion of consultancy – with the exception of John, the occupational situation of most of my respondents

– has been a *sine qua non* of the restructuring of Western capitalism and production around the concept of the 'flexible, market-driven' firm, a current archetype of this process of economic abstraction (Carrier, 1998: 2). The increasing fragmentation and dispersal of the operations and holdings of large, particularly transnational corporations, has created a need for an array of specialized services to cope with the ensuing administrative and developmental challenges (Sassen, 1994). Flexibility has also been interpreted in a tendency for large firms to contract out an array of tasks and services they might once have provided in-house. One result of this structural reorganization has been a marked expansion of the business service sector that includes lawyers, accountants, advertisers, computer analysts and other 'experts' who provide services to these firms. Consultants accordingly advising on such diverse domains as engineering, environmental and financial planning, information systems, management, workforce re-training or urban development, have in common intrinsically peripatetic work lives. As a matter of course, they must be able to adapt to a succession of different organizations for which, each in turn, they are providing temporary consultancy support. Their 'place' of work is therefore serial, subject to a constant recasting in terms of locale, social relationships and theatres of interaction. Disembedding is thus fundamental to the organizational structure of consulting. In turn, this process has been heightened by a trend towards rapid turnover within and between consultancy firms.

According to Monica, a Seattle-based management consultant specializing in high technology who was a salaried employee of a large multinational consulting firm, and her spouse Richard, a systems analyst working for a somewhat smaller multi-establishment firm, consultants were the vanguard for a much more general reorganization of career paths. Monica and Richard had taken the initiative to change jobs several times in the course of their careers, changes that involved long-distance moves across Canada and between Canada and the United States. Some of these job changes, like their move from eastern Canada where they had been educated, to the British Columbia Lower Mainland where Monica had been raised, were spurred by a desire to live in a particular locale. Yet when, only a few years later, Monica decided to change jobs because of her dissatisfaction with management changes, she opted to take up a position which required relocation to Seattle even when she had been offered reasonably comparable jobs in Vancouver. Richard arranged for a transfer between the Vancouver and Seattle offices of the same company. They left friends and family behind. In due course they expected to change their employers repeatedly. Within their fields, Monica claimed, it was fairly common for professionals to change jobs every year and a half to two years:

But I think for consultants as a whole, even the ones who go into industry and don't want to travel any more, it doesn't mean that they'll stay at the job for twenty years. I don't think that's the mind-set at all. I don't think that any consultant really takes it for granted that you're going to have a twenty-year career path and stay with a certain company. So even if they go somewhere else and don't want to travel, they might stay with that company for a few years and go to a different company. I think they're pretty much ready to change all the time.

It is a change in the nature of employment that according to Monica and Richard had affected the more general labour market encompassing a wide gamut of workers. Consultants had simply 'adapted to that change better than maybe some other people in other industries'. And, indeed, a little over a year later, Richard changed jobs again.

Thus, in sharp distinction to the response I noted earlier of some members of my anthropological audience, who thought that the travelling professionals I was describing were exceptional in their acceptance of constant disjunction, for Monica and Richard, these processes of mobile disembedding are an intrinsic and generalized aspect of contemporary work lives. Nor, as Monica and Richard point out, is this an expectation and construction of work that only affects travelling consultants. Whether they travel or not, consultants move constantly, as do an increasing number of workers in a wide range of sectors. But this stress on flexibility is not really a new phenomenon. The expectation that economic roles are subject to a different set of priorities than other kinds of social engagements and relationships, and that rational economic agents are willing to shed social ties in order to pursue career paths, has long been an aspect of the institutional organization of Western capitalist economies. Indeed, one can argue that children in Western countries such as Canada are trained to expect such disjunction as a 'normal' aspect of their life courses.

TRAINING FOR DISJUNCTION

During the late 1980s, I directed a study[3] of a small group of high school students completing their last year of secondary education in a Montreal high school. As the students looked forward with excitement to their graduation, they prepared to say goodbye to their high school friends while they moved onto CEGEP, the next stage of their education. In Quebec, the CEGEPs provide a college education which is intermediary between high school – ending in secondary V, that is, grade 11 – and university. Although there are private CEGEPs, most students attend public colleges where their education is entirely state funded, as opposed to the universities, where tuition fees are payable. Almost none of the Royal Haven students on whom our study focused considered that their group of school friends could survive intact the impending shift from high school to CEGEP. According to Mike:

After high school everyone goes their own way. That is probably the last time that you will see all your friends. After this, it is all new friendships and new people and things. ... There is nothing that you can do about it. You have to accept it. But right now we don't realize it. But it is going to happen. But we don't think about it. And just enjoy the good times that we have now. But after the summer comes, we will keep in contact then. But once school [CEGEP] starts, everybody is going their own way. They are not going to have much time for anything else.

Mike's opinion was echoed by many of his fellow students. Other students expressed regret at the impending break-up of their group of friends; the wish that the relationships could continue on as close as ever, but also the conviction that, whatever one's wishes to the contrary, new involvements would inevitably supersede as a consequence of enrolment in different CEGEPs.

The Royal Haveners' expectation that school friendships would not likely survive graduation reflected their previous experience of such relationships. Within Royal Haven itself, friendships were shaped by class assignments. Students tended to establish friendships from among their classmates. Every year students were assigned to new classes and from year to year, circles of friends tended to regroup accordingly. Thus when Francesca passed around photographs of her 'sweet sixteen' party it was noticeable that the Royal Haven students who appeared in them were not among her circle of close friends in secondary V. Less than a year after the party, Francesca had a reconfigured set of school friendships.

Among the students on which this study focused were a number who had attended Mount school for their first three years of secondary education before switching to Royal Haven in secondary IV. Mount school had been re-organized as an 'alternative' school with a curriculum that emphasized the fine arts. In the first three years of this programme, the school had accommodated general as well as fine arts students, but the general students eventually had to complete their final two years of high school elsewhere and hence had transferred to Royal Haven. Although they often spoke of their former school with longing and affection, the late arrivals at Royal Haven had not maintained contact with other Mount students who had either stayed on in the school's fine arts programme or else transferred to schools other than Royal Haven.

In a city like Montreal, that has a high ratio of renters and a high degree of residential mobility, it was not unusual to find that individual students had to change schools as their families moved house and neighbourhood. More generally within the Canadian school system, it is not unusual to hear parents and teachers expressing the view that transfers between schools or classes are a good learning experience for children, since it will force them to learn how to make new friends. In elementary schools, where for all or most of their subjects, students remain in one class for the duration of each academic session, close friendships between classmates are one of the factors which enter administrative calculations of assignments for the succeeding year. It is quite common for teachers to recommend or parents to request that good friends are assigned to separate classes. Friendship can be viewed as a distraction from paying attention to lessons, a potential challenge to the authority of the teacher and a disincentive to the formation of new relationships.

The shifting patterns of school friendships had therefore taught Royal Haveners that such relationships, while valuable, were highly tenuous and institutionally contingent. The study of Royal Haven, and indeed the structure of the broader school system within Canada, suggest that dislocation of personal relationships has long been structured as routine practice, at least in this country, without the antecedent necessities of long-distance movement. This kind of disruption is not an incidental outcome of some other activity. It is remarkably stable, planned and institutionalized.

DISJUNCTION AND COSMOPOLITAN ADVENTURE

So far, we have been discussing disjunction as a kind of economic necessity, a condition for successful participation in certain kinds of institutional arrangements. But this reading converges in the lives of the travelling consultants with a rather different construction of disjunction, one of fun and cosmopolitan adventure. For, after all, John and Margaret had not opted for a career of business travel because they had no other option. They had quite deliberately structured their work lives to ensure frequent travel. Similarly, overseas travel was a key consideration for Tanya, a professional on salary with the environmental section of a Canadian engineering and consulting company. Her work involved consultation on a variety of infrastructure development projects dispersed over a far-flung swathe of sites all over the world. Each project entailed the assembly of a new team comprising a mixture of professionals who, like Tanya, were salaried employees of the same firm, as well as independent consultants who were hired on a temporary contractual basis. On a number of occasions, Tanya had either rejected or refused to pursue potentially prestigious employment opportunities because they would not have allowed her to continue to work on development projects overseas.

While most people don't use travel to reconfigure their lives as thoroughly as these professionals, very many do use it to achieve a briefer disjunctive abridgement. After all the *sine qua non* of tourism, the most common basis for contemporary travel, is the opportunity it provides for a similar if less consequential extrication from the embeddedness of everyday life, a chance temporarily to escape the myriad activities, roles, obligations, expectations, representations, peers, intimates, adversaries and other consociations that impossibly complicate our usual routines. Escape mixed with curiosity about unfamiliar places and people makes for a powerful thrust towards movement, rendered all the more alluring by the cultural capital which can be conferred by travel. If many of the world's travellers may not be cosmopolitans in the sense Ulf Hannerz imparts to it of genuine 'openness toward divergent cultural experiences' (1996: 103), their journeys may nonetheless be tinged with at least a veneer of fashionable urbanity. Thus a throng of young men and women now take a break from their work or studies to travel the world, supported by means of short stints of work in the locales they are visiting. Europeans, North Americans, Israelis, Australians, South Africans and more crisscross each other's countries and other destinations for months, occasionally even years. Between 1993 and 1996, in the course of several fieldwork trips I made to Grand Cayman,[4] a popular Caribbean tourist and offshore financial centre, I discovered that among the hundreds of young foreigners working in the shops and restaurants of Grand Cayman, are many who are treating their stay as a form of work-tourism.

But I also discovered that it was not only the young and still relatively unencumbered who longed for adventure and escape. The sense that travel could offer an escape from the staleness and stalemates of a sedentary life also figured prominently when a number of expatriate professionals I met explained their motivations for taking up temporary contracts in Grand Cayman. But unlike the transnational consultants referred to above, for these would-be adventurers in Cayman, it was not so much movement which had been enlisted in the development of careers, as that marketable skills enabled them to act on longing for movement and/or change. James had arrived in Grand Cayman from England in 1982. He had seen a job in Cayman advertised in a computer press but this was the first he had heard of this Caribbean island. 'I came not really knowing if I would be living in a mud hut or in comfort.' He had come, he explained for 'the adventure aspect of it, the sun, sea, sand, to see the world'. For James this was his first extended period outside England. 'If Cayman had not been as good, I would have probably dotted around the world.' As it was, conditions were sufficiently good that James stayed on. James had met his wife Joan, another British expatriate, while she was visiting a relative living in Cayman. Eventually, Joan had herself migrated to Cayman. She explained:

I had a very good job in England but I had gone as far as I could go in this job and I couldn't go any further. Life was pretty stale. I was looking for a change, for adventure, something different. I was sick of not earning much money, of not being able to travel ... Having a relative here gave me access to living here for a while without a work permit.

Joan was then able to find a job as a midwife in a Caymanian hospital.

Joan and James referred me to their friends Anne and Greg. Anne, a nurse and Greg, a teacher were also British expatriates in their 30s who had met and married in Grand Cayman. Like James and quite a few of the other expatriate professionals I spoke to, Anne had been drawn to the Cayman Islands by a job she saw advertised in London. The job had captured her attention because it called for a nurse with a background in community health, her speciality. She was interviewed for the job in London and then hired. At that time, she was single. She was looking for a change in scenery but, like James, she didn't even know where the Cayman Islands were. She had to look them up. This was the first time she had worked outside England. She had longed to travel overseas for some time but family commitments had previously prevented her from acting on that desire. When she accepted the offer of a job in Cayman, she had had no particular long-term plans. She figured that Cayman might be a stopping off point to somewhere else. It was only a two-year contract, the salary was very good and she had 'nothing to lose'. 'It was a safe way to take my first step overseas.' She had thought that this experience would allow her to decide which way to go. It would either bolster her courage about living away from England or else demonstrate to her that she was going to be too homesick for this to be feasible. In the end, however, she had not actually committed herself to either option. After three years, she and Greg had left Cayman. They embarked on a year's travel abroad and, because they had bought a round the world ticket, the final destination had to be their point of embarkation, Cayman. What they had intended as a quick return visit and vacation ended up being extended when Greg was offered a new two-year contract in his old teaching job. So they stayed on again, although Anne had experienced difficulty in finding employment. Anne said that she and her husband were feeling pretty open minded about what was going to happen when Greg's contract expired again.

PARADIGMS OF MOVEMENT

Anthropological attention to long-distance movements has generally focused on migration. Recently, anthropologists have noted that global restructuring of trade, finance and production as well as improvements in transport and communication have changed the circumstances of labour migration. The links and disruptions engendered by capitalist penetration into new markets have prompted new outflows of migrants (Basch et al., 1994; Sassen, 1994, 1996). Improvements in communication and transport systems have facilitated the development and management of social networks and commitments crossing state borders (Basch et al., 1994; Guarnizo and Smith, 1998). But these same developments have also impelled an increase in other kinds of movements while at the same time blurring the distinctions between them. Perhaps the greatest increase in transnational movements has occurred in the expansion of long-distance tourism, but the distinction between this form of holiday and business or labour movements is becoming more difficult to clearly delineate. Is the young adult working his/her way around the globe a tourist or a labour migrant? Is the consultant who takes on a temporary contract requiring months, or occasionally even years of residence in a foreign destination, a migrant or a business traveller? .

It would probably be difficult to catalogue comprehensively all the myriad personal circumstances and motivations that are implicated in these forms of long-distance movements, but they are as likely to be informed by a general ethos of movement and personal development that emphasizes social disjunction than one which emphasizes continuity. Many of these movements are not undertaken with the intention of carrying along relationships formed in one context into a new situation. Instead, their predominant orientation is one emphasizing separation, severance, reconfiguration. This emphasis can be framed within a rhetoric of professionalism that associates successful career development with organizational and/or spatial mobility; it can be informed by an aspiration to a more or less profound cosmopolitanism or it can be framed within a discourse of adventure and escape. But in all these stances, it is disjunction, the break, however temporary, with previous relationships and contexts, with the familiar and the local, an embrace of new situations and possibilities that is valorized as a hallmark of this form of movement, not continuity and integration.

The current paradigm of movement predominating in anthropology is more often the inverse, stressing connection and community and hence perhaps provoking the bemusement of some of my anthropological audience to my portrayal of the lifestyles and choices of John and Margaret and their fellow occupational travellers. This orientation towards mobility as connection has been encouraged by several recent influences. First there is the transmigration approach, which has dominated the American literature on transnationalism and is most commonly identified with Basch et al.'s *Nations Unbound* (1994). Here the emphasis is on the transnational connections created when migrants continue to maintain a foothold in their country of origin, even as they participate in nation-building projects in another state. Or, as Luis

Guarnizo argued in a more recent publication, being a transnational 'implies becoming habituated to living more or less comfortably in a world that encompasses more than one national structure of institutional and power arrangements, social understandings, and dominant political and public cultures' (1997: 310). This duality constitutes, he suggests, a 'transnational habitus' linking two states – in his example, the Dominican Republic and the United States – as a *single* sociocultural, economic and political field (1997: 311).

The second has been the use of the concepts of borderlands or borders as metaphors for processes of de-territorialization and cultural connection, and as vehicles for arguing that pastiche, hybridity and boundary transgressions are ordinary processes of cultural production. Or as Renato Rosaldo put it in justifying his argument for an ethnography focused on border zones:

All of us inhabit an interdependent late twentieth-century world marked by borrowing and lending across porous national and cultural boundaries that are saturated with inequality, power and domination. (1989: 217)

Closely related to the metaphorical use of border zones has been the extension of Benedict Anderson's concept of imagined community (1991/1983) to include an ever wider range of socially recognized identities. As the concept has become a more ubiquitous vehicle to represent de-territorialization, it has – as we saw earlier in Appadurai's treatment – been stripped of much of its social and interactive content so that it looks increasingly like little more than a categorical referent, the possibility of attributing social connection without the complications of place, commonality or even regular interaction.

While these efforts are substantial contributions to the more general anthropological interrogation of concepts of place, community and culture, they appear to incorporate a contradictory reading of the very possibility of collective transnational connections as axiomatic, even while seeking to problematize the territorial, cultural and social under-pinnings of these links. Occasional invocations of displacement and ubiquitous intonations of flux and motion notwithstanding, the most striking aspects of these representations of de-territorialized relations is their persistent subtext of unity and stability. Migrants operate in a single continuous field, manage to maintain spatially dispersed family and economic relationships between generations; national borders become porous sites of ongoing syncretism and communities continue to be imagined effectively. We may be willing to acknowledge that the people we are studying are moving, but their moves are insistently framed within fields which bear more than a little resemblance to a familiar representation of peoplehood that we have spent a lot of time criticizing as far too bounded, continuous and internally articulated.

This emphasis almost entirely misses the workings of another dominant ethos that emphasizes disjunction rather than connection, one that, as I have argued above, is consonant with long-standing institutional representations of modernity and capitalist rationality, and is therefore perhaps even more likely to inform the movements of many transnational travellers. There is, after all, something rather odd about this omission on the part of anthropologists given that the construction of their principal methodology has also usually emphasized the fissures of movement. In its traditional rendering, participant observation was supposed to involve a sharp break with the fieldworker's normal involvements, a journey to a far away site and complete immersion in personal face-to-face relationships with a variety of natives over an extended period of time. If anthropologists have recently been questioning this archetype (Amit, 2000; Gupta and Ferguson, 1997a), its persistence over so much of their own disciplinary history should surely make the appeal of similar disjunctive models unsurprising.

What is most disappointing about the anthropological tendency to over-privilege peoplehood in explicating contemporary patterns and conceptions of movement is the resulting failure fully to engage with some of the internal contradictions and costs of separation, flexibility and cosmopolitanism which weave through other travelling accounts. For the ruptures that people can court as a testament to their realism and autonomy can sometimes turn on them in ways they did not expect.

COSTS

The Royal Haven students viewed the impending disruption of their peer group as an unfortunate but unavoidable aspect of institutional transition. Ironically, it is therefore likely that they helped to deliver the future rupture they feared. In contrast, the various travellers who have featured in this account shared with each other a sense that they had voluntarily chosen lives of movement and attendant disjunction. They could have chosen less peripatetic lives. John could have, as he originally intended, restricted his business enterprise to western Canada alone. Tanya and Margaret could likely have elected to work as consultants on local development projects. Monica and Richard could have stayed in or found new jobs in the Lower Mainland of British Columbia rather than Seattle. James, Joan, Anne and Greg had not left Britain out of desperation or destitution but out of a desire to change their lives.

There were personal costs to this choice of which John, the seasoned rover was all too aware. Less acutely, most of the other travellers acknowledged that distance had had its effect on attenuating their relationships with absent friends and family. Yet it is likely that their sense of the aptness of these choices was reinforced by the degree to which their patrons had counted their 'flexibility'. Margaret noted the perks that accrued to her international work: the luxury hotels, trips around the world and payment in US dollars. Towards the end of 1998, Monica was able to contend that, for information technology specialists like herself and her spouse Richard, it was easy to get a job. She had experienced no difficulties in finding a number of positions successively in Ottawa, Vancouver and Seattle. Nor could she really envisage a time when this would markedly change:

I think, especially if we [Monica and Richard] stay very technology-focused as we are now, I don't think so because even in a down-turn economy, people are actually going to implement more systems than they normally would. So I think it's kind of like banking. You're pretty safe either way. I think so.

So Monica was not particularly worried that she still had no more security of tenure in the United States than the two years remaining on her temporary work visa or that she would probably need the assistance of her employer to carry out the process of acquiring permanent residence status: the 'green card'. Three years later, in the light of the world-wide collapse of the information technology sector and tens of thousands of related job losses, Monica's assurance is likely to seem quite ironic. Yet even before this economic reversal, the experiences of expatriate professionals in the Cayman Islands provided due warning that the structures through which rewards are conferred on professionals willing to move jobs and locations can at the same time also confer vulnerability.

In the course of its transformation from a small-scale maritime economy to a major tourist and offshore finance centre, Grand Cayman shifted from being an exporter to a net importer of population. Most of the workers that Cayman recruits are skilled, and most are hired on temporary work contracts. In 1994, 40 per cent of the workforce consisted of foreign workers, recruited primarily from elsewhere in the Caribbean, Honduras, the United Kingdom and North America. As Cayman became more dependent on foreign workers, legal and social distinctions between new arrivals and indigenous residents became more sharply drawn. It became increasingly difficult for expatriates to acquire permanent residence status. Work permits range from a few months to three years in duration but are frequently renewable, and foreign workers can change jobs with the appropriate issuance of new work permits. Employers are, however, legally required to give preference to qualified Caymanians, not only when first filling a vacancy but at each instance of contract renewal. Contract renewal is therefore a time of high anxiety, when the vulnerable legal status of even the most highly sought-after professional is underlined. As Mark, an expatriate working in the cultural sector explained:

> There is enough work to keep me occupied for a lifetime but we do have bouts of 'get the expats out'. There are funny attitudes here. When you get to the point when you could apply for status [permanent residence], they tend to turn down your work permit. It's silly because they don't have to give you status. If someone objects to your work permit, you get turned down.

Stories about well-known expatriates who had faced this kind of political disciplining abounded, as did accounts of foreign workers whose work permits and/or contracts had not been renewed under less dramatic circumstances. Thus Mark was able to tell me about James, who, after 13 years, had been informed he was about to be replaced by a qualified Caymanian and his contract as a computer specialist and manager would not be renewed. Commenting on James's situation, Mark remarked: 'This does seem to be a taking situation. They want you until they've used up what you've got and then they just replace you and you're discarded.' In his own commentary, James claimed that:

> We [expatriates] can't vote, we don't have elected members that have expat interests in mind, no representation, therefore can't change it. If you try and change it, then you come up against the victimization part again and eventually you will suffer for it.

Yet wasn't this kind of exploitation, the inherent disposability of foreign labour, always an explicit aspect of the conditions under which Mark and James, their expatriate friends and family members had been employed? After all, from the outset they had been recruited to fill positions only on a limited-term contractual basis. Why, then, this sense of betrayal, of dismay at the vulnerability that attends even renewable short-term contracts? I suspect that their consternation derives from the unwelcome realization that when Caymanian officials and employers said 'temporary', 'employed only until ...', they actually meant it. When foreign professionals are being actively and determinedly courted to come to the Cayman Islands, recruited in their home countries, wooed with high tax-free salaries, the occasional fringe benefit, the delights of a warm and attractive locale, it seems hard to imagine that, alongside that valorization of skills and experience is an intrinsic definition of the person that provides them as structurally dispensable. It is easier, surely, to see temporary contracts as bureaucratic formalities, easier to assume that how long you work and stay in the Cayman Islands, given the demand for your skills, will be your choice, and a shock to discover that it isn't. And, fast on the heels of this discovery, comes the realization that national, regional and highly local boundaries continue to be crucial features of the global organization of labour, that there may be no going back to the job or employment market you 'escaped' from, that here, too, the choice may not be yours. Your job may no longer be there to go back to, you can be deemed too old, your experience elsewhere may not be judged as valid as local careers, and so on. And in the course of these realizations, the dream of unfettered mobility, of the transnational portability of skills, of the potential for greater agency embedded in the proliferation of contractual work across borders and across job categories, can stand revealed as highly contingent.

CONCLUSION

In an ascendant rendition of modernity, it is flexibility, movement and disjunction that can deliver career success, adventure and sophistication. Aihwa Ong's account of overseas Chinese corporate elites highlights the way in which mobile managers, technocrats and professionals seek 'to both circumvent *and* benefit from different nation-state regimes by selecting different sites for investments, work and family relocation' (1999: 112). By acquiring multiple citizenships and residential locations, these mobile Chinese entrepreneurs seek to ensure their continuing transnational access to economic opportunities and personal security. The kind of border-hopping Chinese entrepreneur 'with no state loyalty has become an important figure in the era of Pacific Rim capital' (Ong, 1999: 136). Ong notes however that:

there may not be anything uniquely 'Chinese' about flexible personal discipline, disposition and orientation; rather they are the expressions of a habitus that is finely tuned to the turbulence of late capitalism. (1999: 136)

Yet, while these Chinese executives appear to share the dominant paradigm which also frames the choices of the travellers I have described, the former are operating in very distinctive circumstances. These Chinese elites are set apart from many other mobile professionals by the sheer scale and size of their holdings and economic activities. Given their ethnic minority status in many of the countries in which they reside or hold citizenship, the political uncertainties engendered by tensions between the various states in which they hold stakes, and the transfer of Hong Kong to China, they have become highly conscious that the security of their citizenship entitlements and transnational investments cannot be taken for granted. Accordingly, they have been both more deliberate in their efforts to develop 'flexible [and transnational] strategies of capital accumulation' (Ong, 1999: 113) and also have the economic and political resources to realize these strategies. However, other less well resourced and less politically and ethnically self-conscious elites who are seeking to practise similar regimes of mobility and compartmentalization will not necessarily be as successful in manipulating politico-economic conditions in different parts of the world to their advantage. Thus, British expatriates arriving to take positions in the small British colony of the Cayman Islands have been surprised to discover the limitations of their entitlements, their professional qualifications notwithstanding. The Canadian consultants I met assumed that the valorization of the sectors in which they were working would hold indefinitely. They had therefore not taken the same measures as their Chinese counterparts for ensuring the protections of multiple citizenships, nor had they been urged to by the governmental or corporate regimes courting them for their mobility. Thus the very pervasiveness of this particular model of modernity can mask the degree to which states and corporations converge in their capacity to discipline workers through the same mechanisms they also use for channelling rewards. The proliferation of temporary work permits across the globe has permitted an extraordinarily diverse stream of workers, more or less privileged, to take up a wide range of job opportunities in many countries. But temporary work permits can also easily be rescinded. Under the banner of 'flexibility', corporate restructuring has catalysed the development of the business service sector and facilitated the strategic movement of employees between organizations. But the same flexibility that allows workers to move at will when their skills are in demand also allows corporations easily to dispense with their services when economic circumstances change. Valorization, as expatriates in Cayman have already discovered, can go hand in hand with expendability. In the Cayman Islands, government authorities facilitate and employers take up the accruing opportunities actively to recruit staff in other countries, but neither public nor private agencies are averse to exploiting the tenuous legal status of most foreign workers as mechanisms for discipline and economic rationalization.

It has probably never been 'easier' to travel the world, for play or work. But much of this is travel without a safety net. It is surely time for us to address the appeals and vulnerabilities of many contemporary forms of mobility within their own terms rather than simply reproducing familiar anthropological frames of community, newly dressed in metaphors of flux and de-territorialization. Something else is happening here and we should be investigating it.

3   THE TROUBLE WITH COMMUNITY

The most common appearance of community within the social sciences, and especially the anthropological literature, has probably been in its most taken-for-granted and unexamined form as a unit of analysis, the location rather than the object of research. But community has also featured as a long-standing vehicle for a broader scholarly interrogation of the dialectic between historical social transformations and social cohesion, and as such was a focus in scholarship as varied as that of Tönnies, Durkheim and Weber writing at the turn of the twentieth century (Chorney, 1990), the 'Chicago School' urbanists of the first half of the twentieth century (Hannerz, 1980; Park, 1925; Wirth, 1938), Oscar Lewis (1965), Young and Willmott (1962/1957) and more recently Anthony P. Cohen (1982, 1985), Benedict Anderson (1983/1991) and Gupta and Ferguson (1997b), to name but a few.

Given this diversity of scholarship it is hardly surprising that, by 1955, numerous definitions of community already abounded in the sociological literature (Hillery, 1955). Nonetheless, one could argue that in spite of this apparent cacophony, much of the analytical querying of community has and continues to revolve around a key dilemma: incorporation. The emergence of state, industrial, urban and now increasingly global structures have all entailed processes of agglomeration that placed successive question marks around the foundation, viability, indeed the very ontology of the smaller groupings incorporated into these larger systems. Attention to these processes of incorporation required that social analysts account not only for the organization of collectivities but for their very existence, efforts which have in turn tended to group around two primary focuses of scrutiny: locality and identity. The problematization of locality assumed its most pressing form in the study of the city. Amongst the dense, diverse and transient populations of large and rapidly growing cities, one could no longer presume social affiliations and relationships from the mere fact of propinquity. People might live alongside each other, cheek by jowl, but the social distance separating them could still be a chasm of class, ethnic, occupational and age differences, a 'mosaic of little worlds that touch but do not interpenetrate' (Park, 1952 as cited in Hannerz, 1980: 26). So urban scholars had to account for the factors and processes that, in certain circumstances, allowed for the emergence of social affiliations and groupings, for social relations to be transformed from aggregation into consociation, or perhaps even communality. The urban ethnography that emerged from this line of inquiry, like its rural counterpart, tended to focus on localized small-scale, face-to-face relations but could not similarly treat place and community as homologous. Instead, it assembled around a much more self-conscious effort to lay out the social impetuses and ground for the production of collective affiliations. Was the basis of community association sentiment or necessity (Suttles, 1968)? Did the conditions of urbanization and industrialization require that primary associations of intimacy and trust cede to more contractual and instrumental affiliations (Wirth, 1938)? What was the role of the extended family (Young and Willmott, 1962/1957), religion (Lewis, 1965; Williams, 1974); livelihood (Wallman and associates, 1982), poverty (Lewis, 1966), neighbouring relations, language (Jackson, 1988/1975), government policy (Wallman, 1982) and, of course, ethnic and racial difference (Epstein, 1958; Mitchell, 1956; Wallman and associates, 1982) in the mobilization of local collectivity?

Another line of inquiry focused on the production of collective identities but for a time this effort, particularly within anthropology, became framed within a dominant paradigm of incorporation: ethnicity. During the 1950s and 1960s, the mounting efforts of anthropologists to contend with 'Third World' urbanization and the emergence of post-colonial states forced cultural difference into new relief. Amidst the diverse, frequently tense and uncertain terrain of these shifting political environments, collective distinctions could no longer be treated as a function of cultural isolation. It seemed clear that notions of difference were being constructed in the midst of intense and ongoing interaction between peoples identifying as members of distinct collectivities and not as an outcome of their separation.

Anthropologists such as A.L. Epstein and Clyde Mitchell, working in the Copperbelt cities of southern Africa, or Abner Cohen in southern Nigeria and social scientists such as Nathan Glazer and Daniel Moynihan in New York City, argued that ethnicity was not simply an outdated survival from pre-modern periods but a response and adaptation to modern urban and state politics (Cohen, 1969, 1974; Epstein, 1958, 1978; Mitchell, 1956, 1970). This reinterpretation of ethnicity proved an especially useful means to reorient the anthropological gaze without radically shifting ethnographic practices. Anthropologists could retain their micro focus while reformulating the status of their ethnographic subjects; now no longer 'small-scale societies' but ethnic groups mobilizing in response to their incorporation into modern state systems.

A wide variety of groups was thus rapidly subsumed under the rubric of ethnicity, from Karen hill farmers in Thailand (Keyes, 1979), to Creole elites in Sierra Leone (Cohen, 1981), to the residents of inner-city London suburbs (Wallman, 1984).

Roger Keesing once noted that '[I]f radical alterity did not exist, it would be anthropology's project to invent it' (1994: 301). The 'new' ethnicity, however, allowed alterity to be reinvented as the deliberate project of the Other, rather than the anthropologist. Like colleagues in other social sciences, anthropologists were not agreed on their explanations and descriptions of ethnicity. Ethnicity was variously offered as a classificatory system for social mapping of diverse and strange urban environments (Epstein, 1958; Mitchell, 1956), as an informal cultural vehicle for promoting common political and economic interests (Cohen, 1974), as strategic calculations of social maximization (Barth, 1969), as a process of individual psychological development (Epstein, 1978), as a boundary between different organizational and cultural systems (Wallman, 1978) and so on. What persisted across these various explanations, across the circumstantialist/primordialist debate was the priority assigned to collective difference in and of itself. Sociality now became an effect of constructed and oppositional categorical distinctions, realized by positing an 'us' versus 'them'.

The tendency of anthropologists to study 'down' and to view themselves as protectors of their ethnographic subjects converged neatly with the inclination of a larger range of social scientists to regard ethnic groups in Western countries, particularly in North America, as subordinate and disadvantaged minority groups competing for scarce resources. It was therefore probably not surprising to find social scientists increasingly inclined, not only to view the perpetuation of ethnicity as a rational response to modernity, but to cloak this form of mobilization in heroic garb. The expanding ambit of ethnicity was represented not (or at least not primarily) as a factor of scholarly representation but as a 'new' phenomenon, a feature of the times (Glazer and Moynihan, 1975). As ethnicity became heroic and the study of it thoroughly modern, ethnic studies became more celebratory than critical. By 1978, John Higham was already complaining about the lack of a critical perspective in American ethnic studies. In 1994, on the occasion of the twenty-fifth anniversary of the publication of his seminal edited volume *Ethnic Groups and Boundaries*, Fredrik Barth chastised anthropologists for regularly operating 'too narrowly as (self-appointed) advocates and apologists for ethnic groups in their grievances' (1994: 24).

The enthusiasm for ethnic studies has sputtered across the social sciences with sociologists consigning it to a symbolic residue (Gans, 1979) or pronouncing its American twilight (Alba, 1981). According to

Marcus Banks, anthropological interests have also moved away from ethnicity to new topics and theoretical interests (1996: 1). And there have certainly been some notable critiques of the broader emphasis on cultural alterity (Abu-Lughod, 1991; Keesing, 1994). Yet the shift away from ethnicity as a paradigm for theorizing and evaluating community and cultural difference may be more apparent than real. The enduring legacy of this conceptual framework is most evident in the persisting convergence of community and ethnicity. As the quotes below indicate, efforts to theorize community have conscripted the emphases on social boundary and identity, the relational and oppositional nature of collective identities which were developed in the study of ethnicity, most notably in Barth's seminal study of ethnic boundaries (1969):

'Community' thus seems to imply simultaneously both similarity and difference. The word thus expresses a *relational* idea: the opposition of one community to others or to other social entities. Indeed it will be argued that the use of the word is only occasioned by the desire or need to express such a distinction. It seems appropriate, therefore, to focus our examination of the nature of community on the element which embodies this sense of discrimination, namely, the *boundary*. (Cohen, 1985: 12)

'Community' is never simply the recognition of cultural similarity or social contiguity but a categorical identity that is premised on various forms of exclusion and construction of otherness. (Gupta and Ferguson, 1997c: 13)

At the same time, the idea of community has been imported into efforts to explain nationalist and ethnic movements:

In an anthropological spirit, then, I propose the following definition of the nation: it is an imagined political community – and imagined as both inherently limited and sovereign.

It is imagined because the members of even the smallest nation will never know most of their fellow-members, meet them or even hear of them, yet in the minds of each lives the image of their communion. (Anderson, 1991/1983: 5–6)

The convergence between community and ethnicity has relied on their empirical 'hollowing out', a mutual shift from an emphasis on actual social relations and groupings to symbolically demarcated categories of identity.

As I will try to illustrate later in this chapter, the legacy of the 'new' ethnicity has also been manifest in recent revalorizations of cultural difference. Just as anthropologists were busily denouncing and distancing themselves from the bounded, ahistorical and homogeneous cultural differences of yore, the invocations of cultural difference and authenticity by 'others' were being interpreted as instances of rational modernity, resistance and empowerment. As long as we didn't take these vernacular summonings of cultural distinctiveness too literally (Gupta and Ferguson, 1997c: 3), it seemed we were free to denounce radical alterity and embrace it at the same time, an intellectual version of having your cake and eating it too, made all the more incongruous because it was offered as an instance of critical reflexivity.

I am not persuaded that a move away from celebrating our own analytical essentialization of cultural differences towards celebrating the essentialisms insisted on by the people we are studying is much of an advance. Nor am I sure how much heuristic progress we can claim for a move away from representations of communities as sociocultural content without broader context, to representations of communities as entirely contextual but empty of social content. When our anthropological progenitors treated ethnographic subjects as self-contained isolates, they were able to evade accounting for the impact of the incorporation of these groups into colonial or imperialist systems of domination and exploitation. Evasions of a similar order occur when contemporary analysts treat contemporary invocations of community as metaphors of difference without accounting for the social implications of these claims. The result is that some fairly reactionary workings of authenticity and exclusion can be oddly lauded as cosmopolitan and progressive. But this most recent evasion is not peculiarly anthropological. Diaspora, multiculturalism, transnationalism: the current vocabulary of categorical alterity is multidisciplinary.

DIASPORA

Amidst the proliferating appearance of the term *diaspora* in a variety of scholarly literatures, two particular trends stand out. In one of these, diaspora appears tacked on to fairly conventional and localized accounts of immigrant populations. Accounts which might once have had 'ethnic' or 'immigrant' as identifying descriptors now rely on the euphemism of 'diaspora' without much in the way of justification or theorization. Tellingly, diaspora often appears more prominently in the titles of such pieces than in the texts they head (for example, Fortier, 1998; Portes and Grosfoguel, 1994; Yon, 1995). In these instances, one would have to wonder whether the term 'diaspora' is being drawn on less for a new theory of mobility and cultural hybridity than for the cachet of fashionability it bestows on otherwise well-trod terrain. Thus, in these instances we appear to have not so much abandoned ethnicity (Banks, 1996) as renamed it.

But there is also another genre of literature which has struggled to use diaspora and particularly the concept of 'diasporic space' to chart new theoretical openings. One of the most influential of these efforts has been

Paul Gilroy's notion of the 'Black Atlantic' (1993). Gilroy employs the concept of a Black diaspora to assert a web of personal, historical and cultural connections that connects the Americas with Europe and in turn with Africa. Staking out the ground of anti-anti essentialism, Gilroy seeks to chart a middle ground between the 'purified appeal of either Africentrism or the Eurocentrisms it struggles to answer' (1993: 190) without giving up on the notion of continuity or community. Instead, he proposes to historicize tradition, to see it as an ephemeral, 'magical' process of connectedness that binds Africa to Black diaspora cultures without ignoring the cultural flows, invention and fragmentation which undo any efforts to assert a linear narrative of cultural continuity. Critical of the tendency of Africentricity to efface intra-racial variations, he instead celebrates hybridization, intermixture, the messiness and inspiration of interstitiality, the stories of love and loss which constitute the communities of sentiment and interpretation making up the Black Atlantic.

As James Clifford has noted, in Gilroy's presentation, diasporic subjects are 'distinct versions of modern, transnational, intercultural experience. Thus historicized, diaspora cannot become a master trope or "figure" for modern, complex, or positional identities, crosscut and displaced by race, sex, gender, class and culture' (Clifford, 1994: 319). But such cautions notwithstanding, diaspora, and particularly Gilroy's version of diaspora, has indeed become just such a trope because it manages to be so quintessentially postmodern without the political fatalism to which this particular intellectual orientation has so often succumbed. It poses diasporas as vigorous 'counterdiscourses to modernity', 'cultures of resistance' (Clifford, 1994: 319) that are at once ethnically particularist and politically open. In the light of a decade at the millennium's end which has seen ethnicity and nationality all too often summoned as the basis for the harshest of brutality, it is easy to understand why Gilroy's vision of a 'response to racism that doesn't reify the concept of race', 'a series of answers to the power of ethnic absolutism that doesn't try to fix ethnicity absolutely but sees it instead as an infinite process of identity construction' (Gilroy, 1993: 223) should be so appealing. But to assert the redemptive and transcendent aspect of diaspora, Gilroy has had to strip it of social relations and turn its ideological bias on its head.

Much of this celebration of diaspora (for example Brah, 1996; Gilroy, 1993) displays very little curiosity about the social dimension of diaspora, that is, how it actually works and is reproduced over time. As a result, these scholars appear little concerned with the possibility that the processes they are celebrating as the progressive *raisons d'être* of diaspora are more likely to be the subject of anxiety, denouncement or denial by its principal stakeholders. But even more socially grounded accounts of diaspora can be subject to similar glosses of valorization. The degree to which expectations of progressive possibilities can shape readings of contemporary diasporic politics is highlighted in a recent article by Pnina Werbner (1998). Werbner is concerned with a sphere of political debate among south Manchester Pakistanis. Restricted to Pakistani men, this sphere had remained closed and largely invisible to the wider public until the publication of Salman Rushdie's *The Satanic Verses*, when South Asians in Britain spearheaded a global mobilization of Muslims against the author and his book. Werbner draws attention to the legacy of anti-Muslim prejudice which was a spin-off of this campaign. She notes the paradoxes of a movement that used threats of violence to enforce demands for respect. She observes the 'internecine fighting, mismanagement of communal institutions and constant appeals for state handouts and recognition which plagued communal affairs' and which resulted in a loss of local control by Manchester Pakistanis over key institutions (1998: 22). She is keenly aware of the 'male stranglehold on the diasporic public sphere'. Yet hers is ultimately a tale of the triumph of diasporic activism, of women newly empowered, of extremists rendered less powerful, of new forms of volunteerism and activism arising from the shards of a shattered alternative civil order. Amidst a set of events and processes unflinchingly observed as redolent of polarization, violent polemic, exclusions and radical disagreements, diaspora still manages to rise transcendent, united through heterogeneity, 'a shared space of dialogue', a context for an activism in which 'passive victims can become the imaginative agents of their own destiny' (1998: 27–8).

Werbner's reading of diaspora as an interpretative community in which protoganists share the premises of their debate even as they take opposed positions in it is very familiar to me. I recognize it because, as I illustrate below, my account of the London Armenian community more than a decade earlier shared this orientation (Amit-Talai, 1989; Talai, 1986). Unfortunately, the celebration of communal resilience which shaped my earlier research staked out an uncritical intellectual stance which this work shared with many of the other studies produced during the heydey of ethnic studies. This tendency is, if anything, even more acutely apparent in the current enthusiasm over the progressive potentialities of diaspora. A new generation of scholars appears to have dampened their own capacity for critical scepticism in a determination to render diaspora as an exemplary transnational space for critical insight and political alternatives (Clifford, 1994; Gilroy, 1993; Tölölian, 1991).

However in the shift from ethnicity to diaspora as master tropes of social diversity and migration, two unfortunate tendencies appear to have been preserved: an inclination towards ever more expansive definitions of the related concept and interpretation of this status (that is, first ethnic and then diasporic) in celebratory rather than critical terms.

Thus, in a trajectory reminiscent of the earlier reworking of ethnicity, the use of the term *diaspora* has now been extended far beyond its classic application to the Armenian or Jewish people, and has been identified as an emblem of the historical moment. If ethnicity was redefined as a feature of modernity, diaspora has become an icon of postmodernity.

Two concomitants of postmodernism's rejection of universal standards and metanarratives are relevant to our present concerns. First, it was associated with a concerted critique of science, objectivity and rationality as a hegemonic language/system of power and social detachment (Abu-Lughod, 1991: 150–1; Scheper-Hughes, 1995: 418). Sentiment and poetics, the perceived antitheses of science, were redeemed as newly authentic. Second, without a universal standard of evaluation, criticism from 'outside' was rendered not only invalid but potentially oppressive, because it represented a struggle not over truth but over the power of contingent and specifically situated perspectives. Diaspora's redefinition as postmodern brought ethnicity back full circle, reinvested once again as a phenomenon of passion and poetry. Now, however, such sentiment is not treated as inferior to rational calculation but as more authentic.

Thus, as Werbner has noted, it is the experiential and aesthetic dimensions of diaspora that have received the greatest emphasis in this theoretical genre; the connectedness of scattered and differentiated individuals is 'magical', according to Gilroy. Magically connected, only tenuously subject to objective political scrutiny, the fragmentation and dispersal of diasporas becomes homologous with the fragmentation and interconnection of the contemporary world. But since diaspora has retained ethnicity's earlier identification with political marginalization or subordination, it has become an emblem for not only the postmodern moment but also a subaltern one. Thus it is possible to see why diaspora is both heralded as being so thoroughly of the moment but at the same time mooted as an 'alternative' public sphere (cf. Brah, 1996; Gilroy, 1993; Werbner, 1998), 'nontotalizing globalization from below' (Clifford, 1994: 325). And it becomes possible to understand, perhaps, why both Werbner and Gilroy would insist on the politically open and redemptive character of diaspora, even when they are respectively aware of the insular nature of the male-dominated south Manchester Pakistani 'public' sphere and the essentialism of Africentrism. This, however, is to attribute progressivism by ascription rather than commitment.

LONDON ARMENIANS: A DIASPORIC ARCHETYPE?

So how does this relate to the tiny pocket of the Armenian diaspora that I observed in London during the 1980s? Numbering, by the most generous of estimates, only 10,000–12,000 persons scattered over many different districts of one of the largest conurbations in the world, the Armenians were not easy to find. When social scientists set out to find ethnic groups, however, they usually succeed. I thus found a much smaller set of approximately 1,500 people who were busily organizing a shifting set of voluntary associations which sponsored a small cultural centre, two churches (one rented from the Church of England, the other a tiny chapel donated by the wealthy Armenian Gulbenkian family), a Sunday school and a wide variety of less regular activities from lectures to movies to music recitals to teas or fundraising dinner dances.

The diasporic dimensions of Armenian ethnicity were acutely apparent in London during this period. London Armenians, who were still largely first-generation immigrants to Britain, originated from over seven different countries. The dispersal of Armenians throughout the Middle East as a consequence of the genocide of 1915 was reflected in the life histories of most of the Western Armenian speakers whose parents or grandparents had been expelled from eastern Turkey. The longest-settled residents had arrived from Cyprus, taking advantage of a temporary offer of full British passports to migrate to London either just before or after the independence of Cyprus. Since such a large proportion of the Armenian community in Cyprus was involved in this movement, quite a few of these former Cypriot Armenians had many members of their extended families with them in London. This was much less often the case for Armenian migrants from other parts of the Middle East who were travelling under less propitious conditions. In Iran, Armenians had formed a much larger minority population. Some had arrived several years before to pursue their studies and found their expected return stymied by the upheaval of the Iranian Revolution; others arrived singly or as nuclear family groups in the lead-up to or in the immediate aftermath of these political events. They didn't have British passports and they sought residence in London at a time of general tightening of the immigration regulations. Most therefore experienced considerable difficulty in acquiring permission to remain permanently in Britain; they certainly had little possibility of bringing other members of their families to join them and they faced the likely prospect of moving on to further destinations, most likely in North America. In spite of the differences between these situations, most Armenians in London, of whatever origins, had experienced the transnational dispersal of significant family members. Mr G,[5] Lebanese Armenian, had a brother still living in Beirut, another living in the United States while his mother moved regularly between three continents visiting her sons in turn.

In the Middle East there had been extensive movements and contacts between Western Armenian-speaking communities in different countries, taking advantage of extensive personal networks as well as organizational connections. Many of the ethnic associations this diverse set of Armenians established in London were branches of transnational organizations with similar offshoots in many Armenian diaspora communities. In London, Armenians often established new branches of associations with which they had been familiar in their country of origin. The three Armenian political movements (the Ramgavar, Hnchaks and Dashnaks)[6] which had been established at the end of the nineteenth and beginning of the twentieth century were present through their affiliates in London as they had been similarly established, if somewhat unevenly, throughout the diaspora. While during the height of the Cold War in the 1950s, the status of the Armenian Caucasus republic in the Soviet Union had been a source of considerable tension among Armenians elsewhere, in 1980s London there was a general pride in the existence and accomplishments of the Armenian Soviet Republic. Films, magazines and books were imported, and scholars, artists and other notables visited the London community from Soviet Armenia. Groups of London Armenians were regularly sent on visits to the Republic. And there was similar regular input from other diaspora communities.

In spite of the extensive personal and organizational resources which had linked Armenians in dispersed diaspora communities before their arrival in London and which continued to connect them with Armenians elsewhere, they were acutely aware of the distinctions which had been nurtured by this dispersal. Armenians originating from communities established through the exile from eastern Turkey spoke the Western Armenian dialect. On the other hand, Armenians from Iran, who were able to trace their presence in that country over some 300 years, spoke the Eastern Armenian dialect also spoken in the Armenian Republic. While the majority of Armenians in London were at least nominally members of the Armenian Apostolic Church, a minority were Catholic or Protestant. The Apostolic services, adapted from originally much longer monastic liturgy, had been variably abridged in different communities and could be affiliated with one of two different Apostolic sees. In London, Armenians had quickly incorporated the general secularization of their host country and few attended church with any regularity. Food, secondary languages and other practices had all been influenced by and varied in accord with, the settlement of Armenians in different countries. The experience, length and future of settlement in London varied between Armenians arriving from different countries in different periods, with different statuses.

This internal differentiation was an explicit aspect of the descriptions provided to me by London Armenians and a key feature in the negative evaluation of the organized community. Divisiveness could be represented as an intrinsic aspect of ancient Armenian history, but more commonly the dispersal of Armenians was named as the source of internal divisions within the wider diaspora as a whole, and within London specifically. In London, the most overt and common distinction was attributed to the differentiation between Eastern Armenian-speaking Iranian Armenians and Western Armenian speakers in general, or the Cypriots who particularly predominated in this latter set. Western Armenian speakers complained that Iranian Armenians had adopted far too many Farsi words into their dialect, making them difficult to understand. Iranian Armenians claimed that their version of Armenian was the more authentic of the two dialects spoken in London. More generally, Armenians with longer settlement in London, most commonly Cypriots, were viewed by more recently arrived Iranian Armenians as being too Anglicized and Westernized, less authentically Armenian altogether. The internal political distinctions which occurred in London as they did in most diasporic communities were also linked to different organizational histories, with Western Armenian speakers establishing affiliates identified with the Ramgavar party while Iranian Armenians established affiliates associated with the only Armenian political party which had held sway in Iran, the Dashnaks. More generally, association control and membership, as well as informal friendship sets, tended to fall along, and to be represented in terms of, Western and Eastern Armenian divisions. The process of settlement in London and in Western countries more widely was hardly expected to repair these divisions since the increased rate of exogamous marriages, decreased proficiency in Armenian among British-born or British-raised Armenians, and limited participation in associational activities were seen as impetuses for further fragmentation and likely eventual assimilation.

Fragmentation, dispersal, transnational contact and hybridity, all features identified with diaspora formations, were certainly therefore denoted, but more often denounced or worried over than celebrated by these Armenians in London. To transcend these differences, to assert a moral and affective national unity, Armenians reached back beyond these contemporary or recent practices to assert the continuity and antiquity of their identity as a people and of their connection to the 'lands' in eastern Turkey. I was surprised to find no small number of Armenians interested in apparently esoteric archaeological and linguistic literature analysing the historical settlement of the Caucasus and Eastern Anatolia regions. It didn't take long before I realized that this interest in apparently ancient history was partly related to a concern to establish the primacy of Armenian claims to territories in these regions, which have also been settled by other peoples. As one Armenian respondent explained:

Armenians tend to be worried about any suggestion that the Armenians were migrants. Because if they were migrants, the Turks were also migrants then they also have a right to be on the lands of Eastern Anatolia. (Amit Talai, 1989: 127)

To assert the indigenous status of Armenians in Asia Minor, seemingly neutral archaeological or philological research was avidly scoured for evidence of a historical legacy that could buttress an existential charter of ultimate origins. Physical distance, dispersal and differentation became expiated by a reaffirmation of the roots of all Armenians, wherever their contemporary locations, in the ancient Armenian 'homeland'. Antiquity and continuity also became, in themselves, constitutive elements in defining the transcendent quality of Armenian ethnicity:

Other ancient nations, like the Hittites and the Assyrians, the Medes and the Babylonians may have waxed and waned, declined into but a shadow of their former greatness, or entirely disappeared but the Armenians have 'survived the ravages of history to the present day...' [began] the London-Armenian writer in his 'perspective' on Armenian history. ... But this concept of continuity refer[red] not only to the people themselves but to their culture. 'Other nations like the Assyrians or the Kurds, there are a lot of them but they have lost their culture', explained Mr. VJ. (Amit Talai, 1989: 128)

Or it was argued that other also ancient nations had not experienced a genocide. So, the continuity and antiquity of culture and people was also a heroic endurance against all odds. A 'historical' narrative was thus invoked as a charter of transcendent and distinctive unity for a dispersed set of exiles who were acutely aware of the differences between them. At the same time, this symbolic codex established a moral obligation for self-perpetuation, for resistance to assimilation, a commitment to carry on this legacy in the name of all who died, so tragically and violently, because they too were identified as Armenian.

The transcendent unity of the 'diasporic' divided Armenians was established through the proclamation and narrative reiteration of a primordial connection. Tellingly, even Iranian Armenians whose ancestors, for the most part, had not been involved in the massacres of 1915 claimed these events and the 'lands' on which they occurred as an intrinsic part of their heritage. These themes of exile, antiquity, homeland, tragedy and redemption are not unique to Armenians. Indeed, they have been adopted, more or less, as the virtual *sine qua non* of diaspora constitutive narratives (Clifford, 1994; Gilroy, 1993). Here I think it becomes important to distinguish between this use of diaspora as a charter of identity and the efforts of an increasing number of individuals to manage personal networks dispersed across region and state borders. The latter have variously and confusingly been referred to under the rubrics of transnationality or ethnoscape, and even diaspora, but this conceptual muddle aside, the efforts of individuals to respond to the scattering of their significant family, friends and colleagues need not in and of themselves necessarily involve either exclusivity or primordial claims of communality. However, primordialism and essentialism are not haphazard or occasional features of the effort to reproduce diasporas as ideological vehicles of identity. They are fundamental to this process. To be able to assert categorical claims of shared identity across the palpable and anxious differences of experience, geography, history and outlook, it becomes necessary to posit an essential, anterior and 'magical' connection. To borrow Gilroy's terms, it is roots and not routes which are, in the course of these efforts, redeemed as the salvation of diaspora. Hence Africentricity was not an accidental diversion in the formation of the Black diaspora. In one version or another, some such narrative would have to be invoked to assert a rationale for the integrity and limits of 'black' connections spanning Africa, Europe and the United States across centuries. If primordialism and essentialism are key elements in the efforts to define the ideological rationale and boundaries of diaspora, it is ironic to see cultural theorists, who have so denounced the exoticisms of the colonial and orientalist gaze, now embrace them as vehicles for subaltern political liberation.

MULTICULTURALISM

A reference to 'revolutionary multiculturalism' in a reading by an American anthropologist (Turner, 1993) drew puzzled looks from some members of my class of university students in Montreal. How could a subject often associated with worthy official platitudes be 'revolution- ary'? The Canadian multicultural policy was introduced as a response to the unintended consequences of the establishment, in 1963, of the Bilin- gualism and Biculturalism (B&B) Commission, a Royal Commission charged with reviewing the participation of French-speakers in Canadian political institutions. Defined thus, the Commission mandate provoked interventions by members of various ethnic associations, who were concerned that people of neither British nor French origins were in danger of being excluded from an effort to entrench a bilingual and bicultural model of Canada. The volume of these unsolicited representa- tions was so large that the Commission eventually produced Book IV of its report devoted to 'The Cultural Contribution of the *Other* Ethnic Groups' (emphasis added) (Abu-Laban and Stasiulis, 1992: 366). In 1971, the Trudeau Liberal government tabled its response to this report in the form of a formal federal policy which confirmed the bilingual status of Canada but within a multicultural rather than bicultural framework. In 1972, a Multiculturalism Directorate was established in the

Department of the Secretary of State in order to implement this policy and related programmes. Successive governments have shifted the placement and standing of the Directorate/Department, but it has managed to persist in some form or another, to continue and develop its relationship with client ethnic associations, all the while largely retaining its junior institutional status.

There are three processes exemplified by these historical events that I want to stress here. First, as has already been well noted elsewhere (Verdery, 1994; Williams, 1989), the formation of ethnic 'groups' is fundamentally embedded within state- and nation-building processes. Second, what excited ethnic mobilization, in this instance, was the perception that an effort was being made to restructure and redefine the Canadian polity. The interveners were not responding to an explicit government initiative to redefine the status of ethnic minorities so much as the *uncertainty* of the potential outcomes issuing from any structural redefinition of the nation-state. Third, the multicultural policy with which the Canadian government responded to the representations prompted by and subsequently interpreted by the BandB Commission, worked to define, contain and manage this ethnic mobilization.

In the light of the events surrounding the establishment of the Canadian multicultural policy, it is not surprising to note that much of the contemporary 'talk' of multiculturalism in other countries has also been associated with a response to, or expectation of, even more profound political and economic reorganization, with interest proliferating as this restructuring extends over a multiplicity of jurisdictions. The status and scope of inter- and intra-national borders, distribution of power, economic systems, state sovereignty and citizenship are thrown into anxious question by the further elaboration of the European Union (EU), the dissolution of the Soviet Union and its political alliances; and lurking behind these uncertainties is the spectre of the violent disintegration of Yugoslavia. In his overview of multiculturalism in a 'New Europe' being reshaped by post-Second World War migration, the EU and the end of the Cold War, Tariq Madood argues that there is an 'emerging recognition that multiculturalism means a new way of being French, a new way of being German, a new way of being British – and perhaps also a new way of being European' (1997: 24). In these, as in the earlier Canadian example, it is not the already recognizable outcomes of these political and economic developments so much as the uncertainties of their long-term effects which seem to be prompting contemporary interest in multiculturalism. What differentiates these two historical instances, however, is the identification of multiculturalism with resistance which sometimes occurs in more recent discussions. In 1971, the Canadian multiculturalism policy seemed far less a symbolic locus of resistance than a belated and fairly token institutional response to the resistance incited by the particular paradigm of nation-building which was exemplified in the mandate of the BandB Commission. In contrast, some of the more recent versions are investing the concept of multiculturalism itself with radical possibilities.

In the United States the specific political focus of multiculturalism was shaped by its integral interaction with the growing popularity and institutional entrenchment of cultural studies as an academic discipline. To the extent that the Americanization of cultural studies largely happened via departments of English and Literature (Knauft, 1994: 133), it is hardly surprising that its multicultural counterpart correspondingly focused on literature and the humanities curriculum. In effect, this meant a focus on a critique of the presumed universality and Eurocentric bias of the humanities 'canon', and a call for the inclusion of other cultural/literary traditions as a matter of course in the liberal arts curriculum. Both sympathetic analysts (Taylor, 1992) and rather more vociferous critics (Narveson, 1995) of multiculturalism identified this orientation with a call for equal recognition of the value of all cultures. However, in defending this curricular reform, Marilyn Friedman argued that an a priori insistence on the equal value of all cultures was not commensurable with the fundamental multiculturalist (and, one might add, postmodernist) scepticism about the possibility of any universal standard (1995b: 110). Without such a standard, rather than ascribing equal value, multiculturalism involved an eschewal of the very possibility of making cross-cultural comparisons of value and an openness to a non-judgemental interest in learning about a multiplicity of cultural and literary traditions. For Friedman, this information constituted a means towards the end of 'respectful treatment of other persons', a moral obligation in a pluralist society like the United States (1995b: 110–11).

And yet the postmodernism which had such an influence on the development of American cultural studies and, in turn, multiculturalism, placed a question mark on the very possibility of this kind of cross-cultural, intersubjective comprehension (Knauft, 1994: 128–9). Postmodernism's focus on the impossibility of dissociating knowledge from the context in which it is produced drew analysis inevitably to the location of the speaker, the 'voice' of this knowledge. Even Friedman was concerned that the 'relevant voices' should speak for a variety of viewpoints (Friedman, 1995a: 9).

Energized by this concern with multivocality, multiculturalism moved rapidly beyond care for the inclusion of a variety of different forms of knowledge or cultural standpoints, to attempts to ensure the inclusion of appropriate voices, hopefully those that had been previously oppressed, excluded, disempowered or simply unrecognized. The concern with who speaks sometimes resulted in a focus on the identity of the writers or artists (Amit-Talai, 1996) who should or should not be included in the multiculturalist curricula, that superseded interest in the content of their expressions. It was an attempt that included efforts to ensure the representation of previously excluded 'voices' among the faculty and students of universities, even a competition for 'star minority intellectuals' (Dominguez, 1994). Resistance, in this version of multiculturalism, started off as a largely discursive resistance to the hegemony of a Eurocentric bias (Knauft, 1994) but quickly became focused on representation. Change the scope of categorical representation and somehow you change the structure of power.

At this point it is possible to note a bifurcation both within as well as between multiculturalism and cultural studies. The protagonists in a version of multiculturalism that was, first and foremost, a politics of identity seemed little exercised about the possibility that the status of the representative 'voices' they were seeking to empower was problematic either in terms of the ambiguous, differentiated and contested nature of particular identity categories, or in the complex relationship between culture and classificatory identity. Such discourses of multiculturalism therefore often yielded a 'rhetoric of "identity politics" based on an essentialist notion of a fixed hierarchy of racial, sexual, or gendered oppressions' (Mercer, 1994 quoted in Knuaft, 1996: 261), an essentialism made all the more ironic given its anti-essentialist postmodernist roots.

Criticisms of this fetishization of identity also came from supporters of multiculturalism. But among the latter, anthropologists such as Terence Turner or pedagogues such as Peter McLaren were careful to direct their criticism against a discourse they characterized as but one variant of multiculturalism. This neoliberal colonization of multiculturalism, McLaren argued, was ominous in its treatment of diversity as something to be struggled for, for its own sake (1997: 296), while Turner argued that 'difference multiculturalism' reduces culture 'to a tag for ethnic identity and a license for political and intellectual separatism' (1993: 414). They were both careful, however, to distinguish this kind of essentialist identity politics from the revolutionary potential of the 'critical multiculturalism' they themselves were espousing.

For Turner, this political philosophy offered a critical reconfiguration of both minority and dominant cultures, a form of participatory democracy which facilitates the inclusion of a multitude of voices but without encouraging the reification and separation of groups. What was revolutionary here was apparently the principle that 'that the protection and fostering of the human capacity for culture is a general human right and, as such, a legitimate goal of politically organized society' (1993: 428). What this meant in terms of political mobilization, what made this

principle 'revolutionary', or how it would yield the empowerment of
'relatively disempowered culturally identified groups' (1993: 427) was
not clear. As Knauft noted, concerted analysis of social power was not
highly developed in either Turner's discussion or in much of critical
pedagogy more generally (Knauft, 1996: 267). McLaren, however,
professed a direct concern with political economy, with a revolutionary
struggle for liberation on the basis of race and gender that incorporated
a critique of and struggle against capitalism. He invoked a notion of
cultural hybridity which had been popularized in recent cultural studies
as a means of resisting the essentialisms of identity politics, but also
argued that care must be taken to ensure that such processes of hybrid
identity formation would be coalitional rather than fragmented and
atomized. The political and racial centre would be destabilized, it
appeared, by an embrace of the postmodern borderland with its emphasis
on cultural fusion, experimentation and dialogue. But here again, how
this was actually to happen was far from clear.

There is a basic contradiction in some of the recent scholarly
enthusiasms for diaspora and multiculturalism. The greater the claims
for their revolutionary and empowering possibilities, the more nebulous
and metaphorical these representations of categorical difference become.
But if diaspora and multiculturalism have no palpable social content or
consequence, then it is difficult to see how they can deliver political
empowerment. At the same time, the very obscurity of these scholars'
revolutionary claims abdicates the social actualization of these identities
to others with less compunction. The result is that some of the more
idealistic interpretations of categorical difference can end up in
partnership with, or at least appearing to legitimate, some fairly brutal
instantiations of ethnic exclusivity.

SEPARATING COMMUNITY AND ETHNICITY

Let me backtrack for a moment to reconsider the initial point of departure
with which I started Part I of this book: the invocation of community to
distinguish a collective connection that is not merely or even primarily
instrumental. Thus the members of a workforce are not likely to feel that
they are members of a community if their relationship is based exclusively
on their formal roles within the organization that employs them. If, on
the other hand, they are able to extend this association into a more
extended, voluntary sociability (lunch conversations, socializing after
work, gossip, etc.) then they may well feel that they, or at least some of
them, form a community. Most of our experiences of communality arise
similarly out of the more or less limited interactions afforded by a variety
of circumstantial associations, with our neighbours, the parents of

children at our children's school, or team-mates, fellow students, club members, conference-goers and more.

Noel Dyck (2002) describes the development of this process of consociation among parents whose children are members of a community track and field club in a British Columbian Lower Mainland suburb. The rapid expansion of suburbs in this area has attracted many newcomers to this particular locale, British Columbia or even Canada altogether. The high cost of housing in this region has typically required two-income households, with earners often commuting long distances to and from paid employment. Thus any sense of belonging in such a setting may be frustrated by the impersonality of suburban living. The particular athletics club on which Dyck's account focuses had expanded rapidly in a few years and, like many other such clubs in this area, had attracted a significant number of parents and children from many countries. In addition to the participation of coaches, athletes and officials, track and field sports require a substantial contribution of parental assistance in order to stage weekend competitions hosted by successive local clubs:

> What parents of athletes have in common is that they are parents who share a common concern with child rearing and also at least some minimal experience with the routines of club athletic involvement which engage their children and them. Being a parent who is situationally recognized as being involved in children's athletics makes one eligible to claim or to be accorded a formal or categorical identity of 'track parent'. Yet beyond this relatively impersonal form of identification lies the possibility of what Sansom identifies as consociate identity which is constructed 'with reference to a person's history of co-participation with others in happenings'(1980: 139). Consociate relationships emerge when individuals become capable of putting names to known faces and telling stories about mutually shared experiences in the world of track and field. (Dyck, 2002: 116)

Usually some of the relationships developed in one circumstance of consociation can extend into other spheres and even become divorced entirely from the original involvement in which it was formed. Thus, for example, it is possible that two parents of children in this Lower Mainland athletics club, in time could develop a friendship that was independent of their involvement in this association. In such a development, the relationship shifts from being principally constituted through consociate membership in a collectivity to a more dyadic link within a personal network. But very often, however satisfying and important these consociate relationships may be, they remain contingent upon continued involvement in the association or activity in which they were formed.

These are forms of community which are conceptualized first and foremost by reference to what is held in common by members rather than in terms of oppositional categories between insiders and outsiders. That is to say, such consociation and the identities deriving from it are built up through the shared experiences of participation in particular associations and events. What matters most, therefore, is what 'we' have shared, not the boundary dividing 'us' from 'them'. In such circumstances, the identity and sense of community arises in the course of, and is conceptualized in terms of particular forms of social interaction. To represent these kinds of social relationships in terms of the social boundaries that define ascribed collective identities is fundamentally to confuse two very different logics of collective identification.

Ascribed categorical identities, whether of religion, race, nation, ethnicity or gender, are conceptualized as anterior to the actual social relationships and activities that may be attributed to them. The category, in other words, trumps the relationship. In sharp distinction to the sociality of the British Columbian athletics club, this kind of ascribed link can be claimed between people who have never known each other and perhaps never will, since consociation is not a prior condition for claiming this identity. Because these identities do not necessarily arise through or are defined in terms of substantive relationships, they rely heavily on symbolic markers. Hence, as Fredrik Barth (1969) observed, the boundary between insiders and outsiders or 'them' and 'us' is often more important than the content which the boundary encloses, and hence, as Benedict Anderson (1991/1983) noted, communion as well as exclusion are both imagined vis-à-vis strangers.

In practice, however, these kinds of ascribed identities often piggy-back on and draw their affective charge from actual relationships of intimacy. Thus, when people talk about being Jamaican or Nevisian, they often have in mind intimate relationships with family and friends (Olwig, 2002). On the other hand, the more far flung the efforts at mobilization, that is, the more distanced from existing intimacies, the more likely they will be dependent on the invocation of categorical oppositions and primordialized notions of moral obligation. And the more likely it will be that the circumstances of mobilization will involve some element of force or compulsion. That is why mass nationalist mobilizations often require situations of violent conflict to be realized and cannot hold indefinitely beyond them. But the brutality of these mobilizations is not only levelled against those excluded. To create unity among people who have little of social substance in common requires an exertion of force against those included as well as those excluded. Hence ethnic mobilization often features internecine fighting and factionalization, and the exertion of informal or organizational pressures to squash open expressions of intra-ethnic dissension. The old canard that ethnic loyalties require an abstention from expressing criticism of ethnic or religious compeers or 'leaders' to outsiders combines both these forms of boundary marking and silencing. For even while it emphasizes the boundary between insiders and outsiders, the promulgaters of this version of ethnic loyalty are usually much more concerned with silencing internal opposition to their views or demands.

It is not altogether difficult to understand why cultural theorists who have characterized contemporary life in terms of movement and fluidity, of interconnection and border-crossing, should be so interested in this form of collective identification. Because the premise of this form of collective identity is not actual consociation, in principle, it appears to be quite portable. It can be moved from locality to locality, take shape in different forms of activities and claim adherence across the divides of region, class, gender, citizenship. It can be decontextualized and recontextualized across a gamut of social situations.

But are all national and ethnic distinctions equally portable? In exploring the creation of transnational family networks among Caribbean emigrants, Karen Fog Olwig notes the continuing grounding of such networks in the island of origin through continued collective rights and investments in territorial loci such as family land or the family house (Olwig, 1997: 24). However, migrants can sometimes lose their rights in these sites as Olwig relates in the story of Edwin who had emigrated from Nevis to Great Britain:

I interviewed Edwin – not very long after the death of his parents and the resultant inheritance of the family home, which they had owned and occupied, by a sister who had remained in the home with them and cared for them. With the sister as the sole owner of the house, Edwin had, in essence, lost the firm anchoring point to which he had returned during his visits on the island. This was particularly the case, because the siblings, as noted, could not agree on how to divide the land. Edwin explained that his father had offered the entire piece of land to him because he was the eldest son, but that he had turned down the offer. He had done this because he felt that all the siblings had helped the parents by sending remittances or staying behind and caring for them, and everybody therefore ought to have a share in the land. Now he was beginning to regret this decision, being left with no land at all, as the siblings differed about how to divide it. The feeling of alienation and discrimination which Edwin evoked to characterize his life in British society, and the unfriendly welcome which he described receiving on Nevis as a British returnee, thus was heighted by the fact that he had lost the firm source of identification and belonging which his parents, their home and land, and the wider family network had constituted for him. (Olwig, 2002: 139–40)

Whether Edwin will eventually invest in another property as a physical locus in Nevis as some other Nevisian emigrants have done, or whether he loses his interest in Nevis as has occurred for some second- and third-generation 'Nevisian' emigrants in New Haven, Connecticut (Olwig, 1997: 32), or whether Edwin will find some other point of collective identification altogether – Olwig notes that he has recently begun to express an interest in religion and to study with Jehovah's Witnesses (Olwig, 2002: 140) – is a chapter in this narrative that remains to be written. But it is clear that this type of transnational connection is much closer to the form of consociation of the British Columbian athletics club than to some of the de-territorialized ascriptions that have often been enlisted under the term of diaspora. It arises through and continues to be socially and meaningfully contextualized in very particular relationships, activities and physical locations.

There has been an unfortunate tendency to merge different dialectics of mobility and collective identification. Thus, as I argued above, a plethora of immigrant groups have now been recuperated by analysts as diasporas. But many transmigrant identities, as Edwin's story indicates, are anchored in and hence are dependent on connections to very specific places and networks of relationships. Remove those connections and it is doubtful that the identification will continue to be meaningful or claimed. This is very different from identities such as Jewish, Black, Armenian, etc., that do not rely on specific networks or even specific places to be claimed. The eponymous 'homelands' with which they are identified are usually a very different order of cultural siting than the family home through which Edwin charted his Nevisian identity. Will the possibilities of imagination unleashed by twenty-first century media allow for some of the transmigrant identities to be re-imagined in diasporic terms? Perhaps. But the increasing importance of 'Black' identity that has been reported for second-generation youths of Caribbean or African origins in London (Alexander, 1996) or Amsterdam (Sansone, 1995) suggests that their experience of racial or ethnic divides is more likely to be signified in quite different categories than the transmigrant identities claimed by their parents.

The presumption within recent literature on migration that transmigrant collectivities will continue to be maintained and reproduced over generations, elides the extraordinary difficulties of sustaining connections that arise within very particular social contexts once these circumstances no longer pertain. It's rather as if the parents of the British Columbia athletics club that Noel Dyck described, continued to gather together even when their children were no longer involved in the club. Some parents may continue to meet, perhaps even an occasional reunion may be held, but in most cases the link and identification will attenuate or fall away altogether, transformed into personal memories rather than consociate experiences. In other words, it is very difficult to maintain a sense of community and identity that arises through consociation when the basis of that consociation is removed. If we treat communities as if they were indefinitely portable and decontextualizable, as if all we need is an email address and a telephone and communality can be sustained indefinitely by people now participating in very different places, activities and networks, then we may end up promoting as cavalier an attitude to the dislocations of movement as Norman Tebbitt's infamous 1980s admonition to 'just get on your bike'. The contemporary capitalist ethos of flexibility abstracts work roles from their broader social contexts, expecting workers to change jobs, homes and regions as the occupational market place dictates. Recent scholarly presumptions of intergenerational transnationality sometimes unintentionally seem to include a similar abstraction of community.

On the other hand, some of the recent celebrations of diaspora have interpreted this very capacity for decontextualization as emancipatory. Summoning adjectives of fluidity, hybridity, postnational, magical interconnectedness, the imagination of de-territorialized 'communities of sentiment' (Appadurai, 1996: 8) is represented as a new 'staging ground for action' (Appadurai, 1996: 7), a diaspora space 'where difference and commonality are figured in non-reductive relationality' (Brah, 1996: 248), 'nontotalizing globalization from below' (Clifford, 1994: 325). But this is to confuse de-territorialization with cosmopolitanism. If the paroxysms of various recent and older religious fundamentalisms should have taught us anything, it is that parochialism is as exportable as the openness to other cultures that Ulf Hannerz identified as the hallmark of true cosmopolitanism. The recent intellectual applause for diaspora is beginning to resemble an earlier scholarly hope that postcolonial nationalisms would deliver a more progressive transcendent alternative to the tribal rivalries fostered by colonial regimes. Nationalism was supposed to resolve the legacy of colonialism, and diaspora is now supposed to resolve the inequalities engendered by globalized capitalism. One can see why the notion that multitudes scattered over numerous political and territorial jurisdictions, should, through the medium of new medias, come to feel a sense of communion with each other, might seem potentially progressive. But the history of nationalism has already indicated that not all notions of brother- and sisterhood are benign. When an ethnic or religious identity is imagined as exerting a primordial moral claim on millions of people that supersedes the demands and alliances of their particular histories, localities, personalities, friendships and consociations, then we had best hope that this 'community' remains restricted to the realms of imagination. For the prospect of massively successful group 'action' in these terms should profoundly alarm us.

AN ETHNOGRAPHIC VIEW OF COMMUNITY AND BELONGING

Over the last three decades, cultural analysts have increasingly resorted to this form of proclaimed categorical, fictive communality as the theoretical model for all forms of community. But some of the most crucial forms of fellowship, of belonging, are barely marked by explicit symbolic icons. They arise when students in a Montreal high school extol the sense of 'family' they came to feel with each other. They are formed when parents of community athletes get to know each other over the course of rainy mornings spent together while their children compete, of long bus trips to competition fields, of endless waits together for competition to start. Or perhaps they develop through even more limited familiarities:

The regular residents of ordinary urban neighourhoods get to know each other by sight. They meet shopping, standing at the bus stop or walking in the street, and over time they learn the public habits and timetables of people they do not know by name and probably never visit where they live. Recognizing and being recognized by others create a sense of belonging in inner-city areas just as much as they do in a rural village although the potential for turning 'traffic relations' into action sets or sources of support may be more crucial to survival in town. (Wallman, 1998: 184)

These forms of fellowship and belonging are intrinsically contextual and therefore often ephemeral. As the secondary V students of Royal Haven (see Chapter 2) realized, leave the school, the athletics club, move out of the neighbourhood and the sense of collective connection is not likely to be sustained.

But some of the personal links that arise through these experiences carry on. Most people are able to transform some of these encounters into more dyadic personal relationships that can be exported into different contexts. Our personal networks are often cumulatively developed over the course of multiple opportunities for consociation, in the process transforming collective experiences into personal intimacies. It is this process that probably most ensures some sense of personal continuity in circumstances of spatial and social mobility, even though it is the least institutionalized and hence structurally the least enduring. Indeed one has to wonder whether what anthropologists have identified as transnational fields or communities are not more often instances of personal networks of family and friendship. Are people forming transnational communities or transnational personal networks?

These are simple observations. Pick up almost any reasonably competent ethnography and you are likely to find that it is replete with accounts of these processes of consociation, of personal amities, of people making places, institutions and associations, at least for a time, into their own. As ethnographers, anthropologists have been remarkably attentive to charting the substance and complications of social connections. It is therefore all the more puzzling to watch them join in a theorization of communality that is so devoid and dismissive of social content.

NOTES TO PART I

1. This project was made possible by grants from the Concordia University General Research Fund as well as the Social Sciences and Humanities Research Council of Canada.
2. In order to preserve the confidentiality of the people who participated in this research project as in all the other research projects refereed to in this chapter, aliases have been used in place of the actual names.
3. This study was made possible by a grant from the Quebec Ministry of Education.
4. This study was made possible by grants from the Concordia University General Research Fund and the Social Sciences and Humanities Research Council of Canada.
5. In order to preserve the confidentiality of people who assisted me in this project, I have used aliases.
6. See Panossian (1998) for an account of the formation of these parties and the differences between them.

REFERENCES TO PART I

Abu-Laban, Yasmeen and Daiva Stasiulis (1992) 'Ethnic Pluralism under Siege: Popular and Partisan Opposition to Multiculturalism', *Canadian Public Policy* 18(4): 365–86.

Abu-Lughod, Lila (1991) 'Writing against Culture', in *Recapturing Anthropology: Working in the Present*, Richard G. Fox (ed.). Sante Fe, NM: School of American Research Press.

Alba, Richard D. (1981) 'The Twilight of Ethnicity among American Catholics of European Ancestry', *Annals of the American Academy of Political and Social Sciences* 454: 86–97.

Alexander, Claire (1996) *The Art of Being Black: The Creation of Black British Youth Identities*. Oxford: Clarendon Press.

Amit, Vered (2000) 'Introduction: Constructing the Field', in *Constructing the Field: Ethnographic Fieldwork in the Contemporary World*, Vered Amit (ed.). London and New York: Routledge.

Amit Talai, Vered (1989) *Armenians in London: The Management of Social Boundaries*. Manchester: Manchester University Press.

—— (1996) 'Anthropology, Multiculturalism and the Concept of Culture', *Folk* 38: 125–33.

—— (1998) 'Risky Hiatuses and the Limits of Social Imagination: Expatriacy in the Cayman Islands', in *Migrants of Identity: Perceptions of Home in a World of Movement*, Nigel Rapport and Andrew Dawson (eds). Oxford: Berg.

Anderson, Benedict (1991/1983) *Imagined Communities*. London and New York: Verso.

Appadurai, Arjun (1990) 'Disjuncture and Difference in the Global Cultural Economy', in *Global Culture: Nationalism, Globalization and Modernity*, Mike Featherstone (ed.). London, Newbury Park and New Delhi: Sage Publications.

—— (1996) *Modernity at Large: Cultural Dimensions of Globalization*. Minneapolis and London: University of Minnesota Press.

Banks, Marcus (1996) *Ethnicity: Anthropological Constructions*. London and New York: Routledge.

Barth, Fredrik (1969) 'Introduction', to F. Barth (ed.) *Ethnic Groups and Boundaries*, pp. 9–38. London: Allen & Unwin.

—— (1994) 'Enduring and Emerging Issues in the Analysis of Ethnicity', in *The Anthropology of Ethnicity: Beyond 'Ethnic Groups and Boundaries'*, Hans Vermeulen and Cora Grovers (eds). Amsterdam: Het Spinhuis Publishers.

Basch, Linda, Nina Glick Schiller and Cristina Szanton Blanc (1994) *Nations Unbound: Transnational Projects, Postcolonial Predicaments and Deterritorialized Nation-States*. Basel: Gordon & Breach Publishers.

Bauman, Gerd (1996) *Contesting Culture: Discourses of Identity in Multi-ethnic London*. Cambridge: Cambridge University Press.

Brah, Avtar (1996) *Cartographies of Diaspora: Contesting Identities*. London and New York: Routledge.

Carrier, James G. (1998) 'Introduction', to *Virtualism: A New Political Economy*, James G. Carrier and Daniel Miller (eds). Oxford and New York: Berg.

Chorney, Harold (1990) *City of Dreams: Social Theory and the Urban Experience*. Scarborough, ON: Nelson Canada.

Clifford, James (1992) 'Traveling Cultures', in *Cultural Studies*, Lawrence Grossberg, Cary Nelson and Paula A. Treichler (eds). New York and London: Routledge.

—— (1994) 'Disaporas', *Cultural Anthropology* 9(3): 302–38.

Clifford, James and George Marcus (eds) (1986) *Writing Culture: The Poetics and Politics of Ethnography*. Berkeley and London: University of California Press.

Cohen, Abner (1969) *Custom and Politics in Urban Africa*. London: Routledge & Kegan Paul.

—— (1974) 'Introduction: The Lesson of Ethnicity', in *Urban Ethnicity*, Abner Cohen (ed.), pp. ix–xxiv. London: Tavistock Publications.

—— (1981) *The Politics of Elite Culture: Explorations in the Dramaturgy of Power in a Modern African Society*. Berkeley: University of California Press.

Cohen, Anthony P. (1982) 'Belonging: The Experience of Culture', in *Belonging: Identity and Social Organisation in British Rural Cultures*, Anthony P. Cohen (ed.). Manchester: Manchester University Press.

—— (1985) *The Symbolic Construction of Community*. London and New York: Tavistock Publications.

—— (1996) 'Personal Nationalism: A Scottish View of Some Rites, Rights and Wrongs', *American Ethnologist* 23(4): 802–15.

—— (2000) 'Epilogue', in *Realizing Community: Concepts, Social Relationships and Sentiments*, Vered Amit (ed.). London and New York: Routledge.

Cohen, Phil (1996) 'Homing Devices', in *Resituating Identities: The Politics of Race, Ethnicity and Culture*, Vered Amit-Talai and Caroline Knowles (eds). Peterborough, ON: Broadview Press.

Dominguez, Virginia R. (1994) 'A Taste for "the Other": Intellectual Complicity in Racializing Practices', *Current Anthropology* 35(4): 333–48.

Dyck, Noel (2002) '"Have you been to Hayward Field?" Children's Sport and the Construction of Community in Suburban Canada', in *Realising Community: Concepts, Social Relationships and Sentiments*, Vered Amit (ed.). London and New York: Routledge.

Epstein, A.L. (1958) *Politics in an Urban African Community*. Manchester: Manchester University Press.

—— (1978) *Ethos and Identity: Three Studies in Ethnicity*. London: Tavistock Publishing.

Fortier, Anne-Marie (1998) 'The Politics of "Italians Abroad": Nation, Diaspora and New Geographies of Identity', *Diaspora* 7(2): 197–224.

Friedman, Marilyn (1995a) 'Codes, Canons, Correctness and Feminism', in *Political Correctness, For and Against*, by Marilyn Friedman and Jan Narveson. London and Boston: Rowman & Littlefield.

—— (1995b) 'Response', in *Political Correctness, For and Against*, by Marilyn Friedman and Jan Narveson. London and Boston: Rowman & Littlefield.

Gans, Herbert J. (1979) 'Symbolic Ethnicity: The Future of Ethnic Groups and Cultures in America', *Ethnic and Racial Studies* 2: 1–20.

Geertz, Clifford (1975) *The Interpretation of Cultures*. London: Hutchinson.

Gilroy, Paul (1993) *The Black Atlantic: Modernity and Double Consciousness*. Cambridge, MA: Harvard University Press.

Glazer, Nathan and Daniel P. Moynihan (1963) *Beyond the Melting Pot*. Cambridge, MA: MIT and Harvard University Press.

—— (1975) *Ethnicity: Theory and Experience*. Cambridge, MA: Harvard University Press.

Goodenough, Ward H. (1971) *Culture, Language and Society: A McCaleb Module in Anthropology*. Reading, MA: Addison-Wesley Publications.

—— (1976) 'Multiculturalism as the Normal Human Experience', *Anthropology and Education Quarterly* 7(4): 4–6.

Guarnizo, Luis Eduardo (1997) 'The Emergence of a Transnational Social Formation and the Mirage of Return Migration among Dominican Transmigrants', *Identities* 4(2): 281–322.

Guarnizo, Luis Eduardo and Michael Peter Smith (1998) 'The Locations of Transnationalism', in *Transnationalism from Below*, Michael Peter Smith and Luis Eduardo Guarnizo (eds). New Brunswick, NJ and London: Transaction Publishers.

Gupta, Akhil and James Ferguson (1997a) 'Discipline and Practice: "The Field" as Site, Method and Location in Anthropology', in *Anthropological Locations: Boundaries and Grounds of a Field Science*, Akhil Gupta and James Ferguson (eds). Berkeley, Los Angeles and London: University of California Press.

—— (1997b) 'Beyond "Culture": Space, Identity and the Politics of Difference', in *Culture, Power, Place: Explorations in Critical Anthropology*, Akhil Gupta and James Ferguson (eds). Durham, NC and London: Duke University Press.

—— (1997c) 'Culture, Power, Place: Ethnography at the end of an Era', in *Culture, Power, Place: Explorations in Critical Anthropology*, Akhil Gupta and James Ferguson (eds). Durham, NC and London: Duke University Press.

Hall, Stuart (2000) 'Old and New Identities: Old and New Ethnicities', in *Theories of Race and Racism: A Reader*, Les Back and John Solomos (eds). London and New York: Routledge.

Hannerz, Ulf (1969) *Soulside*. New York: Columbia University Press.

—— (1980) *Exploring the City: Inquiries Toward an Urban Anthropology*. New York: Columbia University Press.

—— (1992) *Cultural Complexity: Studies in the Social Organization of Meaning*. New York: Columbia University Press.

—— (1996) *Transnational Connections: Culture, People, Places*. London and New York: Routledge.

Higham, John (1978) 'Introduction: The Forms of Ethnic Leadership', in *Ethnic Leadership in America*, John Higham (ed.). Baltimore and London: Johns Hopkins University Press.

Hillery, C.A. (1955) 'Definitions of Community: Areas of Agreement', *Rural Sociology* 20: 86–118.

Jackson, John D. (1988/1975) *Community and Conflict: A Study of French–English Relations in Ontario*. Toronto: Canadian Scholars' Press.

Keesing, Roger (1975) *Kin Groups and Social Structure*. New York: Holt, Rinehart & Winston.

—— (1994) 'Theories of Culture Revisited', in *Assessing Cultural Anthropology*, Robert Borofsky (ed.). New York: McGraw-Hill.

Keyes, Charles F. (ed.) (1979) *Ethnic Adaptation and Identity: The Karen on the Thai Frontier with Burma*. Philadelphia, PA: Institute for the Study of Human Issues.

Knauft, Bruce (1994) 'Pushing Anthropology Past the Posts: Critical notes on Cultural Anthropology and Cultural Studies as Influenced by Postmodernism and Existentialism', *Critique of Anthropology* 14(2): 117–52.

—— (1996) *Genealogies for the Present in Cultural Anthropology*. New York and London: Routledge.

Lewis, Oscar (1965) 'Further Observations on the Folk–Urban Continuum and Urbanization with Special Reference to Mexico City', in *The Study of Urbanization*, Philip M. Hauser and Leo F. Schnore (eds). New York: John Wiley & Sons.

—— (1966) *La Vida*. New York: Random House.

Louie, Andrea (2000) 'Reterritorializing Transnationalism: Chinese Americans and the Chinese Motherland', *American Ethnologist*, 27(3): 645–69.

McLaren, Peter (1997) *Revolutionary Multiculturalism: Pedagogies of Dissent for the New Millennium*. Boulder, CO and Oxford: Westview Press.

Miller, Daniel and Don Slater (2000) *The Internet: An Ethnographic Approach*. Oxford and New York: Berg.

Mitchell, J. Clyde (1956) *The Kalela Dance*. Rhodes-Livingstone Papers, no. 27. Manchester: Manchester University Press.

—— (1970) 'Tribe and Social Change in South Central Africa: A Situational Approach', *Journal of Asian and African Studies* 5: 83–101.

Modood, Tariq (1997) 'Introduction: The Politics of Multiculturalism in the New Europe', in *The Politics of Multiculturalism in the New Europe*, Tariq Modood and Pnina Werbner (eds). London and New York: Zed Books.

Narveson, Jan (1995) 'Politics, Ethics and Political Correctness', in *Political Correctness, For and Against*, by Marilyn Friedman & Jan Narveson. London and Boston: Rowman & Littlefield.

Olwig, Karen Fog (1997) 'Cultural Sites: Sustaining a Home in a Deterritorialized World', in *Siting Culture: The Shifting Anthropological Object*, Karen Fog Olwig and Kirsten Hastrup (eds). London and New York: Routledge.

—— (2002) 'The Ethnographic Field Revisited: Towards a Study of Common and Not so Common Fields of Belonging', in *Realising Community: Concepts, Social Relationships and Sentiments*, Vered Amit (ed.). London and New York: Routledge.

Olwig, Karen Fog and Kirsten Hastrup (1997) (eds) *Siting Culture: The Shifting Anthropological Object*. London and New York: Routledge.

Ong, Aihwa (1999) *Flexible Citizenship: The Cultural Logics of Transnationality*. Durham, NC and London: Duke University Press.

Panossian, Razmik (1998) 'Between Ambivalence and Intrusion: Politics and Identity in Armenia–Diaspora Relations', *Diaspora* 7(2): 149–96.

Park, Robert E. (1925) 'The City: Suggestions for the Investigation of Human Behavior', in *The City*, R.E. Park, W. Burgess and R.D. McKenzie. Chicago: University of Chicago Press.

Portes, Alejandro and Ramón Grosfoguel (1994) 'Caribbean Diasporas: Migration and Ethnic Communities', *The Annals of the American Academy of Political and Social Science* 533: 48–59.

Rosaldo, Renato (1989) *Culture and Truth: The Remaking of Social Analysis*. Boston, MA: Beacon Press.

Sanjek, Roger (1994) 'The Enduring Inequalities of Race', in Steven Gregory and Roger Sanjek (eds) *Race*. New Brunswick, NJ: Rutgers University.

Sansone, Livio (1995) 'The Making of a Black Youth Culture: Lower-class Young Men of Surinamese Origin in Amsterdam', in *Youth Cultures: A Cross-cultural Perspective*, Vered Amit and Helena Wulff (eds). London and New York: Routledge.

Sassen, Saskia (1994) *Cities in a World Economy*. Thousand Oaks, London, New Delhi: Pine Forge Press.

—— (1996) 'Whose City Is It? Globalization and the Formation of New Claims', *Public Culture* 8(2): 205–23.

Scheper-Hughes, Nancy (1995) 'Objectivity and Militancy: A Debate, 2. The Primacy of the Ethical: Propositions for a Militant Anthropology', *Current Anthropology* 36(2): 409–20.

Steinberg, Stephen (1981) *The Ethnic Myth: Race, Ethnicity and Class in America*. Boston, MA: Beacon.

Suttles, Gerald D. (1968) *The Social Order of the Slum*. Chicago: University of Chicago Press.

Talai, Vered (1986) 'Social Boundaries Within and Between Ethnic Groups: Armenians in London', *Man* 21: 251–70.

Taylor, Charles (1992) *Multiculturalism and the Politics of Recognition*, ed. and with an Introduction by Amy Gutman. Princeton, NJ: Princeton University Press.

Tölölian, Khachig (1991) 'The Nation State and its Others: In Lieu of a Preface', *Diaspora* 1(1): 3–7.

Turner, Terence (1993) 'Anthropology and Multiculturalism: What is Anthropology that Multiculturalists Should Be Mindful of It?', *Cultural Anthropology* 8(4): 411–29.

Verdery, Katherine (1994) 'Ethnicity, Nationalism, and State Making: *Ethnic Groups and Boundaries*: Past and Future', in *The Anthropology of Ethnicity: Beyond 'Ethnic Groups and Boundaries'*, Hans Vermeulen and Cora Grovers (eds). Amsterdam: Het Spinhuis.

Wallman, Sandra (1978) 'The Boundaries of Race: Processes of Ethnicity in England', *Man* 13(2): 200–17.

—— (1982) 'Epilogue' and 'Conclusion', to *Living in South London: Perspectives on Battersea 1871–1981*, Sandra Wallman and associates. Aldershot, Hants: Gower.

—— (1984) *Eight London Households*. London and New York: Tavistock Publications.

—— (1998) 'New Identities and the Local Factor – or When is Home in Town a Good Move?', in *Migrants of Identity: Perceptions of Home in a World of Movement*, Nigel Rapport and Andrew Dawson (eds). Oxford: Berg.

Wallman, Sandra and associates (1982) *Living in South London: Perspectives on Battersea 1871–1981*. Aldershot, Hants: Gower Publishing Company Limited.

Werbner, Pnina (1997) 'Essentialising Essentialism, Essentialising Silence: Ambivalence and Multiplicity in the Constructions of Racism and Ethnicity', in *Debating Cultural Hybridity: Multi-Cultural Identities and the Politics of Anti-Racism*, Pnina Werbner and Tariq Modood (eds). London and New Jersey: Zed Books.

—— (1998) 'Diasporic Political Imaginaries: A Sphere of Freedom or a Sphere of Illusions?', *Communal/Plural* 6(1): 11–21.

Williams, Brackette F. (1989) 'A Class Act. Anthropology and the Race to Nation across Ethnic Terrain', *Annual Review of Anthropology* 18: 401–44.

Williams, Melvin D. (1974) *Community in a Black Pentecostal Church: An Anthropological Study*. Prospect Heights, IL: Waveland Press.

Wilson, Thomas M. and Hastings Donnan (1998) 'Nation, State and Identity at International Borders', in *Border Identities: Nation and State at International Frontiers*, Thomas M. Wilson and Hastings Donnan (eds). Cambridge: Cambridge University Press.

Wirth, Louis (1938) 'Urbanism as a Way of Life', *American Journal of Sociology* 44: 1–24.

Yon, Daniel (1995) 'Identity and Differences in the Caribbean Diaspora: Case Study from Metropolitan Toronto', in *The Reordering of Culture: Latin America, The Caribbean and Canada in the Hood*, Alvina Ruprecht and Cecilia Taiana (eds). Ottawa: Carleton University Press.

Young, Michael and Peter Willmott (1962/1957) *Family and Kinship in East London*. Harmondsworth: Penguin Books.

Part II

THE TRUTH OF MOVEMENT, THE TRUTH AS MOVEMENT: POST-CULTURAL ANTHROPOLOGY AND NARRATIONAL IDENTITY

Nigel Rapport

CONTENTS

PREAMBLE

An incident at random: a review by John Gray in the *Times Literary Supplement* of a new book on the notion of trust (Adam Seligman, *The Problem of Trust*, 1997) ponders the possibility of 'a dialectical turn in the ethical life of modern individuality' wherein people no longer believe they are responsible to themselves as individuals (1998: 6). Personal responsibility as a public ideology, Gray expounds (*après* Seligman), grew over the centuries in the West as traditional social roles became less constraining and the authority of social groups diminished. But now, it seems (somewhat ironically), even the authority of an inner conscience is being challenged and further emancipation sought: a freedom from fixed internalized norms of the self; freedom from abiding selfhood. And Gray concludes:

Is Seligman also right that as inner, moral sanctions on personal conduct lose legitimacy, the external forces that maintained social order in a more distant past are making a comeback? Certainly, many people today classify themselves and others – as they did in traditional societies – primarily as members of social groups rather than as individual subjects. It does not matter much whether the criteria of group membership refer to lifestyle, religious belief, economic status, or ethnic lineages. What matters is that the predominant relationship between human beings in late modern societies is often not that of individuals who trust (or fail to trust) one another. ... But if we are entering a world without individual subjects who can trust or mistrust one another, it may not be a world of playful freely floating selves like that dreamt of in postmodernist utopias. Instead it could turn out to be a world of tribes and gangs, where membership is not chosen but fated, and the dominant mode of interaction is not trust among individuals but the making of alliances among groups.

I intend this essay as a fantasia upon Seligman's gloomy predictions and Gray's dystopian images: upon the dangers of individuals eschewing notions of personal responsibilities, and upon the possible alternatives to a world of ascribed membership to 'tribes and gangs', of 'unreflective, herd solidarity', where individuals eschew perspective on themselves and others first-and-foremost as individuals. The keywords of the essay are Freedom, Irony, Identity, Science, Human Rights, Law, Morality, Community, Movement and Globalism.

Woven around these tropes is an attempt to image a world where identity is constructed by the individual, and affirmed by others on an individual rather than a collectivist or communitarian basis. Moving between philosophical conceptions of the person, theoretical constructions of the civil polity and empirical description of the Salman Rushdie affair and its aftermath, the essay represents a quest for 'post-cultural' identity – as both anthropological methodology and morality:

We need an anthropology which does not make a fetish of culture ... . Our predicament is – to work out the social options of our affluent and disenchanted condition. We have no choice about this. (Gellner, 1995b: 26)

4 INTRODUCTION: A THEORY OF MOVEMENT

In his discussion on the best possible relationship between science and non-science (in which he included religion and the arts), Friedrich Nietzsche decided on the image of human beings having 'a double brain': a brain with two chambers lying next to one another, as it were, separable and self-contained, and experiencing different things without confusion (1994: 154). An experience of both science and non-science was necessary for human health, Nietzsche deemed, but at the same time the two had to be kept apart. Non-science inspired and was the source of human strength, while science was the source of truth, direction and regulation; while non-science gave rise to those illusions, errors, fantasies and passions by which human life was 'heated', scientific knowledge served to protect from the pernicious consequences of 'overheating'. If not for non-science, scientific truths would eventually seem commonplace and everyday, and lose their charm; if not for science and the continuing search for truth, the joys of non-science would cause 'higher culture' to 'relapse into barbarism' (1994: 154).

At first blush, Nietzsche's language and his conclusions seem distinctly 'non-anthropological', at least as disciplinary dispensations commonly delineate that term today. However, Ernest Gellner, shortly before he died, came to promote strikingly similar propositions. A culture, Gellner suggested, is a collectivity united in a belief: '[m]ore particularly, a collectivity united in a false belief is a culture' (1995a: 6). For what is particular to a culture is its errors, and commitment to these comes to define a community as a badge of loyalty and belonging:

Assent to an absurdity identifies an intellectual *rite de passage*, a gateway to the community defined by that commitment to that conviction. (1995a: 6)

A cultural community becomes a collectivity holding faith with error.

Truth, meanwhile, that which is disinterred by science, Gellner describes as available to all and valid for all. Science represents a form of knowledge, a cognitive style and an understanding of nature which reaches beyond any one culture so as to transform totally the terms of reference in which human societies operate. Science offers propositions and claims which can be translated, without loss of efficacy, into any sociocultural milieu, and whose application, as technology, provides a means universally of transforming the human condition.

However, science alone is also insufficient. Gellner calls it 'too thin, too abstract, too far removed from the earthy and the concrete' to support most people in a crisis (1995b: 7); it may correctly give on to objective reality but it does not 'warm the heart, or help a man sustain a tragedy, or behave with dignity when circumstances become too much for him' (1995b: 8). In Weberian terms, the triumph of rationality enables a more efficient satisfaction of human wants, but it also drains social life of the mystification necessary to afford efficiency any meaning beyond itself. While science has changed the traditional habit of employing religious doctrine to underwrite our values, then, it can offer little in its place; continually changing itself, scientific knowledge of the world can be expected to furnish few foundations by which rigid moral prescriptions might be legitimated (cf. Geertz, 1957). This spells moral crisis.

What is needed, Gellner concludes, is a healthy admixture or amalgam of scientific order and truth on the one hand and cultural, moral community and faith on the other. Gellner's (half-serious) image is of a 'constitutional religion' (1993: 91), run on a similar basis to a constitutional monarchy, which underwrites community, which retains the ritual and symbolism of an earlier non-scientific age, but is now deprived of real power in its relationship to social life; this runs instead along instrumental and profane lines. Religious institutions may mirror the past only, not the present situation of decision-making, but the non-scientific idiom continues to afford social legitimation, aestheticism and comfort in ways which the realities of scientific knowledge do not.

I would describe Gellner's notion of a constitutional religion as only half-serious because I believe he felt humankind could do better. It could better approach the goal of securing agreement on principles of justice which allowed for the peaceful coexistence in one liberal polity of persons with divergent even incommensurable conceptions of world-view and 'the good life'.[1] Gellner, moreover, felt that anthropology had a significant role to play in the process. For a start, anthropology could seek an answer as to why scientific knowledge was so successful with regard to the domains of nature and technology but not to others, such as culture and morality. Science proved that knowledge beyond culture was possible; indeed, Gellner referred to this as '*the* fact of our lives' (1993: 54), and the starting point of any adequate anthropological appreciation of our shared, global, human condition today:

Our world is indeed a plural one, but it is based on the uniqueness of truth, on the astonishing technological power of one particular cognitive style, namely science and its application. (1995b: 3)

But if knowledge was global in this way, then why not morality? If '[v]alid knowledge ignores and does not engender frontiers' (1995a: 6), then may not anthropology work towards the formulation of a morality similarly beyond community and the particularities of culture? While accepting that a cultural or symbolic domain alongside the technical one of science may continue to be necessary for human comfort, could not this domain nevertheless assume a global provenance and ultimately be subject to reason? Certainly, Gellner thought this *the* necessary anthropological project, however difficult in practice such moral arrangements might be to set up.

The liberal societies of the West Gellner called 'well-matured political systems'. Here – echoes of 'constitutional religion' – 'absolutist symbols, shorn of too much power, coexist amicably with pragmatic, effective powers shorn of too much symbolic potency' (1995b: 9). However, more needed to be done and better could be accrued; human liberty deserved surer foundations than the purely technological and commercial workings of the '"McWorld" – McDonalds, Macintosh computers and MTV music' (Barber, 1996: 140).[2] In the contemporary West, science sat alongside morality (usually in the form of religion or relativism) courtesy of an uneasy relationship of ambiguity or avoidance. A balance was achieved between the moral 'thinness' of science on the one hand and the moral rigidity of religion and the tolerance of relativism on the other hand by no one having to declare their loyalties clearly or finally (to themselves or to others); a person could vacillate between science and non-science according to circumstance without being pressured into selecting one option over the other. However, the relationship was also unstable. Certainly, if the model was to be copied elsewhere on the globe (such as the post-Communist bloc), and if it was itself to be protected from adverse developments elsewhere on the globe (such as the reactionary fundamentalisms of the Middle East), then it needed clarifying and stiffening. A global morality alongside a global science, to repeat, might be expected to share a certain rationality and hence to be mutually supportive, even if remaining different in cognitive style ...

Gellner seemed to like ending paragraphs with three-dot ellipses ... which suggested at the same time a following-on and a lack of ending: flow and movement. I would read into them a movement into the future, when anthropology starts to tackle the sociocultural issues of a world of movement (a flow of people, goods, behavioural forms and ideas around the globe), by way of a consideration of the fundamental place of movement in cognition and the construction of identity, and so elucidate a set of propositions which afford a movement between scientific knowledge and morality.

How, in short, might one move from the world of material security and individual liberty to which the Enlightenment project of scientific investigation has given rise, to a world of rational morality in which all may have faith, all may feel they belong, all may find beauty, comfort, solace and security? While not presuming to provide a definitive response, I wish to take Gellner's questions and his project for anthropology seriously; I want to formulate an anthropological account, descriptive and prescriptive, of interaction in a 'post-cultural world' of science, irony and individuality, of global movement, civil society and morality.

I also want to move towards an answer by theorizing in terms of movement, both cognitive and physical: truth as movement as means for coming to terms with the truth of a world of movement. E.M. Forster has alluded to it as follows:

The business man who assumes that life is everything, and the mystic who asserts that it is nothing, fail on this side and on that, to hit the truth. 'Yes, I see dear, it's about half-way between.' Aunt Juley had hazarded in earlier years. No: truth, being alive, was not half-way between anything. It was only to be found *by continuous excursions into either realm*, and though proportion is the final secret, to espouse it at the outset is to ensure sterility.

This is extracted from the novel *Howards End* (1950: 174 [my italics]), and I am struck by the appositeness for the discussion here of Forster's notion of truth as 'alive', as a balance, and as phenomenological or existential. To 'hit on the truth' entails a process of juxtaposing erstwhile separate sets of information and domains of knowledge, and cognitively bringing them together so that their differences connect. But importantly, this connection does not take the form of a common denomination or generalization, of finding a middle way between. Rather, separate things are kept separate, their integrity respected, and it is only the perceiver who, undertaking an experiential journey into the realms of each and coming to an understanding of each in its own terms, then brings these understandings together in the mind for comparison and collation. These separate understandings never merge into a static synthetic state, never coalesce into a tertian quid; for they are ever derived from and maintained by distinction. And hence the truth continues to be 'alive', and remains something to be found in movement: in moving from one understanding to another.

In what Forster says I find significant possible correspondences with both Nietzsche and Gellner.[3] Science and morality (religion, culture and the arts) represent two distinct domains of human experience, both phenomenologically vital. However, equally vital is that they be somehow brought together and interrelated, if human social life in community is to be blessed with, and benefit from, both knowledge of reality and pleasure in reality. The way to bring them together, moreover, is not fusion or synthesis but by their common individual experiencing and by the writing of a cognitive narrative whereby one continually moves from the experience of one to that of the other.

What Forster and Nietzsche and Gellner all look forward to is knowledge of those sociocultural circumstances in which individuals are prone habitually to make such a journey: to live in movement both physical and cognitive.

5   INCOMMENSURABILITY: POLITICS OR LAW?

There are at least two potential pitfalls in this project, pitfalls of hoary longevity: the attempt to move from 'is' to 'ought', from science to morality; and the attempt to move to morality from moralities. At the least, much wisdom would lead one to suspect that an account of a relationship between science and morality which is clearer and firmer than the ambiguous and uneasy one which Gellner finds presently to characterize liberal society would have to take the form of a continuing negotiation of plural and partial compromises rather than anything more singular or statutory. It would be an inherently 'political' account rather than a 'legalistic' or 'constitutional' one, delivering not so much an ideal or lasting harmony between science and morality, or between one morality and another, as a precarious and provisional settlement among what are deemed to be equally legitimate but are nevertheless inherently opposed and irreconcilable, claims, ideas and interests.

This, in fact, was Max Weber's view of the political nature of social life *tout court* (cf. Gray, 1997). Sociopolitical exchange was, for Weber, an ultimately tragic and antinomic affair because it dealt in conflicts of moral value from which no ultimate mediations could be made without irreparable loss to all sides. Since Weber, many theorists have concurred (e.g. Berlin, 1990; Gray, 1995; Raz, 1990): the diversity of moralities, in form, content and conception, is irreducible, and even the idea of reaching an Archimedean point for universal norms and categories of justice (of unifying all under the aegis of seeming pan-human entitlements such as reason) is merely a hangover from transcendental monotheism. Hence, the realities of sociopolitical life are about balancing competing claims of equivalent moral validity, finding a *modus vivendi* among ways of right that are irreconcilable. Social exchange, in short, is permanently intractable to rational reconstruction, and there is no legalistic or constitutional way around a moral or value pluralism wherein a multitude of incompatible but equally morally valuable forms of life coexist.

THE POLITICAL VIEW

To elaborate upon this political vision somewhat, Isaiah Berlin describes how between the values, ends and truths which human beings take to be foundational, supreme or final there will inevitably be conflict and irreconcilability; in short, 'Great Goods collide' (1990: 17). This is the case, moreover, not only with the values of a succession of civilizations, or of nations and communities with their own distinct centres of gravity at any one time, but of contemporary, individual consociates.[4] To say this is, for Berlin, not necessarily to be relativistic, for adherents to one supreme value can still, if they are sufficiently imaginative and openminded, understand the positions of others (however personally unacceptable they might find them). It is, rather, to be pluralistic: to recognize that there are many different ends that human beings might seek, and for these human beings still to be taken to be rational, capable of mutual understanding, and worthy of sympathy and respect. What is called for in order that those with conflicting final values might live together without conflict is *compromise* (a curtailing of the final end of liberty, say, so that room might be made for that of charity, or justice). But even here, there is no clear solution concerning what to sacrifice to what: no overarching standard or synoptic theory which can guide the criteria of compromise. All there is is a possible softening of collision by political negotiation: by looking at the force of particular claims in concrete situations and arriving at priorities which are far from perfect, final or absolute. We are doomed to choose, Berlin concludes, while each choice may give rise to a new situation with new clashes – and so social life proceeds.

With clash and compromise ongoing, an emphasis on political resolution is crucial, Gray concurs (1995); without recourse to rationality or some other overarching systemic (revelation, the unconscious), a diversity of moralities can only meet via negotiation, compromise and provisionality. Liberal thinkers have often decried political solutions in comparison with legal ones, Gray continues, deeming them ignoble and grubby, and too modest (Gellner himself spoke of them as 'uneasy, unstable and too ambiguous' [1995b: 9]). However, politics is a noble, humble activity, according to Gray, and the opacity, the dissimulation and the bargaining is something that the 'value pluralist' welcomes – as preferential to the clarity or finality of war; whereas any non-opaque, legalistic vision is a mere utopia. Politics affords a moderation of the inevitable enmity between agonistic identities and generates conventions of peace among warring moral communities. In short, in any bringing together of moralities and world-views (of science and morality), the political realm must be seen as primary and the project divorced from any liberal or even democratic conception; politics is war's only abatement.

The political thesis concerning the incommensurabilities of the contemporary world and their necessarily non-liberal treatment is a complex one, however, which bears further unpacking. The core project of the European Enlightenment was, according to Gray, the displacement of customary and revelational moralities by a critical-cum-objective world-view which would form the basis of a universal civilization. The hope was that humankind would shed its traditional allegiances and local identities and unite in a global association grounded in generic humanity and a rational morality. This morality would be secular and humanist (whether contractarian or utilitarian, rights-based or duty-based) and set universal standards for the assessment of human behaviour. In this vision, diverse and rivalrous cultural identities would, in the fullness of time, become ephemeral. Culture was an inessential marker of human difference, and could be viewed as an historically transitory, developmental stage. The destination of cultural differences was thus to flow into a great sea of universal humanity. To the extent that culture survived as a phenomenon within the cosmopolitan civilization, it would take the form of an elective identity in the private sphere, or that of voluntary associations: an epiphenomenon of personal life-plans, individual lifestyles and conceptions of the good.

The fullness of time, however, has shown this evolution not to be so. History has passed the Enlightenment project by to the extent that modern sociopolitical life is dominated by renascent particularisms, militant religions and resurgent ethnicities. Moreover, cultural identities remain very much givens; they are fates not choices, not so much voluntarily constituted as inherited and dependent on others' recognition. Not only does there seem to have been a primordial human disposition to cultural difference, then, but humankind yet possesses a propensity to exhibit distinctive cultural identities. These remain today's most potent political force, identities demanding political embodiment and exhibiting an irreducible plurality. To the extent that one can foresee, the twenty-first century will likely be dominated by conflict between ancient passions: ethnic and religious loyalties, fundamentalist, nationalist, Malthusian convulsions, irredentist claims and secret diplomacies. This has been history's predominant terrain in the past and it looks set to remain so.

All of which makes contemporary liberal theorizing (after Karl Popper, John Rawls, Richard Dworkin, Robert Nozick) devoid of any real understanding of contemporary political life beyond the Anglo-American academic class. For, liberal theory adopts unreflectively the individualist bias of contemporary Anglo-American political philosophy; it deploys an unhistorical individualism and employs an abstract concept of the person voided of any definite cultural identity or inheritance. The rights of individuals thus overwhelm the diverse claims of historical communities – claims, say, to distinct legal regimes regarding abortion, education and pornography – if such claims are admitted at all. The world is portrayed as a society of strangers without deep and diverse cultural attachments. To treat the world of real social and historical phenomenologies, however, rather than the fantastical, timeless verities of metaphysically neutered Kantian selves, is to find people individuating one another and themselves as members of communities not as specimens of a generic humanity. People see themselves not as essential persons with diverse, contingent relationships and attachments but as beings constituted by their historical attachments. Hence, they assert themselves (such as recently in Eastern and South-Eastern Europe) as peoples not persons, whose senses of injustice arise from their membership of oppressed communities (religious, local or national). There are, in short, far more ways of 'being modern' than the Enlightenment envisaged (Gray, 2000: 13).

It is in place of such liberal theorizing, therefore, that Gray offers what could be called the 'politics of value pluralism'. This endeavours to find *modi vivendi* between cultural communities possessed of irresolvable, conflicting and incommensurable claims. The fundamental social and agential units are here recognized to be communities not individuals, and culture is treated in more than a merely banal, sanitized form, as in liberalism; (deep cultural diversity is a feature of most contemporary societies and it will not simply evaporate – to be replaced by either a single, integrated culture or an individualistic non-culture). Value pluralism affirms the validity of a real historical and ongoing diversity of moralities, polities, forms of government, and familial, social and economic life, agonistically constituted often, and containing subordination, exclusion and closure as essential aspects of cultural forms of life. This is pluralism not of the diluted, liberal and individualistic variety, of individual life-plans (amounting to the legal disestablishment of cultural traditions) but of whole ways of life.

Harmonious coexistence between cultural communities, Gray continues, calls for a political settlement which balances claims and interests through negotiated compromise. This latter would afford to distinctive ways of life and separate communities legal recognition; each would enjoy its own distinct jurisdiction, within englobing, plural polities. Such 'legal pluralism' would cause members of distinct cultural traditions to have these latter mirrored in the legal orders to which they were subject and so hopefully offset any (Herderian) need for secession; legal pluralism would amount to the embodiment of a human propensity for cultural diversity in circumstances of global interaction.

As to what forms the political compromises between cultural communities might take and might not take, there is no final saying. Legal pluralism, as a manifestation of value pluralism, means that both within and between cultural communities any number of different arrangements may be arrived at, at different times, so as to keep the peace. The pluralist standard of assessment for a legal regime would be the extent to which it 'enables its subjects to coexist in a Hobbesian peace while renewing their distinctive forms of common life' (Gray, 1995: 140). Here is a (Hobbesian) recognition of politics as an avoidance of war; also a Machiavellian recognition that there is no ultimate progress to be made towards diverse world-views one day meeting in one politico-legal system, only, through *fortuna*, a series of partial, temporary successes in offsetting violence and secession. Hence, legal pluralism may give on to regional alliances between (cultural) nations as sovereign states – such nation-building and alliancing seeming to be the modal political activity of the current age. Or again, the peace may be kept in terms of a negotiated neo-imperial framework, knitting together communities which yet retain their cultural sovereignty. In short, legal arrangements will alter as political conditions and cultures and negotiations between them do. But no such experiments in *modi vivendi* between cultures may be deemed universalistic. Different political and legal institutions are desirable and legitimate in different historico-cultural milieux: from nation-states to ethnic states, federal super-states and empires. Such diversity, moreover, has significant historical precedents (in ways in which an a-cultural liberal polity does not). For instance, the '*weltan-schauung* states' (Moorish kingdoms in medieval Spain, the Ottoman Empire, Anglican England and contemporary Malaysia) managed to combine the propagation of a state culture with religious toleration and pluralism – by subordinating all else to a concern for a negotiated peace among a variety of ways of life. Even freedom is subordinated to maintaining and renewing the latter variety.

Legal separation of this sort is the only way to protect different ways of life from one another and ensure their several continuations, Gray concludes. Where radically different conceptions of the good (and 'Great Goods') are held, then only distinct legal-cum-cultural spaces work, with the provisional compromises of political negotiations between them. Trying, as the United States has, to incorporate cultural differences into one legal framework of unconditional entitlements leads only to a kind of low-level, civil war – between races, between pro- and anti-abortion-ists, and so on. For, within one legal community, law turns divisive issues into absolute victories and defeats. Instead, between different cultural conceptions of the good there can only be the provisional stabilities brought about by contingent compromises. Hence, political negotiation between different legal regimes will give rise to much local variation in *modi vivendi* according to local standards and circumstances. The *modi vivendi* is what can and should be hoped for, not any universalistic concurrence. This is why every erstwhile Enlightenment culture in the world is now faced by a project of re-enchantment of the world – whether via religious fundamentalism or political communitarianism. And while – Gray would agree with Gellner – ultimately these cannot work (since pre-modern modes of thought cannot be revived and an earlier unconscious rootedness of cultural tradition has been lost), still the universalizing, imperialist project of the Western Enlightenment must needs be surrendered. The earth must be shared among radically different cultural traditions, and legal regimes, and political institutions devised whereby these latter achieve recognition and security: their competing claims, their contingency, particularity and irreducible diversity mediated and moderated, and their integrity and differences respected. Political negotiation must be employed to shelter cultures from the impoverishing homogeneity which global markets and technology threaten, and to protect their traditions from externally induced change.

THE LEGAL VIEW

Gray claims that his vision of value pluralism, of ongoing negotiated, political settlements between cultural communities recognized as sovereign legal regimes, is not 'communitarian' (*à la* Alasdair MacIntyre, Charles Taylor, Michael Sandel, Michael Walzer, Amitai Etzioni). He even mounts significant arguments against this way of thinking. To wit (Gray, 1996): the ideal notion of a distinct and separate cultural community is an illusion which misses the rival claims which communities make on shared territory, the conflicting narratives and traditional practices which animate them, and the strategies of exclusion and hierarchy by which they renew their identities across the generations. Meanwhile, operationalizing this permanence of conflict within and between communities are individuals whose identity and belonging are defined by a confusing array of memberships (not only communitarian): individuals strategically deploy 'community' – as stereotype, as inheritance and as ascription – as part of a conflictual will to power.

And yet, Gray himself insists on deploying notions of cultural communities as political actors with rights to separateness and sovereignty. For, however illusory, he continues to employ the fictions of cultural communities as separate and their traditions as distinct. The picture he paints of cultural communities with rights to their own legal regimes has no way of engaging with questions of human rights, and one can imagine it being taken quite happily on board by the architects of ethnic cleansing and apartheid. Before the value of negotiated, political settlements between different 'ways of life' – as a means of avoiding war – it seems that all else can be sacrificed.

Besides, how to apply notions of sovereign communities in a situation where, as Gellner describes it (1995a), cultural communities are in such rapid flux that they lack stable or fixed borders, or clear demarcations, and are so intermixed that even inside a community there is no agreement concerning what that community is (cf. Rapport, 1993)? Even if they succeed for a time in imposing a political ideology, a rhetoric, of solidarity, the truth is that a multiplicity of distinct cultural communities has not been the case for at least 2,500 years – or since the first universalistic religions set out to claim access to transcendental truths (and so laid the foundations of rational universalism). In place of these elusive (and illusive) cultural communities, in short, one has a contemporary world of 'overlapping cultural units, in rapid change, frequently undergoing fission or fusion' (Gellner, 1995a: 6).

Another vision of a multicultural polity is necessary, therefore, and, according to Richard Rorty, possible. Namely, one which treats the realities of 'cultural communities' and their individual 'members' in a world of movement in a *legalistic* frame. Rorty describes how one need not so readily ditch the more constitutional hopes of liberalism (1986, 1992, 1997). For, via what he calls 'postmodern, bourgeois liberalism', Rorty seeks to show that there is a definite way for liberal concerns with the liberties of the individual legalistically to speak to a contemporary world of renascent particularisms, militancies and absolutisms.

Leaving 'cultural communities' simply to do their own thing is historically impossible, Rorty asserts (echoing Gellner). Moreover, it is unlikely that, left to their own devices, communities would come up with a set of arrangements which were mutually self-limiting. Instead one can promulgate an idea of progress as an increasing, legalistic encompassment of diversity: legislating for more unity in variety and more variety in unity. This has traditionally been the liberal-democratic regimen, and it has increasing not diminishing pertinency.

Liberal democracy insists that its own 'a-cultural' (technical and legal) institutions must be privileged, Rorty explains: that the safeguarding of its procedures takes precedence over the substantive claims of any of its different cultural components. As a consequence, a liberal democracy allows for the manifestation of more diverse forms of human life – it is the best manifestation of the poiesis of human creativity – while at the same time embodying the 'most' morality of political forms yet attempted in human society; inasmuch as it enables more freedom of action, and more diverse experiences as versions of human happiness. One should argue, in short, that for the purposes of designing contemporary political institutions, cultural identity and diversity can simply be ignored.

Rorty begins with a statement that takes us back to where we began: to the intrinsic discrepancy between a sought-after scientific meta-vocabulary which takes account of all, and the diversity of contingent cultural languages. Like Nietzsche, Gellner and Forster, Rorty advises against attempting to hold all the sides of our life in a single vision; a love of truth means keeping a balance between being, say, passionate and stubborn (passionate and regulated [Nietzsche]; theatrical and rational [Gellner]; mystical and practical [Forster]), and achieving proportion. For instance, it may be said that 'the demands of self-creation and of human solidarity [are] equally valid, yet forever incommensurable' (1992: xv).

To exemplify his point, Rorty draws upon the dichotomization of values represented by a Nietzsche figure as juxtaposed against a John Stuart Mill. Nietzsche's work represents, to Rorty, the drive towards the private perfection of a self-created, autonomous human life; Mill's work embodies a drive towards the socially just end of making our public institutions and practices less cruel. While there may be no way, philosophically or substantively, to combine justice with self-creation, still, a way can be found *procedurally* to relate and balance the two; so that in a polity which aims to be both just and free, citizens may be as privatistic and aesthetic as they choose so long as they cause no harm to, and squander no chances of, others. Rorty's broad argument in favour of a procedural – constitutional and legal – meeting of cultural communities within a liberal polity takes a similar form to his accommodating an appreciation of both Nietzsche and Mill.

No culture is closer to 'the nature of humanity' or 'scientific rationality' than any other, Rorty continues ('culture is the passionate commitment to illusion' [Nietzsche], '... to false belief' [Gellner]). This includes Western liberalism, which can be regarded as an historically and culturally specific form of rhetoric and practice. But this does not mean that every cultural form is necessarily of equal value. For example, when it comes to engendering a framework, constitutional and legal, moral and rational, by which a diversity of world-views, individual and cultural, can best live together in a global social milieu without intruding too far on one another's privacy or meddling too much with one another's notions of the good, Western liberalism may still be found to offer the best point from which to set out and the best prospect for success. This is the position of what Rorty calls the 'postmodern bourgeois liberal'. It is not a question of enlisting Enlightenment rhetoric concerning human nature to back up one's views, nor of trying to justify liberal ideals through metaphysics, nor of seeking absolute and stable criteria by which differences in value can be adjudicated equably and tolerantly. One recognizes these to be illusions – just as one recognizes that the belief in human equality is a Western eccentricity from which most of the world abstains. Nevertheless, ideals that are local and culture-bound can still be the best hope for the species, and this is precisely the case with the

Western liberal ideals of procedural justice and human equality. Parochial, recent and eccentric cultural developments they may be, but no less worth advocating for that. In short, postmodern, bourgeois liberalism neither needs Enlightenment-like foundations nor fears historical contingency. It might even be argued that an ironic, self-reflective awareness of the contingency of liberal discourse affords an enhancement of liberalism; for here is reason extended to the Enlightenment itself. Finally, a recognition of the fragility of liberal beliefs justifies a new commitment to them and adds fervour to working towards their being adopted in other parts of the world.

Western liberalism is not just one more example of cultural prejudice and bias, Rorty insists, because, unlike these fundamentalisms, what liberalism would have everywhere adopted are not substantive beliefs but procedures. Enshrined as legally and constitutionally sacrosanct, these procedures take the form of institutions which safeguard the rights of individuals to hold cultural conceptions of the good which may be incommensurable and conflicting, and promote the ability of individuals to acquire, and keep on acquiring, such diverse conceptions. Tolerance of diversity is, indeed, the source of the Western-liberal sense of moral self-worth; the culture prides itself on always extending the range of its sympathies and its heroes are those who enlarge its capacity for toleration. According to liberal procedural justice, all individual citizens are treated alike. Hence, doctors should cure irrespective of lifestyle, and lawyers defend irrespective of guilt; teachers should teach irrespective of who will best use or most agree with what is taught, and civil servants process cases irrespective of plaintiffs' particular attributes. Anthropologists, meanwhile, Rorty expounds, as with 'Geertz's other connoisseurs of diversity, are ... expected and empowered to extend the range of society's imagination' – the range of those 'conversational partners' with whom people can imagine having a conversation (Rorty, 1986: 529).

Rorty's vision of liberal democracy is built upon clear dichotomies between 'justice' and 'love', and between public and private. There is a domain of public justice which proceeds according to certain legal practices which are foundational to the society, and there are any number of domains of private love which proceed according to their own tenets, except for their necessary respecting of public procedures. This means that while one tolerates as co-citizens and potential consociates any number of individuals with any number of world-views, there is no need for one to share anything substantive with them. There is no attempt, that is, to reconcile the demands of love and those of justice, and to create within liberal society some kind of super-community or *Gemeinschaft*; justice is seen to be sufficient. In public one haggles away with people with whom one might never wish to share a private moment; one is polite before retreating to the sanity of the private club of one's peers. Civil society of the liberal-democratic sort thus comes increasingly to resemble a global collage: a meeting of world-views through universalistic procedural rules alongside a commensurate retreat into exclusive clubs of belonging and evaluational agreement. In other words, here is a juxtaposing of Nietzschean private narcissism against Millian public pragmatism, held together by mutual respect for legal-constitutional procedures.

The initial route to such a liberal-democracy on a global scale, Rorty agrees with Gray, is via conversation: via the strategic use of any and every rhetorical device so as to move the democratic process forward. However, there is a point to this conversation (it is not an end in itself), and that is inculcating people within a certain legal-constitutional framework. And this, in turn, may call for a cultural change in line with two key values of liberal democracy which are non-negotiable: individualism and irony. The liberal believes that, in effect, Mill had the last word on individual liberty and social control: only harm to others justifies restraints being put on individual freedom. And while questions of what is 'harm' and how different harms are to be weighed up can never be finally settled, the principle remains that it is the individual who is the potentially aggrieved party, and a common susceptibility to being harmed and suffering pain which calls for all individuals to be recognized as potential fellow citizens of a liberal polity. Cruelty to the individual is that which the liberal would above all avoid, and the imaginative ability to see individual strangers as fellow-sufferers is the basis upon which a sense of human solidarity can be worked for, created and achieved (cf. Shklar, 1984).

Not only is it individuals who act and suffer, but also individuals who are responsible for creating, selecting and maintaining cultural traditions and communities. It is, Rorty feels, 'our glory' as human beings that we come to voluntary decisions about which social practices to adopt (1997). Moreover, this gives to liberal society a certain, characteristic form whereby it is anticipated that individuals will choose and choose again, while respecting the different, contingent choices of others. This calls for what Rorty refers to as a certain 'ironism': a 'reaction against inherited final vocabularies' (1992: 88). Not only does one recognize that the choices one is now making might not be one's final ones, and need not be those of others, but also that questions of finality are out of place because different vocabularies have different pertinency at different times and for different purposes, and that one is oneself involved in their formation and re-formation. Certainly, the postmodern, bourgeois liberal recognizes the contingency of his or her most cherished values, beliefs and desires – that these do not reach beyond time and chance – even though they seem appositely to suit the present mood.

Admittedly, the individual ironist, in seeking to remove arguments of absoluteness from final vocabularies, is potentially very cruel; it can be seen to humiliate certain others (traditionalists, absolutists, fundamentalists) to relativize the substance of what they consider most sacred. However, such redescription is a necessary step to membership of the liberal polity and fostering respect for its sacrosanct procedures. Indeed, Rorty concludes, if the fundamentalist refuses such ironism – and thus threatens the possibility of diverse final vocabularies being juxtaposed together in a condition of mutual respect and voluntary adherence – then the justifiable recourse is to force: justified by the knowledge that ultimately the liberal way is better and richer, allowing for a broader array of notions of human actuality and potential.

6   EDUCATING FOR LIBERAL DEMOCRACY

Richard Rorty is under no illusions concerning the revolutionary change in sensibility which procedural justice and substantive irony, as the public traits of a civil society, amounts to. If the shift from religiosity to secularism has proceeded over a number of centuries, is still ongoing and is periodically beset by reactionary counter-reformations, then the shift to postmodern bourgeois liberalism, as a global form of polity, might be equally gradual. For the paradox of 'getting rid of God and of grammar' (Nietzsche) while keeping as sacrosanct a method of rationally asserting and adjudicating their (good) riddance – of believing liberal democracy to be the best means of peaceful co-habitation between a diversity of world-views while at the same time recognizing 'liberal democracy' to be one of those world-views – is a difficult notion to accept.

It is for this reason that education plays a special part in the life of the citizenry of such a liberal democracy. It is not, as Gray satirized, that liberal theorizing posits the natural existence of an abstract individual, voided of any definite cultural identity or inheritance, but that it is an ideal actor of this kind which a liberal education sets out to encourage. Transcendence above any one cultural position can be taught and aspired to, instilling irony and doubt concerning any final vocabulary, any timeless verities beyond the human-individual ability to keep on creating and experimenting with these.

Education in and for a liberal democracy sets out to achieve a number of things. It seeks to place the individual in a position where he or she is able to criticize and choose between the values, rules and practices of different cultures. In the same way that the liberal polity bases itself on a set of extra- or transcultural procedures which ensure and regulate the diverse expression of a variety of substantive cultures, so a liberal education seeks to provide each individual citizen with a transcultural method and knowledge, a rationality, whereby each can subject those cultural expressions to searching and ongoing scrutiny. Education thus liberates the individual from the 'despotism of custom' (Mill), and seeks to overcome the tyranny of a passive individual consciousness and imagination constrained by a lack of knowledge of cultural variety, process and choice.

For, the aim of a liberal education is not the maintenance of distinct cultural traditions but the fulfilment of individual citizens: citizens free to choose a form of life – or a variety of forms at once or over time – and thus to develop their own intellectual and emotional capabilities; individuals free to practise forms of life, and invent their own, with as much self-determination as does not interfere with the freedom of others. If the individuals are immigrants from another regime (traditionalist, absolutist, fundamentalist) then they should be taught the irony and the doubt whereby they can free themselves from the contingency and particularity of cultural tradition by appeal to universal, rational norms of judgement. They should be opened up to that debate wherein every point of view is brought into communication with every other. In all cases, education should be geared towards facilitating individuals' movement: both the cognitive movement to self-fulfilment, to making the best of themselves, to creating their best selves; and the social movement to affiliating with or making the cultural communities of their choice. These will be 'personal communities' (Phillips, 1993: 190) not ascribed ones, selected and maintained on the basis of voluntary contacts and contracts.

'DEMOCRATIC INDIVIDUALITY'

The close links between the procedures of a liberal democracy and the education of a certain kind of individuality are made most explicit in the writings of George Kateb (1968, 1981, 1991).

The legal-constitutional procedures of democracy – the 'due process' of law (the separation of powers, checks and balances, judicial review, and a written fund of statutes) and the electoral system – are intrinsically valuable, Kateb suggests. The procedures accommodate, embody and express certain values, and also attain valuable outcomes. These values coalesce around the notion that the individual is the moral centre of society – a figure deserving of respect because he or she is a person with the capacity to suffer, and also the capacity to be a free agent and create. Furthermore, the values and procedures of liberal democracy give on to a form of life which Kateb (drawing on the work of the nineteenth-century American 'Transcendentalists', Emerson, Thoreau and Whitman) calls 'democratic individuality' (1991: 187). This, he feels, represents liberal democracy's highest justification and constitutes the essence of its claim to moral superiority over other cultural forms.

For instance, the political arrangements of liberal democracy conduce to individuals' ability to glimpse the merely conventional nature of all cultural conventions. In particular, the electoral procedure is a key to liberating individuals from servility to conventions and to fostering autonomy and an independence of spirit. For, if all important political offices are filled only for a limited term and only after scrutiny and appraisal and after contested elections (according to rules of electioneering which are changeable), then the mystique of authority is to an extent removed. Furthermore, if elected governments consequently prove to be confused and partisan (as most are) and frequently to lose their dignity, then these reminders of official inefficacy liberate individuals from feelings of inferiority or docility. It might be said that governmental indignity is the chief purpose of government, since it affords individuals the opportunity to keep and increase theirs. Finally, the fact that after an election at least one of the parties which thought to stand for the whole (and to govern) loses, and is thus sanctioned, promotes a sense of moral indeterminacy concerning which of a diversity of versions of events is correct; it also promotes a toleration of difference, toleration which might spread into other relations. For, in the same way that diversity is seen to give way not to one rightness but to continuing contest, so individuals can come to see themselves as enclosed within no one system of relations – not even the one they currently espouse. The electoral procedure thus helps towards a self-consciousness which also distances individuals from themselves, from what each individual currently does and is. If the granting of authority to others is voluntary and contingent, then all other relations in life can come to seem similarly so.

The procedures of liberal democracy are important, in short, Kateb argues, for setting up a certain moral ambience, for sponsoring distinctive moral phenomena, and for helping foster certain traits of character and individual ways of being in the world. Liberal democracy does not posit singular notions of a 'good life', only lives that are not bad because they are their individuals' own: not oppressed, degraded, invisible or held in contempt; not 'enclosed', as elsewhere by 'status, group, class, locality, ethnicity, race' (Kateb, 1991: 188). Liberal democracy intends to 'open life up' and dissolve 'the whole suffocating network of ascribed artificial, or biological but culturally exaggerated, identity' (1991: 188). Here is legal-constitutional recognition that everyone equally has a life to lead, and the right to lead it: to say and do their own things, and to be like others only after some thought and as a matter of choice. Moreover, democracy encourages the growth of individuality by unsettling everything for everyone: so that the manifestation of absolutism in social life, of 'unironical performance', takes on a 'grotesque' aspect (Kateb, 1984a: 351).

These ways of being-in-the-world exist in places other than postmodern liberal democracies but they are not likewise sponsored, rewarded and publicly enlisted. And while one cannot argue that there is a one-to-one relationship between type of political authority and of individual character, or that specific traits are always achieved in democracy or always exercised, nevertheless, the moral distinctiveness of liberal democracy is that, in promoting certain values, it tends to strengthen certain traits. These include the emergence and definition of the individual self: as the bearer of unearned rights and of self-imposed duties, as claimant, as owner of himself, as freely associating, as self-conscious, self-choosing and self-made, as freely contracting, and as transcendent of traditional role and convention.

Three elements of character, in particular, characterize, for Kateb, democratic individuality: *free-thinking, self-reliance* and *empathy*. If the encouragement of democratic individuality is what constitutional democracy is finally for, then these three traits add up to a life in such a democracy of expression, of resistance and of responsiveness. Self-reliance begins with the individual desire to be different, experimental, unique; to be secret, undefined and mysterious, and not part of someone else's game; to think, interpret and judge for oneself and be unbeholden to others; to be assertive and go to one's limit; to experience wildly and live fluidly and diversely in many roles; in short, to shape one's own life, to achieve one's own sense of self, 'to be reborn as oneself' (Kateb, 1991: 190). What is implied is restless and improvisational attachment to existence whereby one is at home in movement. One may never stop, never arrive, and always be in the process of becoming, but one is not living timidly as if no alternatives existed, and one is never allowing oneself to be ascribed a conventional role or to being seen as its function. One aims to live authentically as oneself rather than in imitation, and even if only fitfully achieved, a deliberate self-possession enables one to fight off conventional prejudices, and to define oneself as existing at a distance. Individuals realize their self-reliance by saying and thinking their own thoughts, creating their own openings to the world as distinct from the numerous world-views conventionally available. 'When I am my best self, nothing social, not even intimate or domestic love, can be allowed to interpose itself as supreme' (Kateb, 1991: 196). The strain to be oneself may be almost as much as that to conform, Kateb recognizes, and dignity is not without its costs, whether loneliness, a sense of unreality as one improvises one's own values and rejects ascribed ones, or a sense of contempt and disappointment at others' conformity. Nonetheless, the self-reliant thinking of individuals expressing their own unique perspective on the world represents the soil, the fruit and the flower of liberal democracy, and gives rise to a riot of colours, unplanned and unencompassable in terms of any one means of formal integration.

If liberal democracy makes the life of contemplation and thought possible, so that it is '[e]veryone's vocation ... to philosophize' (Kateb, 1995: 170), then this should also give rise to a strength of character and a habit of free-thinking which leads one to resist the oppressive exercise of power, whether directed against oneself or others. Accordance with custom and convention tends to condition one to accept oppressive practices while the practice of government tends to induce and reward conformity. Free-thinking, however, conduces towards an abhorrence of indifference to, or involvement, in cruelty that derives from thoughtless convention, from tribalism, and from a herd mentality (with its tendencies to stampede and trample). Independence, even disobedience, therefore, are the hopes of liberal democracy, and an interminable chastening of authority. Beginning with oneself, moreover, and what one means to do, democratic individuality embodies a recognition of everyone else's right to be independent likewise and for this right to be protected.

Taking others seriously as individuals, finally, respecting their rights to their own free-thinking, gives on to a particular form of connectedness. It is a kind of generous receptivity, of preparedness to take what is different on its own terms, coupled with an empathetic attempt to imagine that difference. Democratic individuality is therefore not egotism, Kateb insists, and while self-reliance and free-thinking cause a certain distance between people, distance as something mutually respected can give rise to a higher form of connectedness. Hence, while individuals in a liberal democracy will not live for or as others, they will live with others, and seek to react responsively to their differences, and empathize with their hurt.

While one cannot legislate for democratic individuality, for individuals exhibiting self-reliance, free-thinking and empathy in their lives, Kateb concludes, one can put in place certain legal and constitutional frameworks: one can educate in such a way as to inculcate a certain character and practice of doubt, of openness, of scepticism, of irony. Kateb speaks of the benefits of 'a culture of moderate alienation' (1984b: 118); it is not coincidental, he feels, that anti-humanistic political philosophies, both modish and traditional, seek to deny the authenticity and the force of individual inwardness, self-consciousness and integrity. For, it is individual shallowness and docility which accompany notions of sociocultural groups as natural and discrete, closed, certain and fixed, and which in turn give rise to religious zealotry, idolatry and infantilism, bigotry, xenophobia, fascism, war and barbarousness.

It is also the case that democratic individuality does not make for sociocultural coherence and well routinized and rehearsed social life. Continuity is sacrificed and community membership episodic; group 'members' are recognized as accidental aggregations of free agents connected, temporarily, by choice rather than fixedly by the past, blood or faith. For individuals will take themselves, both seriously and playfully, to be at once 'in and out of any game'. Rules and partners will change, and only the playing, the legal right to play and the constitutional conditions of playing, will remain.

Contra Gray, freedom need not be subordinated to the continuation of a valued way of life if freedom is that way of life. Educating for liberal democracy amounts to a transcendent ironization of values – irony being the highest value – under the aegis of legal-constitutional procedures which guarantee the individual the continual right to ironize.

7 THE IRONIZATION OF LIBERAL DEMOCRACY

Nietzsche described a 'revaluation of all values' as his formula for humankind's supreme 'coming-to-itself'. The cognitive act which he called for was an ironic one; the human quality he was calling upon, and raising into a supreme value itself, was irony. Besides its literary meaning, of certain figures of speech (antiphrasis, litotes, meiosis) where there is an inconsistency or contradiction between what is said and what is meant or apparent, irony can be understood as compassing a certain cognitive detachment, recognizing a certain displacement; indeed, it paves a royal road to appreciating displacement as an infinite regress. Irony may be defined (ironically) as: 'never having to say you really mean it' (Austin-Smith, 1990: 51–2), or never accepting that words mean only what they seem to say. Treated more broadly, I would include in its definition, first, an ontological premise that individuals may never be cognitively imprisoned by seemingly pre-ordained and pre-determining schema of cultural classification and social structuration. For, secondly, and existentially, individuals everywhere have some appreciation of the malleability and the mutability of social rules and realities, and the contingency and ambiguity of cultural truths. Hence, thirdly, and descriptively, individuals may always practise a certain detachment from the world as is for the purpose of imagining alternatives.

In unmasking the world as an ambiguous fiction, indeed, irony plays with the possibility of limitless alterity. Here is an ability and a practice, enduring and ubiquitous, by which individuals may loose themselves from the security of what is or appears to be and creatively explore what might be. Here is a process by which human beings may render even the most cherished of their values, beliefs and desires open to question, parody and replacement. However momentary the impulse, irony represents a celebration of the fictive nature of all such human inheritances and the imaging of other worlds.

IRONY AS UNIVERSAL

George Kateb, we have seen, was careful to avoid positing a one-to-one relationship between type of sociocultural milieu and type of individual cognition and way of experiencing; there was no saying that the ironic perspective associated with democratic individuality was a way of being in the world particular to liberal democracy. It was rather that under the latter conditions, ironization was legally recognized and constitutionally enlisted. For others, however, the ironical stance or attitude is something historically and culturally specific. Ortega (1956), for instance, suggests that the ability to become detached from the immediacy of the world and treat it ironically is a manifestation of the technological revolution in human civilization. Entering an intense, inner world in which ideas are formed which are then returned to the world as a blueprint for its reconstruction represents a concentration which humankind has created for itself painfully and slowly. The growth of irony has followed a growth in science, and the freedom not to be obliged inexorably to concern oneself with reacting to things as they are but temporarily to ignore the latter in favour of a created self and a plan of action. In short, irony as that detachment by which the world becomes anthropomorphized, a reflection and realization of human ideas, is a technological by-product.

Oppenheimer (1989) argues that an ironic consciousness attaches itself to the provenance of certain literary forms. He finds irony present in Socratic dialogue, and also in the poetics of classical Rome, but thereafter, through some seven centuries of the Dark Ages, it disappears. Only with the rise of the sonnet in Rome of the twelfth century is there an ironic renaissance. The sonnet might be described, he contends, as the lyric of 'personality' and the 'private soul' for with its invention comes a new way for people to think as and about themselves. Irony as we presently appreciate it is a matter of that introspection and self-consciousness which the possible silent reading of the sonnet literary form caused to be fashionable, conventional, esteemed, and hence possible.

Giddens (1990) makes the argument that only modernity, that recent sociological condition characterized by capitalism, industrialism, cosmopolitanism and the massification of complex society, is characterized by an ironic detachment. Indeed, the presumption of this reflexivity – including our sociological reflection upon our reflexivity – is an intrinsic part of modern social practice. We constantly examine and reform our practices in the light of incoming information about those practices, which thus alters the character and constitution of the practices we next examine. Irony, in short, is part and parcel of the process of structuration by which modernity reproduces itself and knows itself.

Appadurai (1991), finally, sees irony as part of the 'cultural economy' of contemporary globalization. The de-territorialization of ideas, images and opportunities brought about by mass communication enables people to lead complex lives more of projection and imagination than enactment or prediction. The balance between habituality and improvisation shifts, such that fantasy becomes a social practice in even the meanest, poorest and harshest of lives, and conventional cultural reproduction succeeds only by conscious design and political will. People no longer view their existence as a mere outcome of the givenness of things, in short, but as an 'ironic compromise between what they [can] imagine and what social life will permit' (1991: 199).

Notwithstanding the above, I am convinced, *à la* Kateb, that the cognitive displacement and detachment of irony is a universal human trait, capacity and cognitive resort. Always and everywhere it is possible to find 'individuals engaged in the creative exploration of culture' (Goody, 1977: 20), intellectually distancing themselves from existing conceptual universes and looking at them askance. Always and everywhere, individuals are prone and able to 'detach themselves', to question the value and justification of the roles and practices in which they are currently implicated, and to envision themselves with different relationships and preferences:

[T]he human condition actually is more or less a constant: always in face of the same mysteries, the same dilemmas, the same temptation to despair, and always armed unexpectedly with the same energy. (Berger, 1994)

Or, more technically put:

This is the ground of anthropology: ... We can pretend that ... the people we are studying are living amid various unconscious systems of determining forces of which they have no clue and to which only we have the key. But it is only pretence. (Rabinow, 1977: 151–2)

Any notion of a binary divide between those (intellectual individuals, times and places) with irony and those without, Jack Goody concludes, is a nonsense (cf. Shweder, 1991: 14). In Victor Turner's words:

[T]here were never any innocent, unconscious savages, living in a time of unreflective and instinctive harmony. We human beings are all and always sophisticated, conscious, capable of laughter at our own institutions. (cited in Ashley, 1990: xix)

An ethnographic endorsement of this position is provided by Richard Handler and Dan Segal's (1990) examination of the novels of Jane Austen. Writing in and of a time and society (early nineteenth-century England) where irony might seem a far cry from a conventionally stable, unambiguous, axiomatic and homogeneous way of life, Austen shows no ironic 'reticence'. Readily ironizing any claims of a seemingly integrated and bounded sociocultural system to give on to a singular or unitary truth, Austen affords her readers an appreciation of the normative, the institutional and the principled in culture (here, the implicit cultural principles of genteel English society of marriage, courtship, rank and gender) as symbolic forms always subject to, and needful of, creative interpretation: to independent manipulation and individual re-rendering. Handler and Segal dub it 'alter-cultural action'. Clearly, for Austen, the schema of cultural classification and social structuration, being arbitrary, and being recognized to be arbitrary, may be seen less to regulate conduct or ensure the unconscious reproduction of an established order than to give communicative resource, significance and value to what Handler and Segal describe as her characters' 'serious social play'. Rather than norms which are taken literally, conventional etiquette and propriety become matters for metacommunicative comment and analysis – and hence are displaced – in the process of individual constructions of situational sociocultural order.

In short, the writings of Jane Austen are a celebration of the 'fiction of culture' and individuals' creative potential for alter-cultural world-making: of the enduring human disposition to render all sociocultural norms ultimately contingent. Furthermore, what is true for Austen's language is true for language as such: it is 'of its very nature, an ironic mode' (Martin, 1983: 415), imbued with the multiple ironies of there being no certain or necessary accordance between the linguistic meanings of different individuals, or between those and the way the world is. And what is true for Austen's age is true for all. Hutcheon notes (1994: 9) that the historical claim to be an 'age of irony' is a repeated one, but perhaps equally or more true is its denial; for the social milieux in which the cognitive freedom (scepticism, creativity, idiosyncrasy) which irony flags, the will to complexify, multiply and call into question sociocultural realities and the practice of doing so, are welcomed, are at least balanced by a blinkered absolutism or fundamentalism in which the substance of inherited verities alone is validated. But whether it is celebrated or negated on the level of public convention, irony exists as a cognitive proclivity and practice, embodying a certain imaginative movement from the world(s) as is, a certain reflection upon the latter and differentiation from it.

IRONY AS ENDEMIC MOVEMENT

Not all such cognitive movements, reflections and differentiations need be identified as ironic. Irony amounts to cognitive movement as a endemic mode of being; it represents, as I said, something of a royal road to recognising infinite regress, infinite revaluation of values. Certain other cognitions might partake of part of this movement, then, but not its habituation. Conversion, for instance, can be said to entail a cognitive shift or move such that one looks back at a position from which one has now become displaced – from which one has displaced oneself – due to an original sense of 'meaning-deficit' in one's life and a need for revitalization (Fernandez, 1995: 22). However, this does not amount to displacement as an ongoing cognitive resort, as a conscious way of being: to being as an endemic becoming. And yet this latter seems to be essential to irony; it is a living with displacement, and a refusing to take any value as absolute, as free from revaluation, except the value of revaluation per se.

E.M. Forster was once described as having a 'whim of iron' (Trilling, 1951: 11), refusing to take anything too conclusively, too seriously, too fixedly, except the proclivity to reconsider, to change and move on, as such. In arguing on behalf of self-reliance, meanwhile, Ralph Waldo Emerson (1981) felt that ongoing self-examination, a continual distancing of oneself from one's self, instilled an inner iron whereby an individual could withstand the descriptions others made of him, and so go on thinking his own thought. A self-examined self is set at a distance from the immediacies of present experience and thus is kept safe from presentist critique. It is removed from the seeming sacredness of extant traditions and engaged with what is ultimately 'sacred': the integrity of its own mind. The self-reliant, self-distant individual lives from within and belongs to no particular time or place: he or she is their own centre; their nature, their mind, is its own measure. 'Every true man is a cause, a country, an age.... Where he is, there is nature' (Emerson, 1981: 148, 147).

If Emerson's Romantic language sounds dated (in need of being taken ironically), then this should not detract from its truth. There is an individual capacity to transcend present ontologies and epistemologies, present appearances, and insist on the reality of its own being and becoming. Irony is part and parcel of this individual force which 'insists on itself' and proceeds continually to create and to live its own truth. Moreover, this is a continuous process because every truth reached is recognized to be contingent and perspectival, and bound to be left behind in a progression of meaning which is without limit.

8 HUMAN RIGHTS AND LIBERAL DEMOCRACY

If the individual who ironically resists the temptation to cherish particular values, beliefs and desires over and above their continuing revaluation is existentially free, then, as Kateb averred, he or she can still be greatly helped by certain legal-constitutional arrangements, by the procedures of a liberal democracy, which recognize and champion that free ironism. More specifically, the exercise of ironism benefits from the legalism of 'human rights': laws which 'allow for the free exercise of choice as to [the individual's] involvements and protect against unreflective, herd solidarity' (Phillips, 1993: 191).

Human rights, in the past fifty years, has become 'one of the most globalized political values of our times' (Wilson, 1997: 1). And yet, most anthropological literature has isolated itself from mainstream discussion. It has tended to regard the legalistic language and the institutional frameworks of much discussion of rights as falling outside its professional scope (cf. Messer, 1993), and questions of better or worse practices as value-judgements which go against its professional ethos (cf. Wolfram, 1988). While 'human rights', as discourse and as international law, has enjoyed enormous growth, anthropology has remained relativistically aloof, if not sceptical.

Even when they have found themselves, perforce, within the human rights arena, anthropologists have been loath to pass judgement on what might be meant by such notions as the right to 'life', to 'adequate food, shelter, health care and education', to 'privacy and the ownership of property', to 'freedom from slavery and genocide', to 'freedom of movement', to 'freedom of speech, religion and assembly'. Even practices such as 'female circumcision' or 'excision' (clitoridectomy and infibulation), anthropologists have insisted, must needs be treated as a 'problem' by those affected before cultural outsiders may intervene and provide information for change; for 'rights' only exist when claimed or perceived within a society as a particular cultural form.

This stance may be regarded as anachronistic, if not irresponsible and reactionary: a 'tragic' perversion of anthropology's liberal roots

(Washburn, 1998: 178–82). In a 'post-cultural' world, a world where '[t]he "fantasy" that humanity is divided into [discrete groups] with clear frontiers of language and culture seems finally to be giving way to notions of disorder and openness' (Wilson, 1997: 10), anthropologists often remain committed to an autonomous notion of culture, to relativism and communitarianism. They continue to believe that, as canonized by the 1947 statement of the American Anthropological Association executive board (penned chiefly by Melville Herskovits), it is upon 'a respect for cultural differences' that respect for all other social and individual characteristics should be based; therefore, 'individuals are free only when they live as their societies define freedom' (1947: 541). A 1998 Declaration on Anthropology and Human Rights, formulated by the American Anthropological Association Committee for Human Rights, further elaborates that 'concrete human differences' – cultural differences – rather than the abstract uniformity of Western legalism must underlie any approach to human rights since it is these differences which first and foremost define humanity and its capacities (Greaves, 1998: 9). While human rights might come to be 'inevitably linked to the work of anthropologists', indeed, while 'concern for human rights is a proper and sometimes unavoidable concern of the professional anthropologist', the ethical responsibility anthropology possesses translates as 'commitment to the equal opportunity of all cultures, societies and persons to realize [a capacity for culture] in their cultural identities and social lives' (1998: 9). This is in the context of a 'global environment' seemingly 'fraught with violence which is perpetrated by states and their representatives, corporations and other actors' intent upon limiting 'the humanity' – the cultural capacities – of cultural others. Finally, the Declaration reads:

People and groups have a generic right to realize their capacity for culture, and to produce, reproduce and change the conditions and forms of their physical, personal and social existence, so long as such activities do not diminish the same capacities of others. Anthropology as an academic discipline studies the bases and the forms of human diversity and unity; anthropology as a practice seeks to apply this knowledge to the solution of human problems.

As a professional organization of anthropologists, the AAA [American Anthropological Association] has long been, and should continue to be, concerned whenever human difference is made the basis for a denial of basic human rights, where 'human' is understood in its full range of cultural, social, linguistic, psychological and biological senses. (Greaves, 1998)

Not only, in this tautological viewing, does culture yet appear as some self-contained, *sui generis* phenomenon in human life – culture realizes a capacity for culture in the form of cultural identities – but, as propounded in the original 1947 statement (1947: 543), human culture can also be expected to contain an inherent moral rectitude; one might always expect cultural groupings to get along with one another in relations of mutual respect, and one might thereby wish for 'underlying cultural values' ultimately to overcome the (immoral) machinations of politico-legal systems (cities, states and super-states) and their functionaries. Little wonder that, as Richard Wilson puts it, anthropology is often regarded by human rights' theorists and activists as 'the last bastion of cultural absolutism' (1997: 3): a version of 'Romantic' reaction to the Enlightenment cult of progress (Gellner, 1995b: 95).

THE LOGICS OF HUMAN RIGHTS

A number of different ideal types of human rights may be identified, and the 'competing normative logics' (Falk, 1980) by which they are defined. For much of the past two centuries, the prevailing logic, in the West, has been what might be termed 'statist'. That is, nation-states have demanded the right to their own sovereignty and their own juridical and political equality. According to this logic, the rights of their citizens are internal or domestic matters, and it is not the prerogative of members of other states to intervene.

Statist logic developed out of 'hegemonic' logic. This is the reasoning that 'virtue' is a manifestation of power; 'might is right', and it is the right of the more powerful to interfere in the affairs of the less powerful so as to maintain their interests and their (more virtuous) version of right. In its turn, however, statist logic has had to vie for its privileged position, in political debate of recent decades, with a number of other logics. There is a 'supra-national' logic, which lodges judgement of rights with institutions such as the United States (UN), Nato or the European Union (EU); they now claim the power to determine the rightness of states. There is also a 'transnational' logic pertaining to non-state, non-governmental organizations such as Amnesty International, Human Rights Watch or the Worldwide Fund for Nature, which claim the right to monitor behaviour on a global scale whoever the protagonist. Then again, there is a 'populist' logic which rejects the necessary authority of states – if not all such self-perpetuating institutions – and seeks to derive rights instead directly from 'the people'; this might span a range of examples, from Bertrand Russell's pacifist War Crimes Tribunal to fundamentalist and terroristic organizations such as Hizbollah or Islamic Jihad. Finally, there is what Falk (1980) refers to as a 'naturalistic' logic of rights, claiming that they inhere in human nature and therefore should be recognized universally and take precedence over all other (institutional) claims.

While the above logics may be placed in an historical framework, it is important to recognize that all continue to contest for space and allegiance on a world-political stage today. And while the criteria for distinguishing between their appeals are many, perhaps the crucial one for present purposes concerns the units in which they see rights as inhering and to which harm can be done: from groups and collectivities on the one hand to persons and individuals on the other. As an ideal type, statist logic sets out to protect collectivities from infringements against their rights (as does a supra-national logic) while naturalistic logic is focused on individuals, and transnational logic falls somewhere in between. This distinction then correlates with a further important one, between relativism (statist, supra-national) and universalism (naturalistic).

Inasmuch as anthropology has seen its pedagogic mission as the furtherance of respect for 'other cultures' – argued for the rights to cultural difference, and posited cultural differences as the grounds for all others – its engagement with the discourse of rights can be seen to have been of a logically collectivist and relativistic kind.

HUMAN RIGHTS AND ANTHROPOLOGICAL RELATIVISM

The thinking behind anthropological relativism is well rehearsed (cf. Crawford, 1988; Downing and Kushner, 1988). It has been said that ethnography evinces no universal notion of 'humanity', and no commonality among those notions that do exist concerning the distribution of rights, duties and dignity. It has further been said that there is no universal 'individual' – that unified human subject with a knowable essence whom a naturalistic logic posits as the bearer of rights – only socially constructed persons. Those notions of 'human nature' and of 'rights' deriving from the fact of being human which do exist are historically and culturally bounded, and there can be no essential characteristics of human nature or rights which exist outside a specific discursive context.

In particular, it is argued, the UN Universal Declaration of Human Rights of 1948 was a charter of European, post-Enlightenment, liberal-humanist political philosophy which came to be formulated in the wake of the Second World War and the Holocaust. It can be seen as a continuation of Kantian attempts to establish an Archimedean point that provides rational foundations for universal norms of justice; and it ought to be understood as part-and-parcel of the expansion of capitalism – a means for individual profiteering enterprises to proceed unencumbered by communitarian obligations, traditional custom or localized morality. In its application – in Western interference in moral issues internal to other cultures – the Universal Declaration has been responsible for a particular normative blindness towards indigenous peoples and their collectivist narratives of land ownership, political determination, selfhood and so on. Meanwhile, Western governments, such as that of the USA, feel free to absent themselves from UN bodies, such as Unesco, when they feel too much emphasis is being placed on collective rights or too much attention being given to the rights of peoples. A strengthening of group interests at the expense of the human rights of individuals is decried by these Western governments as the so-called 'socialist bias' of non-democratic societies.

Moreover, the argument continues, what are the so-called 'human rights and freedoms of individuals' as distinct from rights which people practise in the context of cultural, national and spiritual communities? To enjoy individual human rights requires community rights; individual rights cannot be exercised in isolation from the community – individual rights to join a trade union or to enjoy their culture, for instance, necessitate rights of groups to preserve their trades unions, their culture. Even in a liberal, Western democracy, individual rights are not absolute or immutable: they are balanced by the rights of others and by the interests of society, so that freedom of expression, of association and assembly, for example, are subject to the maintenance of national security, public order, and health and morals. In short, 'man loses his essential humanity' when removed from his communities (Moskovitz, 1968: 169–70), whence comes the inherently anthropological proposition that cultural rights have been implicit in any other rights from the start.

If, however, there is today a demand or a desire for anthropology to exercise ethical judgements, then an appreciation of cultural relativism need not stand in the way. Cultural relativism simply demands that such judgements always be made in cultural contexts and take account of local *habituses*. For rights cannot be seen as anything but particular cultural forms, and notions of human rights as somehow existing outside or beyond distinct cultural realms is logically and empirically impossible. Notwithstanding, most, if not all, societies have propositions concerning some rights or others, however differently they might be perceived and formalized and the claims operationalized. Hence, one can say with anthropological accuracy that 'human rights' propositions rightfully imply claims to specific goods and privileges by specific groups in specific places and times.

As with rights, moral judgements per se pertain to particular socio-cultural contexts. European genocide, then, is not equivalent to tribal head-hunting or infanticide, cannibalism or feuding, because questions of violence must relate to cultural logic, technology and scale. This means, in practical terms, anthropologists supporting a devolution of power to less powerful yet culturally distinct groups, and advocating their being given 'fair treatment'. Towards the objective of maintaining if not increasing cultural diversity, anthropologists can support the rights of groups to reproduce their own culture, and argue that this be seen to be as fundamental as the right to genetic transmission. One might describe a right of Third World peoples currently to express themselves in nationalistic terms, for instance; in so-called 'third-generation rights' (cf. Prott, 1988), are contained collective assertions by these peoples of the right to self-determination, to protection from genocide, to permanent sovereignty over natural resources, to socioeconomic development and to peace and security which grow out of the senses of group solidarity of various developing populations.

A variety of cultural logics might give on to a variety of notions of 'human rights', in short, but anthropologists can still support and defend the universal rights of cultures to those logics as such. Cultural relativism is after all allied with the universalism that cultures are the foundational human right.

AN ALTERNATIVE ANTHROPOLOGY OF RIGHTS

Equally well rehearsed are the arguments against anthropologically relativistic thinking. To wit: it has morally nihilistic, politically conservative and quietist consequences; the noble goal of understanding others in their own terms slips into a legitimation of inegalitarian and repressive political regimes, and facilitates acquiescence to state repression. Indeed, if groups really possess complete moral autonomy then none can be criticized by members of another. Non-Westerners cannot criticize Western colonialism, and non-Muslims cannot criticize a religious death-warrant against a British novelist (the 'Salman Rushdie affair') – both being products of cultural logics. International charities and aid agencies have no right to operate proactively, and there is no way justifiably to operationalize an antipathy towards slavery, female circumcision, gas chambers or gulags, or any other form of intolerant illiberalism or totalitarianism, beyond one's 'culture'.

Inasmuch as many of the cultural groupings whose practices relativists would seek to defend are themselves far from relativistic or respecters of diversity, whether internal or external, the relativist perforce commits a sin at second-hand: endorsing anti-relativism. Indeed, if no overriding values and criteria for judgement can be posited outwith cultural groups, if truth only exists internally to a culture and its norms, and diversity is 'terminal', then there is no place for the relativist to articulate his or her own position concerning cultural sovereignty; human commonalities must be claimed if only to defend the universal rights of cultural difference, and to explain and describe this diversity at the outset.[5]

Looked at empirically, bridges have always been built between cultural worlds throughout history, and individuals have always refused to be constrained in their choices by their groups' conceptual boundaries and systems. Indeed, it is often today the so-called beneficiaries of cultural distinctiveness who most want to be rid of what keeps them from exercising the choices they see others enjoying. 'What is this "culture" concept?', the anthropologist-cum-administrator-of-refugees, Lisa Gilad, reports being repeatedly asked at immigration offices in Canada, and 'What about my rights as an individual [woman]?' Why, Gilad continues, do we maintain the anthropological stereotype that individualist thinking and social criticism are Western prerogatives and are not as firmly rooted in, say, tribal milieux (cf. Burridge, 1979), in Islam (cf. Amin, 1989), or in Japan (cf. Macfarlane, 1992)? And she concludes: 'What, then, about the obligations of communities and states to their individual members?'; 'What about respect for these latter?' (1996: 82–3).

In short, arguments for cultural relativism are logically inconsistent: inevitably imbued with inconsistencies and a self-contradicting meta-narrative (cf. Gellner, 1993). They also imply a modelling of society and of culture that many would now describe as outmoded. That is, society and culture are depicted as things-in-themselves: as reified and as onto-logically secure. They are modelled as entities not processes, hermetically bounded and discrete, internally integrated, orderly and homogeneous, the basis of all similarities and differences between people, the ground of their being, the bank of their knowledge. This illusion of holism might have been legitimate currency in nineteenth-century nationalism and in Durkheimian sociology (cf. Barth, 1992), but it is of little account in contemporary contexts of globalization: of synchronicity, hybridity and creolization. Mechanistic, social-structural notions of society and culture as organically functioning and evolving wholes must now give way to existential notions of human groupings as purposive political entities (ethnicities, religiosities, localisms, occupational lobbies) which live on as sets of symbols and interpreted meanings in the minds of their members. As Wilson sums up: 'bounded conceptions of linguistic and cultural systems' are out of place in a world where 'culture' may be characterized as 'contested, fragmented, contextualized and emergent' (1997: 9). Here, the more appropriate watchwords are entropy, randomness, multiplicity, contradiction, unpredictability and muddling through (cf. Rapport, 1997a, 2001).

'Culture', in this situation, may not be raised as a rights-bearing entity over and against human individuals. Individuals may have rights to cultural attachment and belonging and rights to membership of one or more cultures (of their choosing), but cultures do not have rights over individuals or members. On this view, 'female circumcision' is a violation of: (a) the right to freedom from physical and psychological abuse, (b) the right to health and education and (c) the right to corporal and sexual integrity (Boulware-Miller, 1985: 155–77). More generally, the noble anthropological goal of seeking to understand others in their own terms cannot be employed as an excuse to avoid making moral and ethical judgements. Furthermore, individuals have the right to resist and opt out of the norms and expectations of particular social and cultural groupings and chart their own course. For instance, an individual's rights freely to choose a marriage partner take precedence over a group's rights to maintain cultural patterns of marital preferences – even if it is argued that these norms are basic to a definition of the group's identity. As the testaments of refugees and asylum-seekers make known, many individuals have recourse only to suicide in order to avoid being forced into unwanted relationships, and it is the responsibility of the anthropologist to support those disenfranchised individuals who find themselves under the power of others (cf. Gilad, 1996). However that power might be locally framed and legitimated (as that of elder kinsmen, religious leaders, traditional bigmen or chiefs, contemporary cultural brokers or 'connoisseurs'),[6] here are relations of domination which anthropology should oppose. Moreover, even though the framing of these conceptions of individuals taking precedence over groups, of individual freedom *contra* cultural hegemony, derive from Western liberalism, still the UN International Bill of Rights to which they have given rise (comprising the Universal Declaration of Human Rights [1948], the International Covenant on Civil and Political Rights [1966] and the International Covenant on Economic, Social and Cultural Rights [1966]) is the best framework we have by which we might hope to make decisions on globally appropriate action. It suggests that 'moral imperatives know no national boundaries' (Doyal and Gough, 1991: 97); it sets out to delineate that which is morally unacceptable in any sociocultural milieu, and it proceeds towards universal standards of need-satisfaction and freedom of choice and movement between different forms of life.

Finally, if the discourse and law of human rights are manifestations of liberalism as a modern political philosophy, then its opposition is no less political or ideological. To decry the seeming atomism of individually conceived human rights – in contrast, say, to notions of collective attachment, common good, public interest, patriotism, group loyalty, respect for tradition and so on – is to extol the virtues of communitarianism: to wish to replace a politics of individual rights with a politics of common good and an emphasis on collective life and the supreme value of the community. This has long had its (equally Western) social-philosophical exponents, from Tönnies and Durkheim ('[T]o experience the pleasure of saying "we", it is important not to enjoy saying "I" too much',

Durkheim, 1973: 240), to contemporary communitarian thinkers (MacIntyre, Taylor and so on). However, as an ideology it can also be critiqued (cf. Phillips, 1993).

As with the aforementioned illusory notions of society and culture as *sui generis*, communitarianism can be said to represent a backward-looking myth of a situation of cognitive and behavioural commonality that never actually existed. Put into practice, communitarianism is often hierarchical and always exclusionary with regard to those who do not belong – women and slaves, savages, pagans, Jews, Communists, homosexuals. In sociological usage, moreover, the ideology represents an attempt to 'colonize' the consciousness of individual members so that the latter are pressed into the matrices of sociocultural groupings and identified with them completely; individuals come to be treated analytically as incidental to their social relationships and cultural institutions. But to ignore individual consciousness in this way, to seek simply to read it off from sociocultural forces and forms, is to exaggerate individuals' vulnerability to these latter and to underestimate their resilience. As Anthony Cohen sums up, this amounts to both flawed social science and to complicity in processes of ideological hegemony. Instead, Cohen counsels:

[we might] make deliberate efforts to acknowledge the subtleties, inflections and varieties of individual consciousness which are concealed by the categorical masks which we have invented so adeptly. Otherwise, we will continue to deny people the right to be themselves, deny their rights to their own identities. (1994: 180)

Individual self-consciousness always informs sociocultural process; as analysts and ethnographers we must endeavour to uphold people's rights to their own awareness. In this way we might contribute to the 'decolonization' of the human subject (Cohen, 1994: 192). To say that it is impossible to consider individuals as bearers of rights independently of group memberships and identities, moreover, is to risk blinding oneself to those iniquitous failures of social arrangement from which liberalism has served as an escape, and to rob human beings of their best protections against abuses of power.

To insist, as liberalism does, that the individual is the benchmark of justice, to believe the morally independent individual to be the ultimate source of value, is also to direct the focus of attention away from notions of bounded groups and towards interpersonal ties: to 'personal communities' not ascribed ones, chosen deliberately, and chosen again, by individuals. If community is important in peoples' lives, then this, to repeat, ought to be seen as personal and voluntary community – whether of friends, neighbours, family, co-workers, co-ethnics, co-religionists – from which individuals are free to come and go. '[I]t is attachment rather than membership that is a general human value', as Phillips frames it

(1993: 194), hence the preferability of a political philosophy which protects the rights of attachment and detachment as such, rather than particular (types of) attachments. Individual actors are 'the anthropological concrete' (Augé, 1995: 20) and they must remain free voluntarily to adopt or reject any number of community personae.

This is 'post-cultural' inasmuch as it posits individuals as ontologically prior to the cultural milieux which they join and form. It is individuals who are seen as animating, maintaining and transforming cultural truths. Furthermore, whatever might be the cultural rhetoric or ideology of the community concerning 'personhood' – concerning the esteeming of individualism or its negation, and the proprieties of personal public expression – a post-cultural wisdom recognizes the universal fact of individuality. That is, there is a universality of individual consciousness and particularity underlying cultural rhetorics of collectivity and homogeneity. In their true light, cultural communities are neither organisms nor machines, neither objective structures nor 'social facts', but symbolical constructs, 'worlds of meaning', which owe their continued existence to their continuing use and re-creation 'in the minds of their members' (Cohen, 1985: 82). Individuals come first, both ontologically and morally, and that which cultural communities formally contain – their traditions, customs and institutions – depends for its continuation, its meaningfulness and its value on the contractual adherence of interacting individuals. While, rhetorically, cultures and communities may represent themselves – to themselves as well as to others – as homogeneous and monolithic, as a priori, then, this is an idiom only, an 'imagining' (Anderson, 1991). Beneath these gestures in the direction of solidarity, boundedness and continuity, the reality is of heterogeneity and multiplicity: of individuals using the formal, superficial samenesses of symbol systems and institutions towards the construction and realization of individual identities and gratuitously diverse world-views. Cultural communities exist as 'mêlée of symbol and meaning cohering only in [their] symbolic gloss' (Cohen, 1985: 20): an assemblage of individual life-projects and trajectories in momentary construction of common ground.

Cultural communities do not exist in themselves, in sum, do not possess their own energies, momentum or agency, and it is less than truthful and more than dangerous for anthropologists to maintain that they do – however these communities, and their members, might ideologically know themselves (cf. Hinton, 1998). Attachment to a community should be seen to be a matter of individual choice not necessity or duty (an achievement not an ascription), and the existence of communities be regarded as an expression of ongoing negotiation between individuals and not evidence of an organism choosing (and otherwise coercing) its member parts.

In an interdependent, post-cultural world, human rights represents a discourse offering shared standards of human dignity, and with possible procedural implications for forms of global governance. It is necessary for anthropologists to advocate the right of the individual citizen to his or her own civil freedoms *against* cultural prejudices, *against* community statuses, and *against* the language embodied in the latters' self-expressions. Human rights possess universal resonance and relevance, and their advancement is a universal responsibility.

A COMPARATIVE ANTHROPOLOGY OF HUMAN RIGHTS

If globalization finally bankrupts relativistic arguments, then this is not to say that the global situation becomes one of either standardization or Westernization. Rather, the situation is of global forms being animated, brought to social life and made culturally meaningful, by an endemic process of local and individual interpretation. Thus, out of global relatedness, new diversities are always being constructed. Postmodern liberalism, to repeat Rorty's characterization, is a matter of certain legal or constitutional procedures being kept sacrosanct rather than something substantive.

Indeed, this is perhaps nowhere more visible than in the case of 'human rights'. In human rights discourse and law, a global form can clearly be seen to be given a diversity of local formulations. Two major transformatory processes are found to be at play: the vernacularization of a set of international legal institutions, and the globalization of local cases of dispute. In 'a confusion of legal tongues' (Geertz, 1983: 220), local, national and transnational codes now overlap and intermix, such that there is no 'traditional culture' which is not an ongoing construction by people who find themselves in a pluralistic sociocultural context.

It is precisely this tension between the local and the supra-local which a 'comparative anthropology of human rights' should set out to study: 'how a transnational discourse and set of legal institutions are materialized, appropriated, resisted and transformed in a variety of contexts' (Wilson, 1997: 23). Notions of human rights come to be seen as the results of concrete social struggles, embedded in local normative orders, while yet caught in translocal webs of power. Anthropologically to represent human rights violations, then, is not necessarily to give in to absolute perspectivism where any representation is as good as any other. Rather, anthropology can judge the appropriateness of particular renditions of concrete examples of violation according to the context of their expression and intended reception. Thus a comparative anthropology of rights can contextualize without relativizing.

More specifically, as Wilson outlines (1997), an anthropology of human rights might provide thick descriptions of existential situations, evidencing how experiences of brute existence in particular contexts come to be translated into human rights narratives. In this way anthropology can restore the richness of subjectivities immersed in complex fields of social relations and show rights to be grounded, value-laden features of social life and bound to purposive agents. Here are human rights not merely as instrumental mechanisms but as expressive too: constructing local identities, classifying and legitimating claims to self-determination and sovereignty, embodying relations of force and struggles for power between competing interest groups.

Hence, while the spread of human rights discourse might seem tantamount to the imperialistic interjection of a Western cultural regime, a vibrant diversity and creativity undergirds this seeming globalization such that indigenous rights movements can be found appropriating the discourse as a suitable form for the expression of a grounded local identity. Notwithstanding, human rights can be seen to provide a symbolic form of common denomination whereby many different individuals and groups can interact, and a legalistic procedure guaranteeing their equitability. Anthropologists might chart how human rights are founded, possessed and transformed as complex strategic situations unfold on the ground. Indeed, amid this diversity, the thick description of anthropological accounts might have a significant part to play in the role of guarantor.

HUMAN RIGHTS IN A POST-CULTURAL WORLD

At the outset of their provocative book, *Anthropology as Cultural Critique*, Marcus and Fischer posed the question: 'How is an emergent postmodern world to be represented as an object for social thought?' (1986: vii). 'Culture', as the purported ground for anthropological analysis, they argued, no longer remained viable in a world of global interdependence; cultural differences no longer really figured. That is, liberal-humanist notions of general humanity now took political precedence over a highlighting of autochthonous difference, while 'Orientalist' critique challenged the perpetration of any form of 'othering'. Global penetrations of systems of communication and technology meant that the once distant 'exotic' informant and lay reader of anthropological texts now became coevals, while the extensive movements of populations (labour migrants, refugees and tourists) made the cognitive landscapes of an increasing number of people a global one. To talk 'culture' in this setting rather than some form of 'global ecumene' (Hannerz, 1992) could be seen, Marcus and Fischer concluded, as a Romantic revelling in inessential minutiae or as an obfuscatory denial of the nature of contemporary social reality (1986: 39). It was not that the global ecumene represented an homogeneous social space, rather that difference was more than ever an internal relation: of wealth, localism, ethnicity, religiosity, sex and gender *within the one, global social arena and proto-polity*. The question for anthropology in this post-cultural environment was both how to write the meeting of internal differences and how to right it.

Rorty (1986), it transpires, has provided the anthropologist with good pointers towards answering this question, and at the same time differentiating the work of the anthropologist from the ethnocentric project of the missionary. Anthropological advocacy, Rorty suggests, has long been among the principal vehicles of recent moral change and progress. It is the case that the expanding of people's moral imagination, through anthropological 'narrations of particularity', has long had the effect of more and more different sorts of people being possibly included in 'our community' as 'one of us'. The anthropological writing of difference Rorty connects closely to the process of appositely treating difference – with its practical 'righting'. For when the anthropologist 'connoisseurs of diversity' have begun to demonstrate to their audience the global reach of our common humanity, the flaming moral torch may be passed on to those Rorty calls 'guardians of universality'. These are officers of the liberal polity whose responsibility it is to ensure that once the alien has been admitted into the social milieu, it is treated properly and fairly. 'Guardians of universality' are the doctors, lawyers and teachers, the ombudsmen and civil servants, whose vital brief Rorty calls 'procedural justice' (1986: 528); this entails endeavouring to balance the competing demands of diverse, incommensurable perspectives while not serving the exclusive interests of any one. By courtesy of the connoisseurs of diversity, one may liberally admit many individuals into the polity, but then one need not expect necessarily to share their sense of what is ultimately or even proximately meaningful, one ought not seek to convert them to one's own perspective; and one does not wish to have them missionize either. All that is demanded is a common respect for the procedural institutions of the polity. Indeed, these procedures must be treated as sacrosanct (as we have heard): they take precedence over the absoluteness of freedom of belief, which might otherwise cause an overthrow of the procedures and the freedoms of others. They also take precedence over specifically communitarian beliefs, for they presume a human equality which pertains not merely to different cultural beliefs and social practices in the abstract, but to their individual carriers, creators and users in the flesh. Irrespective of culture and community, quite independent of the contingencies of particular languages, individual human beings are equal in respect to their ability to be creative and their liability to suffer; and on the basis of this equality alone, 'there is something within human beings which deserves respect and protection' (Rorty, 1992: 88).

This ideal polity is to be brought about, Rorty concludes (in concurrence with Kateb), by globally 'maximizing the quality of education, freedom of the press, educational opportunity, opportunities to exert political influence, and the like'. Ideally this should inculcate a 'free and open encounter' between individuals engaging in undistorted, 'domination-free communication' (1992: 67–8; and cf. Clay, 1988). Given open communication and free discussion, Rorty is assured, people would not abide by (or expect others to abide by) concepts of the person or self, and of self-esteem, which ultimately cause harm to the individual; females would not agree to genital mutilation nor males to suicide-bombing, and no individual would condone the certainties of cultural absolutism or religious fundamentalism and the cruelties which inexorably follow. Through these liberal procedures, in sum, individuals can be expected to seek to make the 'best selves' for themselves that they can, not to allow this potential to be curtailed by cultural, social or linguistic norms (whether this curtailment is self-inflicted or imposed), and to grant others the space to do likewise (Rorty, 1992: 80).

Notwithstanding the ideal-typical – not to say, idealistic – nature of his project, Rorty's programme (like Kateb's) raises a number of *realpolitische* questions. How is one to 'maximize the quality of education' in a fundamentalist regime? How is one to inculcate 'domination-free communication' in a totalitarian milieu? One of the global facts of contemporary social life, as Gellner reminds us (1993), is that if 'Western culture' (including ideas of rationality, liberal democracy and human rights) claims to be a meaning-system which possesses relevance for all, then through reactionary measures as diverse as religious fundamentalism and female circumcision, ethnic militancy and Romantic localism, many other forms of life determine to make sporadic war against the West as best they can. One therefore ought not to expect a peaceful accommodation to Western ideas, however ultimately democratic and beneficial, and anthropologists should equip themselves for arenas of vicious contestation.

But then, both in terms of writing this situation and of righting it, an anthropology of human rights can offer an important step forward. In highlighting the discourse and the laws surrounding human rights as 'transnational juridical processes' (Wilson, 1997: 9), a possible common denominator is offered among a global diversity of individuals and groups; anthropologists can advocate human rights as perhaps 'the world's first universal ideology' (Weissbrodt, 1988: 1). That is, human rights, as discourse and as law, can be seen as a specific, concrete form of Rorty's 'sacrosanct procedures' on which a global liberal polity and justice may be founded. Here is a symbolic form in which the tensions between global and local identities may be played out – in which such differences are respected – without thereby losing sight of the ideal of reaching consensus concerning the legalized freedom of individual practice and belief. Anthropology can describe how 'human rights' can be and is already being adopted as a resource in manifold local situations: a means by which sociocultural identities both come together and remain distinct.

While there may be a flexibility in its interpretation, there are also limits imposed beyond which 'violations of human rights' are readily identifiable. As a legal procedure, 'human rights' might say little substantively about the fundamentals of belief which the discourse expresses, but it does not say nothing. As Wilson spells it out (1997: 8–9), it does not countenance the maintenance of 'inegalitarian and repressive political systems', it does not entertain 'international acquiescence in state repression', and it does not place culture on the level of supreme ethical value. To the contrary, in this 'post-cultural world' the focus, as we have seen, is firmly upon culture as optional resource, as a trope of local belonging, employed by individual actors on a global stage.

Describing the need to imagine a 'post-national state' in Europe, Paul Ricoeur (1996) has suggested an appreciation of human identity as a recounted story; in a global society, fluid and inclusive, it is an entanglement of our own and others' stories which transpires. We must do more than merely acknowledge these stories which our polity now 'shares', Ricoeur continues, we must take responsibility for them – others' just like our own. For, while it might be that the 'inalienable character of life experiences' means that we cannot directly partake of the lives of others, nevertheless, by a respectful exchange of life-narratives we can imagine our way in and we can sympathize. Indeed, it is through the genuine labour of such 'narrative hospitality', for Ricoeur, that new symbolic forms might be instituted which do not replicate the closure and the structure of totalizing communities. Such institutionalizing would recognize the ineluctably polyglot and mobile nature of identity, in debt to the past but always in partnership with innovation, and would legalize this. For, if the process of the reinterpretation of identity is endemic, then the conditions of its taking place must be safeguarded.

By writing existential narratives – rich in subjectivities and interpersonal relations – concerning human capacities and their fulfilment (and the diminishment inherent in their violation), anthropologists can demonstrate the advantages of people the world over engaging with human rights discourses and law for the effecting and expression of a diversity of identities. This version of narrative hospitality might 'restore local subjectivities, values and memories as well as analysing the wider global social processes in which violence is embedded' (Wilson, 1997: 157). In an anthropological dissemination of narratives of human rights, we can play our part in effecting a global polity of individuals free to believe in and practise a diversity of identities which they ongoingly create and ironically inhabit.

9 UNIVERSALISM AND RELATIVISM IN THE GLOBAL ECUMENE

Ernest Gellner spoke of the 'well-matured political systems' of the liberal West (1995b: 9), as we have heard, where efficacious scientific practice and knowledge sat alongside cultural faith and spectacle (however ambiguously). In best effecting the satisfaction of human needs and of liberating humanity from material want, in proceeding towards 'the goal of human liberation' as such, it was not only true to say that some choices in human world-view and behaviour were better than others, but also that one choice was pre-eminent. This was the liberal West: the meaning-system which had developed and accommodated itself socio-culturally to the power of science – and the meaning-system which had made the anthropological appreciation of other meaning-systems possible. It was absurd to pretend that all such meaning-systems were cognitively equal, or to deny this superiority in an attempt at expiation for supposed, past (imperialist) sins: 'cognitive relativism is nonsense, moral relativism is tragic' (Gellner, 1995a: 6). People may be equal but their cognitive claims are not.

In saying this, Gellner was, of course, extending a venerable Enlightenment tradition of Western thought. All people and minds are equal, Descartes prescribed, but not necessarily all cultures or systems of meaning. Moreover, all minds could attain to a unique objective truth if they forswore cultural indoctrination and employed a method of independent rational justification and reconstruction. This 'science' should assume an authority over all other forms of knowledge, Descartes felt; and the 'scientist', the individual agent who accepted voluntary cultural exile, taking in bits of information from the world and processing these into a cognition efficacious in pursuing certain practical goals (through a calculus of means and ends, and a weighing of cognitive claims against known data), would then be rewarded by finding himself or herself on the path to truth. This was a truth, finally, whose meanings could impress themselves as correct on any human minds untainted by the cultural blinkers of custom and example, irrespective of their cultural origin; the *cogito* was a premise and promise of escape.

118

Inheriting from monotheistic religion the notion of singular truth, and that by following certain procedural prescriptions concerning how the world was to be approached, this unique truth could be investigated and approximated to (even if not ultimately possessed), Enlightenment rationalism was itself followed by a Romantic reactionariness and relativism where truth was a matter of position and perspective. A Cartesian opting out and transcendence of sociocultural bounds, by individual, private and independent thought, was declared impossible, as was the desired-for scientific knowledge and perspective beyond community. The belief in finding a universal form of rationality in any time or place, in uncovering features and capacities of human being common to people everywhere which do not derive from culture or circumstance and are not distinctive to certain sociocultural groups, was declared wrong and politically suspect: chauvinistic and imperialistic.

This Romantic reaction gave on to German nationalism, according to Gellner (1995b: 14), emphasizing the priority and homogeneity of cultural community, its traditions of knowing and being, its territory and its people (*das Volk*), in opposition to the so-called bloodless, cosmopolitan universalism of French (Napoleonic) governmentalism, of British capitalism and of Jewish mercantilism. It likewise, according to Stocking (1992: 361), gave on to the cultural relativism which has helped constitute an enduring 'epistemic dualism underlying modern anthropology': between an Enlightenment impulse towards a universal *anthropos* and a Romantic impulse towards a relative *ethnos*.[7] Finally, it can be seen to have given on to the current communitarian opposition to the individualistic values of liberal democracy. John Gray's criticisms of Rorty, for instance, take the latter to task for attempting a political marginalization of culture in the development of a world cosmopolitan society. For Gray (1989: 169–70), to seek to privatize culture, to relegate it to the associational realm and deny it embodiment in political institutions, is simply an Americo-centric attempt to represent Western modernity as a universal sociocultural condition and form, and to see the United States as a timeless, world model; freedom and individualism, Gray is mindful, carry little weight with those who rate a renewal of a valued way of life more highly – and who must be deemed equally 'modern'.

Elements of a critique of Romantic relativism have already been adduced in this essay: its logical inconsistencies, and its descriptive inaccuracies of 'cultural communities' as isolated, bounded and sovereign wholes. What I now intend is an ethnographic treatment of a particular, ongoing state of affairs – the 'Salman Rushdie affair' – as an empirical exposition of the dangers of relativism in countering human rights abuses. The story of a British-based writer incurring the imposition of a *fatwah*, a religious death sentence, issued by an Iranian Muslim leader,

Ayatollah Khoemeni, on 14 February 1989 after the publication of a novel, *The Satanic Verses* (1988), as well as the ensuing institutionalizing of a 'Network of Refuge Cities' by 'the International Parliament of Writers' (in the wake of feeble public posturings of the British Parliament), is a phenomenon, I shall argue, which calls for an appreciation of the global ecumene: of relativistic dangers and of legalistic potentials. It also provides a case-study good to think with in the imaging of global spaces and sociocultural stages across which individuals might demand the right to pass, and the necessary legal procedures to have in place by which those rights might be safeguarded.

THE INTERNATIONAL PARLIAMENT OF WRITERS

The International Parliament of Writers (IPW) was inaugurated in 1993, by a group of authors (of both literature and science), concerned, as they put it in one of their first newsletters (IPW, 1994), that:

writing was today a crime in numerous countries around the world (Algeria, Iran, Nigeria, China...), and that, in recent years, many individuals had paid with their lives for exercising what was their basic human right to write, and to have others read what they write.

Hence, the IPW would represent an institution in defence of writers and artists the world around – their works, their persons and their languages. It would assert the autonomy and sovereignty of literature over and against political, economic and dogmatic institutionalism of all kinds, and promote a new kind of universalism. For, after all, as Jacques Derrida phrased it, 'writing' should be seen to include a universal creativity and narrativity (1998: 1; also cf. Rapport, 1994: 19):

The term 'writer' concerns all those who express themselves, including those who are threatened in their ability to give testimony by speaking or writing.

Salman Rushdie penned 'A Declaration of Independence' for the IPW (14 February 1994) which stated:

Writers are citizens of many countries: the finite and frontiered country of observable reality and everyday life, the boundless kingdom of the imagination, the half-lost land of memory ... and – perhaps the most important of all our habitations – the unfettered republic of the tongue.

It is these countries that our Parliament of Writers can claim, truthfully and with both humility and pride, to represent. Together they comprise a territory far greater than that governed by any worldly power; yet their defences against that power can seem very weak. The art of literature requires, as an essential condition, that the writer be free to move between his many countries as he chooses, needing no passport or visa, making what he will of them and of himself.

... The creative spirit, of its very nature, resists frontiers and limiting points, denies the authority of censors and taboos.

... Today, around the world, literature continues to confront tyranny – not polemically – but by denying its authority, by going its own way, by declaring its independence. ...

Our Parliament of Writers exists to fight for oppressed writers and against all those who persecute them and their work, and to renew continually the declaration of independence without which writing is impossible; and not only writing, but dreaming; and not only dreaming, but thought; and not only thought, but liberty itself. (1994: 2)

Salman Rushdie became Honorary President of the new IPW, while Wole Soyinka is currently the President, and among the Administrative Councillors (Vice-President, Treasurer, Secretary-General, etc.) are: Jacques Derrida, Breyten Breytenbach, Hélène Cixous, John Michael Coetzee, Jürgen Habermas, Pierre Bourdieu, Adonis, Anita Desai, Vaclav Havel, Emile Habiby, Toni Morrison, Edward Said, Margaret Drabble and Harold Pinter.

The first action of the IPW was to campaign for a Network of Refuge Cities in Europe: 'A network against intolerance and for the protection of menaced and persecuted writers' (IPW, 1995b) – in effect, havens for writers whose right to creation (if not their right to life) was under threat in their home communities. The Network of Refuge Cities was seen as a practical means to show solidarity with persecuted writers, and as the embryo of a system through which to reintroduce diversity, otherness and dialogue within and between cultural (legal and economic) exclusivities in the world, and hence to fight a growing sense of extremism in Europe and beyond. For not only artists but art itself, the play of imagination and the practice of creativity, was seen to be under threat.

The IPW's Charter for Refuge Cities was adopted by the Congress of Local and Regional Authorities of the Council of Europe on 31 May 1995, on behalf of 400 conurbations within the Council's 36 member states; all were asked to participate in the network. On 21 September 1995, the European Parliament also voted through a resolution in support of the Network. The first city formally to sign a treaty with the IPW as a place of artistic 'asylum' was Berlin – the place where exiled Jewish and Russian artists had settled in the late-nineteenth and early-twentieth centuries, but also, of course, a place tainted by book-burning and the Nazi atrocities of the 1930s and 1940s. Under the terms of the treaty, the Refuge City pays an annual charitable subscription to the IPW (as a contribution to the management of the Network) and also offers an annual grant of residence and accommodation (including travel, social security, child care and other municipal services) to threatened artists whom the IPW proposes and the city accepts. Berlin, in 1995, began to provide a stipend and housing for Taslima Nasreen (hounded out of

Bangladesh by religious fundamentalists) and Mohamed Magani (hounded out of Algeria). Besides finances, the city endeavours to facilitate the artist refugee acquiring legal status not only to reside in the city but to settle in the host country if desired. For, as the 'Charter of the Cities of Asylum' expounds (IPW, 1995b: 5), enshrined in the European Charter of Local Self-Government's emphasis on subsidiarity is the role of local authorities, especially cities, to promote 'local democracy'. This includes fostering human rights and broadening the net of social, political and cultural inclusions.

To date, the Network is composed of more than 20 cities and a number of urban regions, each hosting one or more artist refugees engaged in creative writing and broadcasting, and giving testimony to abuses of human rights in their past milieux. Included in the Network are: Berlin, Frankfurt, Strasbourg, Basse-Normandie, Amsterdam, Venice, Tuscany, Barcelona, Lleida, Bern, Salzburg, Vienna, Stavanger, Kristiansand, Goteborg, Oporto and Brussels (where, since 1998, the IPW has been based). Beyond Europe, Nagasaki, Durban, Mexico City, São Paulo, Passo Fundo, Buenos Aires, Québec, Montréal, Gorée and Lamentin are also signed up. The Pompidou Centre (Paris) and the Parliament House (Mexico City) have declared themselves 'Places of Asylum', meanwhile, and Caen, Barcelona and Paris have instigated centres for research collating data on censorship and on attacks on 'the freedom of creation', and exploring their parameters. An annual Congress of Cities of Asylum maintains communication between these signatory bodies, and there is a website and a journal. The IPW continues to urge its individual members to propose their own home cities as Refuges 'and so redraw the map of exile in the world' (IPW, 1995a).

'Members' of the IPW are all those individuals who have paid a (modest) annual subscription. This fee goes towards the running costs of the secretariat of the Parliament (based in Strasbourg), towards endowing a fund for persecuted writers and artists, and towards the publication of the newsletter, entitled *Litteratures*, at a price of 30 French francs (which members are also asked to help distribute). Presently, through grants, the IPW has an operating budget of US $150,000. Ultimately, however, the aim is financial independence and, towards this end, in 1997, Salman Rushdie suggested the founding of a chain of shareholders across Europe whereby 1,000 donor groups would each contribute $100 per year and so assure the IPW of an annual $100,000. Subscribers to the IPW are assured that their gesture of solidarity 'manifests the living proof of an active network of citizens who can see themselves and their values in the actions of the IPW'; for, 'the defence of the right to creation is a matter for everyone' (Rushdie, 1997).

THE SALMAN RUSHDIE AFFAIR

One of the major events preceding the setting up of the International Parliament of Writers (and its ironic mimicry of statist terms and offices) was the sentence of a *fatwah* incurred by Salman Rushdie from an Iranian head of state after his publishing of the allegedly 'blasphemous' *The Satanic Verses*; the *fatwah* then being followed by a series of orchestrated riots around the world, and murders of those seen to be furthering the book's dissemination. Only in 1998, after extensive politicking by a new British (Labour) government and by the European Parliament, was there a partial easing of the situation with the Iranian government stating that while it could not rescind the *fatwah* (since the religious edict had been issued by the now-dead Khomeini) as a government it intended no harm towards the person of the novelist, nor wished any to be perpetrated by others in its name. Political rhetoric and *realpolitische* instrumentalities aside, the affair is clearly not over, however, nor the tragedy of Rushdie's altered life-circumstances averted, or even his personal security assured.

Much, meanwhile, has been said in commentary upon the Rushdie affair (Ruthven, 1990; Weldon, 1989), including pronouncements from anthropologists. In particular, an article published in *Current Anthropology* by Pnina Werbner (1996), and given 'the *Current Anthropology* treatment' of itself being commented upon by a number of further writers (B. Parekh, P. Van der Veer, R. Hefner and others), neatly encapsulates the anthropological debate, its tenor and perspectives. The Salman Rushdie affair, Werbner begins (1996: 55), set 'a global writer, publishing house, novel and readership' against 'a global religion and leader'. In particular, British Muslims (the group among whom Werbner undertakes ethnographic research) saw themselves as victims of a racist conspiracy, of violence and discrimination, leading to the Council of Mosques organizing a public burning of the book in Bradford, as well as other civil disturbances around the country. It was said – and one of Werbner's own commentators (A. Kidwai) concurred – that the publication of *The Satanic Verses* constituted an instantiation of a 'liberal fundamentalism' which, while allowing that minority groups may be alienated as a result of matters of race and class, could not respect the experience of such groups in the matter of religiosity and 'blasphemy' (Werbner, 1996: 75; also cf. Madood, 1989, 1990).

Of what precisely, then, did the book in conceptual terms consist? Werbner describes it (and her commentators in large part agree) as an imaginative exploration of cultural communication across disparate aesthetic traditions, both religious and secular. In particular, it juxtaposes an Islamic aesthetic of the sublime against a modernist aesthetic of dialogic genres of narration and plural truths. But it does this from within a Western tradition, to the effect of construing a modernist version of Islam as a tolerant, universalist, liberal, system of genres. *The Satanic Verses*, in short, represents a humanistic, modernist text, exploring the nature of religious belief and certainty with a view to depicting a religion of freedom, and to counselling against dogmatic singularity. Rushdie sought to work out a secular ethics for Islam and to reject the fundamentalistic stress on purity and ritualized praxis. Against contemporary Islamic attempts at cultural apartheid and monolithic holism, therefore, his book images a new organic whole comprising a veritable hybrid of Islamic and Western mythology. Only in such a hybrid form could religion hope to escape moral certainties, monistic visions of the good, and repressive limits to interpretation in aid of dogma.

Rushdie's emphasis on an epistemological pluralism of truths derived from a sense of religiosity as being based on private, individual apperception and belief. Religion should not depend on 'truth' publicly validated and sustained so much as meanings individually created. This would make all moral choices inherently tentative and based on truths posited by individuals devoid of absolute guidance – which should, in turn, make for a more tolerant world. In short, Rushdie prescribed a liberal credo that would offer the individual personal values in a moving world, and take forward an Enlightenment (Cartesian) programme of continuing faith in human beings as sources of rational creativity. In *The Satanic Verses*, he desacralized the sacred in order to sacralize the profane: everyone (Muslim or other) was sacred in their capacity to transcend themselves and their worlds.

Of course, this message would not be well received by the illiberal or anti-liberal, by relativists and dogmatists whether of a religious persuasion or a social-scientific one. Besides the Bradford book-burners, then, Werbner also alludes to anthropological critique of Rushdie's enterprise such as from (New York-based) Talal Asad. For Asad (1990), the Rushdie affair represented the perpetration of symbolic violence by an intellectual-cultural elite upon plebian masses, the latter being 'betrayed' by Rushdie (an assimilated Indian promoting bourgeois ideas against his own people, culture and religion). It was also the continuation of a 'long tradition of Christian anti-Muslim polemics' (Asad, 1990: 252). Together this meant a Western maligning of a Muslim working class and its so-called 'self-appointed', 'semi-literate' and 'irrational' critics – critics, it was further said, who did not possess the aesthetic sensibility to read a book properly, only to decontextualize snippets and interpret them in terms of some pre-modern religious morality. In this way, Asad concluded (echoing Kidwai, above), Western liberals succeeded in coercing others by fundamentalistically imposing upon them their own anti-religious feelings.

Asad's kind of argument resonates with Bourdieu's critique (1984) of Western (Kantian) notions of universal taste in general, Werbner suggests. Western art and literature has, since the Enlightenment, served as a kind of religious dogma, according to Bourdieu, and under the moniker of 'good taste', hegemonic and monopolistic types of distinction have been exported world-wide. Far from 'pure' and 'detached' judgements, however, rooted in reason and understanding, these aesthetic notions are the original expression of an emerging European middle class. Taste and distinction, Bourdieu concludes, form an economic, social, political, moral and sensual whole.

Werbner is not happy either with Asad's or Bourdieu's formulations, however, because such 'class analysis', as she puts it, fails to read the empirical situation aright, and it does not accord either the aesthetic or the religious its own, true imaginative power. This, at least, was something that Rushdie recognized and respected in his writing. The response to *The Satanic Verses* by British Muslims and others, Werbner suggests, was that of another, distinct aesthetic and moral sense; here was a confrontation between two 'high cultures' or world-views, not between high culture (bourgeois, elitist) and low (working-class, mass). This being the case, what, nevertheless, is to be done? And Werbner is determined that something should be done to overcome the differences between the sides. She is not content, that is, with the relativist-anthropological position according to which there is no middle way between two such discrete and opposed aesthetic-cum-moral world-views – no one true interpretation of the novel, no universalist, rational discourse possible between Muslims' and Western secularists' different language-games and rules of interpretation – so that all one can hope for is a translation which points up the differences, and teaches about 'self and other'. Werbner is not content, in other words, to conclude that all one can do is treat the Salman Rushdie affair as an event of political disagreements and compromise. For, however much gratitude Werbner feels to a community of British Muslims which hosted her anthropological studies, and however much she might feel that the Rushdie affair and the wider social malaise it gave on to has its roots in Western colonialist and post-colonialist policies, she still wants to be empowered anthropologically to pursue cultural critique: to overcome the distance between Muslim and Western aesthetics, and support those legal-reformist movements which she finds to be equally intent upon overcoming the dogmatism, irrationalism and hypocrisy of these distinct traditions from within.

The pointers Werbner offers towards this end echo terms and debates which this essay has already addressed. There should be attempts at a 'multicultural politics of recognition and of cultural dignity', she suggests

(1996: 68), borrowing from Taylor (1992), via a constructive dialogue of interpretive disagreements. Rational debate can still take place from within different cultural traditions of inquiry, she agrees with MacIntyre (1988), by way of 'empathetic acts of conceptual imagination'. In this way, and even though speaking from within one tradition while hoping to engage another, one can seek, with Habermas, to re-establish a modified Kantian domain of universal taste.

THE NOVEL AS INTERNATIONAL FORM

Plainly, I share Pnina Werbner's universalist vision. I would also favour a legal over a political solution, as outlined, and support a multicultur-alism which takes as its lodestone the dignity of individual citizens over and against the groups and traditions they happen currently to patronize. The lesson of the Rushdie affair is not merely or only to critique from within different so-called cultural traditions of aesthetics and morality but to break the conceptual hold which 'cultural traditions' are said to have over these matters.

Moreover, I take support for this position from Salman Rushdie's own words (1991). Echoing arguments made above concerning human rights as or 'transnational juridical process' and 'universal discourse', Rushdie describes the novel as an international form of human being, and literature per se as 'self-validating' (1991: 14). Clearly, these judgements are as much prescriptive as descriptive; it is to be wished-for that the novel be accepted as a form of expression which has universal valency and is to be taken on its own terms, but Rushdie's own predicament catalogues demonstrably the reactionary regimens ranged against it.

The arguments which Rushdie uses for making his claims are, however, very instructive. To say that a piece of literature should be judged in its own terms, he elaborates, is to say that its justification lies not with its author's worthiness to write it, but wholly with the quality of what has been written. What has been written, in turn, concerns a construction of human reality. This is perhaps why writers and politicians are so often natural rivals, Rushdie opines, because each determines to make the world in their image. The piece of literature can thus represent a way of denying the official, political version of truth; while an array of such literary pieces increases the aggregate of what it is routine to image in and as the world. Through literature one comes to enter reality from ever new angles such that what eventuates is a kaleido-scopic not holistic vision. Readers and writers of literature find their world-views to be plural and partial, and their perceptions to concern fractured not singular wholes. In its turn, this gives on to an apprecia-tion of the provisional nature of all truths, of all certainties about the human world, and of the ongoing and individual creative sources of these truths. Human beings, Rushdie concludes, are

[p]artial beings, in all the senses of that phrase. Meaning is a shaky edifice we build out of scraps, dogmas, childhood injuries, newspaper articles, chance remarks, old films, small victories, people hated, people loved; perhaps it is because our sense of what is the case is constructed from such inadequate materials that we defend it so fiercely, even to the death. (1991: 12)

The latter reaction is the wrong one, however, not the best one might inculcate or hope for. Indeed, a 'ghetto mentality', cultural apartheid, in which one separates off one truth from others, and one's own truth from another's, is a most dangerous trap. Life is at its most free when the imagination remains most free to choose matter from everywhere and anywhere in its construction of human reality. We must endeavour to open up our worlds to one another, to move continually between worlds, and thus to cross-pollinate our truths. From Rushdie we hear another version of what Ricoeur termed 'narrative hospitality'.

10   EXISTENTIAL ANTHROPOLOGY

What may be drawn from the Salman Rushdie affair, and from Rushdie's own words, in the context of this essay so as to take the argument forward? Regarding the partiality of meaning which Rushdie describes, I have written elsewhere about the randomness of the creative process and the freedom or arbitrariness with which the imagination is wont to select those construed items from which meaningful worlds are constituted (2001; also cf. Brodsky, 1988: G2). But Rushdie's words do not only give on to literary concerns; I would read implications in them which are also *realpolitische*, practical and prescriptive.

'Those who begin by burning books end by burning people', Heinrich Heine famously quipped, looking both backward to medieval religious fundamentalism and forward to modernistic, political-cum-nationalistic ones. (To sentence a novelist to death seems a terrible anachronism, remarked the opening edition of *Autodafe* – a new journal of the International Parliament of Writers, published in five languages in five countries [IPW, 2001] – but the Rushdie affair has been followed by the assassination of the Algerian Tahar Diaout, the arrest of Bei Dao in China, of Yashar Kemal in the Middle East [also the stabbing of Naguib Mahfouz], and the legal murder of Ken Saro-Wiwa in Nigeria.) Milan Kundera (1995) reiterates Heine's point, criticizing his readership for taking insufficient account of the lessons that European history holds and guarding against its reprise. Saddest of all aspects of the Rushdie affair, according to Kundera, when 'theocracy went to war against modernity' and targeted the modern era's 'most representative' expression, the novel, has been the incapacity of modern Europeans to defend and explain to themselves and others the art of the novel, and thus some of their society's most basic values. It was as if 'Europe, the "society of the novel" [E.M. Cioran], ha[d] abandoned its own self' (Kundera, 1995: 29).

The links which Kundera draws between 'Europe', 'modernity' and 'the novel' he had earlier elaborated upon (1990) as involving an aggregation of liberal notions and values. These included: tolerance, a questioning, doubting spirit, an appreciation of the elusiveness of truth, the multiplicities of perspective and the contingencies of knowledge, and a respect for the irreplaceable uniqueness of the individual. As Kundera summed up (1990: 164–5):

> That imaginative realm of tolerance [where no one owns the truth and everyone has the right to be understood] was born with modern Europe, it is the very image of Europe – or at least our dream of Europe, a dream many times betrayed but nonetheless strong enough to unite us all in the fraternity that stretches far beyond the little European continent. But we know that the world where the individual is respected (the imaginative world of the novel, and the real one of Europe) is fragile and perishable. ... [I]f European culture seems under threat today, if the threat from within and without hangs over what is most precious about it – its respect for the individual, for his original thought, and for his right to an inviolable private life – then, I believe, that precious essence of the European spirit is being held safe as in a treasure chest inside the history of the novel, the wisdom of the novel.

The political implications of the Rushdie affair, in short, are far-reaching. They concern the freedom of the (European) individual to imagine new truths, social arrangements wherein ambiguities surrounding individuals' diverse conceptions of the true are endured, and legal procedures whereby a complexity of ambiguous, individual truths are accommodated. All this bespeaks a world beyond dogmas of 'good and evil' – clearly distinguished and certain – because the spirit of complexity which imbues the novel and inspires the (European) society of the novel will ever be incompatible with a totalitarian universe of absolutes and finalities. In the quest for being, its 'discovery' and 'conquest', Kundera concludes (1990: 14), no peace is possible between the novelist and those who know with certainty and forever. The only absolute 'good' is the individual's procedural right to continue seeking and defining it.

THE EXISTENTIAL INDIVIDUAL

The stress given by Rushdie to human beings building edifices of meaning on shaky foundations from fragments of experience, and from Kundera to our discovering human being by way of ongoing, ambiguous and perspectival assertions of individual truth, both resonate with what I have described as a main intent of this essay: a coming to terms with the truth of a contemporary world of movement through an appreciation of human truth as movement. Rollo May sums up the idea nicely (1958: 60):

> World is never something static, something merely given which the person then 'accepts' or 'adjusts to' or 'fights'. It is rather a dynamic pattern which, so long as I possess self-consciousness, I am in the process of forming and designing.

All this, moreover, has a distinct 'existentialist' ring – a word I have referred to in this essay ('existential' situations and narratives, 'existential' freedom and movement) but not thusfar elucidated. Existentialism (after Kierkegaard, Emerson, Nietzsche, Husserl, Jaspers, Sartre and Heidegger) emphasizes a conception of human life not as an assemblage of static substances or mechanisms or patterns, but as something ever emerging and becoming (cf. May, 1958: 12). Human being, as Sartre put it (1972), is characterized by a going beyond: beyond a situation or status, beyond circumstances and conditions that are current. This applies both to individual identity and experience ('a flow of confusing multiplicity and indeterminacy' [William James]) and to those sociocultural worlds which individual consciousness constructs.

Existentialism, as a philosophical conception of the person, would appear to have significant possible consequences both anthropologically speaking and politically. An anthropological awareness has begun to be formulated (cf. Rapport, 1997b; see also Douglas and Johnson, 1977; Jackson, 1989, 1996; Kotarba and Fontana, 1984), and a political enterprise I should like to adumbrate now too. By way of a commentary upon Sartre, I shall outline the possible foundations of both an 'existential anthropology' and an 'existential politics'; I shall hope to explicate how existentialism affords a way of construing identity (in a social science as in a polity) in a post-cultural or post-classificatory fashion.

Sartre writes as follows (1997: 44–6):

Our point of departure is ... the subjectivity of the individual ... not because we are bourgeois, but because we seek to base our teaching upon the truth. ... And at the point of departure there cannot be any other truth than this, *I think, therefore I am*, which is the absolute truth of consciousness as it attains to itself. Every theory which begins with man, outside of this moment of self-attainment, is a theory which thereby suppresses the truth, for outside of the Cartesian *cogito*, all objects are no more than probable. ... [T]here is [an absolute] truth which is simple, easily attained and within the reach of everybody; it consists in one's immediate sense of self.

In the second place, this theory alone is compatible with the dignity of man, it is the only one which does not make man into an object ... – that is ... a set of predetermined reactions, in no way different from the patterns of qualities and phenomena which constitute a table, or a chair or a stone. ...

Furthermore ... [there is] a human universality of *condition* ... all the *limitations* which *a priori* define man's fundamental situation in the universe. His historical situations are variable ... [b]ut what never vary are the necessities of being in the world, of having to labour and to die there. These limitations are [at once] [o]bjective, because we meet with them everywhere and they are everywhere recognizable: and subjective because they are *lived* and are nothing if man does not live them – if, that is to say, he does not freely determine himself and his existence in relation to them. And, diverse though man's purposes may be, at least none of them is wholly foreign to me, since every human purpose presents itself as an attempt either to surpass these limitations, or to widen them, or else to deny or to accommodate oneself to them.

Some of Sartre's phraseology may seem old-fashioned, also sexist and self-satisfied; it can appear the credo of the secure and resourceful bourgeois, able to reflect on the self, to determine 'his' relations to the conditions or circumstances of his life, and to lay claim to a certain lifesome dignity. Indeed, this has led some anthropologists to reject such an existentialist orientation *tout court*, on grounds of political naïveté if not of sociocultural relativity. However, such a reading is superficial, and mistaken; by his words Sartre succinctly points up a number of important truths. Let me elaborate upon a number of his phrases in turn:

'I think, therefore I am ... is the absolute truth of consciousness'

Descartes' attempt to isolate a knowing subject as a foundation for a scientific exploration of the world has been heavily criticized in recent (anti-Enlightenment) social science, as we have heard. The search for a *res cogitans*, a discrete substance and process of cognition, has been seen as responsible for setting up a number of misconceived dualisms, such as mind versus body, thinking versus feeling, reason versus emotion, thought versus action, individual versus environment, man (society and culture) versus nature. However, Descartes' description of consciousness can be improved upon relatively easily without being discarded, by adding such words as 'feel' and 'imagine', 'sense' and 'dream', 'evaluate' and 'experience', to 'think'; and by portraying the knowing being as always situated, as a body in a certain time and space (cf. Cohen and Rapport, 1995).

Hence: 'I think and feel – I experience – at a particular moment, and therefore I am at that moment'.

'... outside of the Cartesian cogito, all objects are no more than probable ...'

What individuals know with most immediacy, clarity and certainty is what their senses inform them of, what they experience firsthand. Indeed, this is the only thing of which they have certain knowledge. They know what they sense but they cannot know the accuracy of those senses and measure them against an absolute standard because they 'are' their senses and not something over and against them. They can test, improvise and experiment with what their senses tell them, but these procedures also call upon their senses to effect and measure. They can compare what their senses tell them with what others' senses tell them, but still these efforts entail their sensual interpretation of the information they glean from (what they interpret to be) others. In short, individuals' senses of self and world are the beginning and, in a way, also the end of knowledge. They are certainly the paradigm of knowledge, and give on to a sense of certainty that is never equalled in other forms of knowledge – however much they might inspire the wish for such comprehension. As Roy Wagner concludes (1991: 39):

> nothing could possibly be more clear, distinct, concrete, certain, or real than the self's perception of perception, its own sensing of sense. It is the very archetype, the inspiration, of everything we have ever imagined for the objective.

And yet such knowledge remains hermetically sealed within the personal microcosm.

Hence: 'I am certain of my own cognitions at a particular moment (and therefore I am) but I am not so certain about anything else.'

'... the necessities of being in the world, of having to live, labour and to die there ...' is a universal human condition

The notion of 'independent existence' Whitehead (1925) famously decried as a philosophical misconception; entities are more properly understood in terms of the way they relate with the universe. In the Heideggerian terms which have become popular in environmentalist anthropology, human beings can be said ever to dwell within worlds of nature and of sociocultural exchange (cf. Ingold, 1986; Weiner, 1991). However, this dwelling does not detract from human beings' individuality. For our being-in-the-world courtesy of individual bodily mechanisms of cognition and perception is such as always to make of the world something other, always something interpreted. One comes to see, to construct, the world and its objects in certain ways which have proven personally 'valuable' over time (cf. Edelman, 1989: 184), and one learns to recognize signs and symbols by which is expressed the experience of dwelling in the ('same') world of other sentient beings. But these signs and symbols remain ambiguous, and the world and its objects ever something refracted through the prism of a situated consciousness. Ambiguity, doubt, incoherence and multiplicity are the nature of the universal human (not to say animal) condition, dwelling alongside fellow sentient creatures, dependent upon one another and the remainder of the organic and inorganic universe for the environmental conditions of one's life (even for the transient agglomeration of chemicals that underwrite one's bodily existence), and yet never certain concerning one's meaningful construction of that universe, its rectitude or sharedness. Meaning is a personal, subjective, internal perception (cf. Rapport, 1993).

Hence: 'I experience and become myself (I am) at particular moments while dwelling within environments comprised of other, similarly cognizing, beings and inorganic, non-beings; and while there is a relatedness, even a mutuality, to all this matter, I know of it only as an interpreted other.'

Being in the world and relating to its conditions is a subjective phenomenon because the world and its conditions 'are nothing if individuals do not live them'

Whatever may be the ultimate nature of earthly physical reality, human beings gain access to it only through their senses. Moreover, this is not a passive or reactive exercise entailing the reception of external stimuli but rather the pro-active testing of original models and the adjudicating of consequences. To 'interpret' the world in this way is not only to give it meaning, then, but also form: to construct it, its objects and events in a certain way. In the world of human being, as Bateson has it (1958: 96), the Berkeleyan motto cannot be faulted: 'To be is to be perceived.' Moreover, it is important to emphasize that it is the individual who is the 'energy source' behind this act of worldly perception or interpretation (Bateson, 1972: 126). Knowledge is individual and subjective, deriving from individuals' sensitive bodies, and the drive, the work and the habitude behind this are exemplifications of individual agency. This is especially important to recognize with regard to habit. Worldly order which they find valuable or satisfying, individuals tend to maintain. They also tend to maintain certain orders in common with those others with whom they dwell in 'an' environment – human and animal, organic and inorganic; (in an habitual way of farming, for instance, individuals will find themselves in symbiosis with human neighbours, with animals, domestic and wild, with crops and with soils). However, these orders do not acquire their own energy or momentum; they are always inert unless continually worked and made meaningful by their individual users. Should they cease to be considered valuable, they cease to exist. These common orders (languages, social structures, eco-systems) are always ambiguous, always means by which a diversity of understandings and motivations are synthesized by common forms and practices which allow a diversity of gratifications. Moreover, they tend to be temporary and transitory, so that after a time individuals construct orders anew and old environmental arrangements and alignments die.

Hence: 'I experience and become myself by dwelling at particular moments in particular environments; but those environments (and that self) exist only so long as I continue to construe them in a particular way and practise them as such.'

Individuals are responsible for determining whether to attempt to surpass the conditions they construe around them or to accommodate themselves to them

Individuals construe the world as they take it to be; nothing is certain but their own consciousness of self, but they construct the world in a way which proves valuable (successful, meaningful) for them. Once they have done so, individuals must also determine how to react in relation to this world. This is a decision which nothing and no one else can make for them, because the decisions and behaviours of others must still be cognized and perceived, interpreted and made meaningful, within the world-views of the individuals concerned. Hence, individuals can be affected by the decisions of others, if they are something of which they take notice, but not determined. There is no alternative to individuality, in short, no certain or direct access to another consciousness or to the world 'as is', and there is no other source of an individual's meanings but individuals themselves. Hence their responsibility for deciding how to react to the world they have made: to do as before (maintain a habit) or to create anew; to try to fit in with what seem to be the expectations and aspirations of others (be a 'good family member', a 'loyal client', a 'pious co-religionist') or to cut a different path for themselves (as 'poet' or 'rebel' or simply 'Jean-Paul Sartre'). Objects and events which they construe within their environment may affect their decision – say the wishes, deeds and words of other individuals – but these cannot determine their decisions; there can be no external determination because the world beyond the individual is always something other to them which they are ultimately responsible for construing. Even trying to fit in to a social group or accede to others' wishes is a creative act of individuality. Individuals, as Sartre concludes, are inevitably 'free', of guidance as of determination (cf. Burridge, 1979).

Hence: 'I experience and become myself by dwelling in particular environments, and I am responsible at every moment for deciding how to act (and be) in relation to my cognitions, and where to take the world around me.'

The appreciation of individuality succeeds in not having humanity appear objectified

Human knowledge is something to which individuals subject the worlds they construe around them. There is no escape from individuality in human life, the latter being ever a subjective condition; human individuals are always subjects: always agents and always exercising their agency. Indeed, there is no other source of human agency but individuals. In search for relief from, or denial of, the burdens of responsibility in their lives, individuals sometimes imagine other sources – gods, ancestors, natural forces, linguistic grammars, cultural traditions, unconscious histories, social conditions – but these are fictions, and serve as puppets in the hands of their human users. This denial of responsibility, turning oneself into an object created, construed and controlled from without, Sartre calls 'bad faith': living one's life 'inauthentically'. What it is also important to say is that it too is an instantiation of individual agency and subjectivity; here are individuals making themselves into certain kinds of object. An existentialist appreciation of human life becomes 'humanist' at that point when it is felt that individuals can do better for themselves than spend their lives falsely objectifying the fictional, and perhaps they can be influenced towards more truthful construals of their condition.

Hence: 'I experience and become myself in particular environments at particular moments, and in recognizing my responsibility for the above I abide by my individual integrity: I accede to the dignity of my individuality.'

ANTHROPOLOGY AND INDIVIDUALITY

To become human is to become individual, Clifford Geertz once expounded (1973: 52), and we become individual in an environment of sociocultural forms and patterns in terms of which we give form, order, direction and point to our lives. The crucial question which this begs is the precise relationship between sociocultural forms and the individual lives lived by them. Becoming human and individual in an environment of sociocultural forms is neither becoming 'the same' as others, or even necessarily comparable, nor is it becoming in a deterministic or directly influenced fashion. In becoming individual in certain sociocultural milieux, energy, agency, intention and interpretation remain the property of the individual, self-conscious subject.

This has often been overlooked or negated in anthropological writings, where a system of forms is foregrounded to the almost total exclusion of their individual usage (creation, animation, interpretation, re-formation). Indeed, the intrinsic dichotomy between the individual and the world is often eschewed as a peculiarity of 'Western' sociocultural milieux, and hence as methodologically and analytically inapplicable. This is indefensible. At best it confuses individuality with individualism; and while the latter might be said to define a particular sociocultural form of behaviour (the pursuit of self-distinguishment), the former concerns a condition which is a human universal: by virtue of a unique consciousness, each of us perforce engages with the world as other and

possessed of distinct perspectives upon it. Such individuality remains consequential whether or not individual consciousness is an item of
collective discourse, whether or not individual reflection is publicly
eschewed, and whether or not individual distinctiveness is something
the institutionalization of a fund of common behaviours does its utmost
to obviate. No process of socialization or enculturation overcomes the
separateness of the individual body and brain, the phenomenology of the
ideating, acting, breathing, eating, mating, dying, birthing subject.
Individuals experience and interpret (and interpret themselves interpreting) and therefore they are.

Treating individual distinction as a matter of sociocultural discourse,
however, has allowed much anthropology to pass over individual agency
and responsibility even where diversity is admitted into the analysis. For
the diversity now becomes that of opposed social-structural interests, of
competing status groups, of contradictory mores, of situational roles, of
circumstantial norms, of a disequilibriated social organization, of a
complex system of values and beliefs, of a social system in change. It is
collective sociocultural systems that become the sources and guarantors
of meaning, and sociocultural forces to which individual 'members'
perforce respond and of which their behaviour is an expression. That is,
individual distinction and diversity disappear as individuals are decentred
from analysis, dissolved into various systems of convention which are
said to be operating through them, constituting their beings.

In much anthropology, in short, individuals become collective
constructs. Psyches become defined and realized by society: universes of
discourse reflecting social positions (cf. Berger, 1970: 375). Selfhood
becomes allocated from sociocultural repertoires for use in certain collectively structured worlds of experience: pegs on which items of
collaborative manufacture can be hung for a time (cf. Goffman, 1978:
245). Roles played become allotted and determined by society, representing bundles of obligatory activity (cf. Goffman, 1972: 76–7). Even
imaginative explorations become emanations of certain pre-given and
pre-structured life-worlds of socialization (cf. Psathas, 1973: 8–9); it is
not individuals who think through their fantasies, but fantasies which
think through them, unbeknownst and outwith their control (cf. Lévi-
Strauss, 1975: 20). Diversity is thus socialized and enculturated, and
thereby sanitized; it is not the individuals who are diverse so much as the
working parts of the complex social systems of which they are
components and conduits. Their diversity is itself governed and part of a
replicated pattern. In fact their diversity becomes an absence of diversity,
of individual difference, and a triumph of cultural order. For culture, on
this view, is essentially a set of 'control mechanisms', as Geertz phrases
it (1983: 44–5): symbolic devices – plans, recipes, rules and instructions

– which act like computer programs, reducing the breadth and indeterminateness of individuals' potential lives to the specificity and narrowness of their actual ones (cf. Gellner, 1995b: 50).

Such modelling is existentially fallacious; it offers only a pale version of the ambiguities inherent in human life and the complexities of individual interactions in sociocultural milieux. Nor is it sufficient to say, as some apologists are wont to do, that social-scientific theorization is committed to holistic explanation and so is bound to seem out of place, anaemic, in the context of the individual and particular case (cf. Culler, 1981: 16). Because it is from individuals, and individuals in interaction, that any comprehension of sociocultural milieux proceeds; it is individuals who remain the anthropological concrete, and they who provide what A.J. Ayer dubbed 'final testimony' to the existence of a common sociocultural world (1968: 256–7).

Far from entities with mechanisms and dynamics operating in their own right, what is socioculturally institutional and systemic is made up of a complex and continuous interlinkage of individual actions, deriving in turn from how individuals define and decide to meet the situations in which they find themselves. The large-scale system of cooperation or conflict (the community, kinship group, class uprising, political confederation or religious sect) may be broken down into smaller-scale interactions between interpreting individuals in any number of settings and situations. Even if, *in extremis*, the sociocultural milieu has come to be seen locally as a machine, a super-organism with a separate existence, then this state of affairs should be described as the ongoing construction of the individuals who serve it. It is they who remain responsible for this 'phantasy' of groupness, as Laing depicts it (1968: 81), and for the 'bad faith' (Sartre) which is ever necessary for its maintenance.

This includes anthropological representations of seeming groupness. Generalizations and classificatory collectivizations are what Michael Jackson (1998: 201) dubs 'defenses against impotence': magical attempts to conjure an illusion of knowledge and transcendent truth in the face of complexity, contradictoriness and situationality. Signifiers such as 'society', 'culture', 'class', 'ethnicity', 'gender', 'habitus' and 'structure', employed as isomorphs of the fluxional world, give us momentary satisfaction and senses of order and control, even mastery and authorship; but they are linguistic illusions (cf. Bockhorn and Bockhorn, 1999). Such concepts pertain to particular contexts in which people live their humanity and their individuality, but they do not describe or compass the essence of these latter.

To get beyond 'identity thinking' in terms of such essentialisms (Jackson, 1998: 200), is to 'decolonize', to dislocate, the individual human subject from its common anthropological representations; conceptually to liberate it, in short, both from overdetermining cultural conditions and overweening social institutions (discourse, language-game, collective representation, social relationship, habitus, praxis), and from their holistic and hegemonically minded social-scientific commentators. Anthropological analysis should retain respect for individual cognitive processes and, to this end, apprehend that ambiguous interface between aggregation and individuality. It should take into account both the individual agency which brings sociocultural milieux to life and also the common sociocultural forms and practices by which individuals coordinate their activities and world-views within these milieux. In this way, an anthropological appreciation might be reached of sociocultural milieux as encompassing and composed of individual difference, indeed, in a significant way constituted by it: by self-conscious individuals making an ongoing diversity of meaningful worlds through which they continue to move.

11   EXISTENTIAL POLITICS

If individual consciousness and agency is seen as responsible for creating and maintaining the diversity of cultural worlds, then anthropologically to 'decolonize' the individual human subject also entails the anthropologist proclaiming the value of the former as a prerequisite of the latter. It becomes an anthropological duty to explain that individuals make communities and create traditions, likewise to champion those social environments in which such individuality is recognized and respected, and to declaim against those which bury individual worth under a weight of so-called traditional or revelational or institutional knowledge and practice. Anthropology, in other words, becomes, at least in part, a political enterprise with a moral agenda. What I would attempt in the final part of this essay, therefore, is an anthropological portrayal of a polity based on a morality of individual sovereignty: a polity with a constitutional identity which is post-cultural, post-classificatory.

Anthropologists have been guilty, I have argued, of treating cultures and societies as if they were things-in-themselves or *sui generis*. They have been content to generalize in terms of vulgar categorizations such as 'tribes', 'castes' and 'ethnic groups', 'social structures' and 'communities', and derive individual identities (if at all) from supposedly deterministic ideological frameworks. This I would describe both as a travesty of the truth and a dereliction of social responsibility. It is a mistake (factual and moral) for anthropology to take cultural ideologies of collectivity, homogeneity, boundedness and distinctiveness at face value, and to further translate this into so-called rights of cultural difference; a serious failing for anthropology to describe and prescribe community – its relative cultural reality – without admitting the universality of underlying individual consciousness and creativity. Likewise, instead of simply lending their advocatory efforts and support to the 'third-generation rights' of cultures and communities to their distinct traditions and religions, anthropologists could work towards an accommodation between such claims to sovereignty and self-determination and the underlying – and overriding – rights of individuals.

What can be argued is that individuals are more than their membership of and participation in cultural collectivities. For it is

individuals who make and maintain cultural worlds – remake them continuously through their creative cognitions – and it is individuals in
interaction who make and maintain communities. The latter are less
objectivities than the subjective realizations of those who symbolically
articulate and animate them at particular times and places. Cultural
communities are symbolizations which exist by virtue of individuals'
ongoing exchanges.

What kind of community, then, might an anthropological morality
point to? In a word, an open or 'voluntaristic' one (Phillips, 1993: 190).
Voluntariness entails anthropologists employing what Rorty (1992:
89–90) calls 'ironic redescription' of cultural communities; to the extent
that cultures claim absolute legitimacy and revelational knowledge,
absolute discreteness and difference from others, and to the extent that
communities lay absolute claim to individual members' loyalty,
thoughts, feelings and lives, these claims can only be taken ironically.
For individuals come first, both ontologically and morally, and all that
cultural communities contain – their traditions, customs and institutions
(their 'priesthoods, secret societies, and schools' in Popper's [1980] dis-
tillation) – should depend for their continuation and their value on the
voluntary, contractual adherence of individuals. Idioms and ideologies of
cultural absoluteness may serve as convenient flags and badges of
belonging, and may be instrumental as currencies of internal exchange,
but anthropologists ought not to describe or prescribe them as anything
more real, nor as having any ontological or contractual primacy.
Absolutist claims pertain merely to Gellner's 'theatre of culture' (1993:
91), while the real science of individual consciousness, of the creativity
of the individual mind, of individual rights to pursue their imaginative
potential, must be seen to undercut them.

PERSONAL NATIONALISM?

[A]ny movement that attempts to transcend (to relegate to the background) the
struggle for individual sovereignty, to place greater importance on the interests
of the collective – class, race, gender, nation, ethnicity, vice, or profession – seems
to me a conspiracy to rein in even further an abused human freedom. (Vargas
Llosa, 1998: 59)

In arguing for an appreciation of what he terms 'personal nationalism',
Anthony Cohen (1996) denies that the logic of national and international political economies need necessarily translate into those who deem
themselves members of such entities sharing a homogeneity of identity.
To the contrary, the upsurge of often militant collective identities which
we have witnessed, in Europe say, over the past few centuries – nation-

alistic, ethnic, religious, regional and so on – and continue to witness today (in Europe and beyond) owe their power and conviction to the grassroots phenomenon that it is these collectivities that *individual members*, separately and distinctively, feel to be the most advantageous medium for the expression of their whole selves. It is in the community voice that individuals best recognize their own experiences and mentalities, and by way of collective symbols that they think through and express their individual identities. In short, it is through the nation (et cetera) that they accrue 'a compelling formulation of self' (Cohen, 1996: 802, 1985: 107–9).

I do not doubt that this 'personal nationalism', the inventing and investing of a collective entity with individual meaning, can be true (cf. Rapport, 1994; also Devereux, 1978). But I think it has dangers; I also think that, as Emerson might have said, a reliance on self, and the self's own voice, for providing 'the most advantageous medium for the expression of self' is a better hope. All forms of collective identity and community identification, as (*litterateur* and politician) Vargas Llosa has pithily described above, eventuate in the setting up of impersonal institutions whose 'own' interests can be construed as distinct from and superior to those of their members – individually or severally considered. However innocuous or innocent-seeming or altruistic or idealistic are the virtues associated with the collective, however much the feelings which bind one to fellow community-members are of solidarity and love, the other side of the patriotic coin is 'the denigration of what belongs to someone else, the desire to humiliate and defeat others, those who are different from you because they have another skin colour, another language, another god, even another way of dressing, another diet' (Vargas Llosa, 1998: 169). And Vargas Llosa, concludes:

[B]ehind your speeches and banners exalting this piece of geography blemished with boundary stones and arbitrary borders, in which you see the personification of a superior form of history and social metaphysics, there is only an astute *aggiornamento* of the ancient primitive 'fear of separating from the tribe, of no longer being part of the mass, of becoming an individual. ... The umbilical cord that connects you across the centuries is called terror of the unknown, hatred for what is different, rejection of adventure, panic at the thought of freedom and the responsibility it brings to invent yourself each day, a vocation for servitude to the routine and the gregarious, a refusal to decollectivize, so that you will not be obliged to face the daily challenge of individual sovereignty. (1998: 169)

One need not agree with Vargas Llosa's explanation for the continuities of the 'irrationalism' of collective identities and community loyalties (or his narration of convention and the group as something prior from which the individual must make an effort to separate himself and decollectivize) in order to share his sentiments.[8] Human beings can do better than patriotism, and their societies can be based on a legal recognition of identities which are other than collectivistic or classificatory: namely treating the sovereignty of moving individuals.

RIGHTS TO MOVEMENT AND THE URBAN REFUGE

The other side of the coin of a contemporary world of particularisms, militancies and absolutisms is a world of movement: of migration, 'multiculturalism', hybridity and creolization. As Gellner expounded (1993: 79), the reactionary despotism of fundamentalist regimes (from Iran to Afghanistan to Sudan) develops in the context of an opening up of the world to science and to choice as implemented by Western, liberal and laissez-faire regimes. (For some, indeed, such fundamentalism is a form of religion born out of contradictions in contemporary capitalism: the ideology of flawed, failed consumers who seek an escape from individual responsibility and choice [Bauman, 1998].)

The experiential implications of a world of movement and sociocultural choice is something that anthropologists are now, of course, deeply involved in charting (cf. Rapport and Dawson, 1998: 3–34). In a mirroring of the psychological processes by which, according to the likes of Rushdie and Brodsky, the individual ongoingly creates meaning in his life by constructing a pastiche out of a diversity of momentary cognitions ('a shaky edifice built out of scraps'), there is now a recognition that sociocultural processes also entail the juxtaposition of a diverse array of behavioural forms.[9] As canonized by Lyotard (1986):

[E]clecticism is the degree zero of contemporary general culture: one listens to reggae, watches a western, eats McDonald's food for lunch and local cuisine for dinner, wears Paris perfume in Tokyo and 'retro' clothes in Hong Kong; knowledge is a matter of TV games ...

and echoed by Bradbury (1994):

Today ... it is no accident that London Bridge now stands rebuilt in the Arizona desert, that Russian radios play American songs, or Italian studios make spaghetti westerns, that Americans eat hamburgers, and Hamburgers eat hot dogs ... . When we think of our times as 'Postmodern', what we generally mean is this sense of ever-refracted, depthless, despatialized history, this sphere of random and pluralistic quotation, this merging of myths and motifs that suggests we live in a culture beyond culture.

For Nietzsche (1994), this coincidence of the characteristics of pastiche in both psychological and sociocultural domains was no accident. The 'wandering encyclopedias' of the modern-day, as he psychically described his consociates and himself, were inhabitants of an 'age of comparisons' which existed as a social-evolutionary stage between 'folk' cultures and nations (*Voelker*) on the one hand and on the other a more 'refined' age which would be better again. In this present age of comparison, there was a great stirring both of internal motives and of external motion: a 'whirling flow of men, [a] polyphony of strivings' (1994: 29). This characterized not only artistic creativity and consciousness, with styles of the arts imitated one next to the other, but also 'stages and kinds of morality, customs, cultures'; a psychic striving was giving on to a sociocultural advance. The outcome would be an evolution in refinement and a heightening of aesthetic feeling, Nietzsche was convinced, due to the multiplicity and openness of comparisons and selection being made between experiences of better and baser versions of both art and society.

Whether or not one is convinced by Nietzsche's evolutionary portrayal, the currency of notions of pastiche, as both psychological descriptor and sociocultural, is an appositely existential image with which to begin considering legal arrangements in contemporary polities; polities which might be based on individual members' accruing identities and meaningful environments for themselves through an ongoing series of individual interpretations. The place I would begin sketching in the lineaments of an existential politics would be with the individual's right to a continuing diversity of freely chosen identities and the juxtaposing of these.

For it should be the right of individuals to construct identities for themselves of their own interpretation and ongoing selection, and it should be a duty to respect this right in others. In neither case need the identities thereby accrued abide by any exterior standards of singularity or consistency or constancy or appropriate form; in both substance and form, it should be the right of individuals ongoingly to construct identities for themselves which are matters of individual decision alone. It should also be a right for the ways in which they are known by others not to negate their decisions of self-identity. In Cohen's words (1996: 806), it should be an individual's right to 'command' their own identity or sense of self, and it is 'an infringement of that right for the anthropologist or anyone else to treat [that] self, however it is described, as a mere reflex of some larger structural condition', as externally derived or determined.

On the face of it, such emphases on individuals' rights to their own identities (and for these to be the basis of how they are known by others) and on their duties to respect these rights in others, are basic to the legal arrangements of most Western democracies. They were famously espoused by John Stuart Mill's prescriptions (1972: 79) for 'representative government', and they were famously enshrined in the American Constitution. The rights are not without limit – they are balanced by duties towards other individuals – and just as the legal procedures of the liberal polity take precedence over the rights of cultural communities to self-expression, so the rights of the individual do not extend to changing the legality of human rights. Individuals have rights to their own identities but not to a limitless expression of these; part of the contractual apparatus of belonging must be a promissory statement by the individual (as self-identified) to the polity to abide by these limitations.

In mutuality with the duty to abide by the legal procedures of the polity and uphold (often implicitly stated) contracts of 'good citizenship', the state endeavours to supply through its institutions a nurturing or at least neutral environment in which individuals' potential freely to decide upon their self-identity is respected and cushioned. This environment commonly comprises, *inter alia*, safeguards concerning the individual's health, education and security. As children, individuals' growth towards autonomy in manifestations of self is anticipated and allowed for, as well as tutoring in the examples and the differences of others, and as adults a continued expression of autonomy in matters of identity is expected.

Notwithstanding, an enshrinement in law of such rights and reciprocal practices does not necessarily eventuate in their routinization – as we are unfortunately aware from our everyday lives. The paradox of instituting universal and non-partisan procedures for treating in a democratic fashion the diversities and idiosyncrasies of individual identities, indeed, has been deliberated upon by a diversity of liberal commentators, from Georg Simmel to E.M. Forster. It is a 'sociological tragedy', according to Simmel (1971: 351ff), that individuals' fluctuating, diverse and continually developing life processes come to be manifested in relatively stable conceptual and categorial forms: in terms of public identities which are fixed, monothetic, even stereotypical. For, while it is by way of stable conceptual and categorial forms – languages and ideologies – that individuals come together in social exchange, these synthesizing phenomena also generalize, abstract and distance individuals from one another's changing inner lives: we expect to know others in the very categorial terms which keep us apart.

Democracy warrants only 'two cheers' (out of an ideal three), Forster concurs (1972: 54), because (as we heard from Rorty) love fails to figure as a force in democratic public life or affairs. In the private life of democracies, of course, love flourishes, but so frighteningly full and complex have open, liberal societies become – full of people one does not and cannot know, and cannot even seem to like ('like the colour of their skins, say, or the shape of their noses, or the way they blow them or don't blow them' [Forster, 1972: 55]) – that love, entailing a close and mutual personalism, does not operate. In a setting where we cannot personally know so much, something much less perfect than love is called for, namely, tolerance. Admittedly, tolerance entails the virtue of imagination, of all the time putting yourself in someone else's place, but, Forster concludes, it is a dull substitute for love (which Forster would count as the greatest of all goods). The public procedures of law and justice, in Rortian terms, are empty of the personal warmth of the private club.

According to Herzfeld (1993: 1), there is some inevitability to these commentaries on life in the liberal-democratic nation-state; not only, he contends, does 'a rejection of [individuals'] common humanity, a denial of their identity and selfhood' often coexist with stated democratic and egalitarian ideals but these failings can be seen to be in a way officially sanctioned. The reason Herzfeld would give is the inexorable reification and indifference of bureaucratic authority. The apparatus of the liberal nation-state claims to be universalistic and respectful of 'the indexical contingency of everyday social life' but in fact the impulse to efficiency of its institutional-administrative workings make it selective, partisan, and interested more in 'the iconic homogeneity of its own eternal being'. The functioning of the state, in other words, is only a small remove from the 'tribe' mentality out of which it evolved but which it purports to eschew. Here are the same self-worshipping rituals, the same symbolic subordi-nation of smaller identities to an encompassing collective good and the same deployment of a kinship-like discrimination between own and other: the transmogrification of individuals into citizens who embody the national image and outsiders who embody difference. The outcome is variable – from petty, bureaucratic capriciousness and bloody-mindedness, to power-grabbing, to genocide – but always, Herzfeld concludes, a far cry from the ideal – even, paradoxically, from the demo-cratically acceptable.

My reading of these critiques is that the manifestations of groupism – people seeing others and themselves in classificatory terms, as first and foremost, group members or representatives; people reading off others' identities in their own terms, by way of criteria external to the people themselves; people with 'the same' identity ganging up; people with 'opposed' identities seeking to nullify one another – are difficult to overcome. However individually orientated the nation-state of liberal democracy sets out to be and claims to be, collective identities become superordinate, become 'imperative' in Barth's terms (1969), such that nationalism or ethnicity or familism or religiosity or regionality or class status become the prism through which all else is read and known. Even 'humanity' becomes a category, inasmuch as one cannot legislate for individuality, make universal policies for individuals, or operate univer-salizing procedures – from language to law – which do not render idiosyncrasies as stereotypes.

And yet I would say that groupism and impersonalism need not be the case (cf. Rapport, 1997b: 12–29). In between the tragedy of formalism (Simmel), the institutionalization of indifference (Herzfeld) and the dullness of tolerance (Forster), there is the possibility of measures being put in place whereby the accruing of identity by one person does not intentionally or unintentionally negate the practice of accruing by others, and whereby others can come to know how to read the individual (recognize individual identities) in terms which that individual creates, or at least validates. In part this is a matter of education; one educates for liberal democracy and in the manner of 'democratic individuality', as we heard Kateb describe it, so that a celebration of individuals' choices and achievements is encouraged, and the 'colonization, massification, or anonymization of the human subject' (Cohen, 1996: 803), by way of classificatory procedures and collectivization, are disparaged. In part it is a matter of a political conceptualization and the legal routinization of individual identity, in the light of anthropological insights concerning the necessary place of movement, multiplicity, originality and change in that identity.

In practical terms it is this that the International Parliament of Writers has sought to conceptualize and routinize in its Network of Refuge Cities, it seems to me: the city being deliberately chosen as the social milieu in which a postmodern liberal polity imbued with a personal ethos might hope to be instituted (cf. Rapport, n.d.). Ancient democracy was born in the *polis*, it is argued in the IPW literature (Lopez, 1995: 5), European towns and cities have acted as sanctuaries since the Middle Ages, and it is a 'civic conscience' which might still hold out the best chance of protection to the individual and the free expression of their artistry. The city can provide 'a community with an unshakeable faith in the democratic values of freedom and law' (IPW, 1995b: 7). If, as Bourdieu puts it (1995: 6), the IPW should act as a research laboratory for new forms of action against international, political and religious tyranny, and the unchecked power of money and the media, then the Refuge City serves at least as a trope with which to image a reinvention of democracy. In the face of the closedness and fixity of states and the reactionariness and institutionalization of censorious opinion, in the face of new persecutions emerging in the gaps between the authority of states – 'arbitrary', terroristic expressions of life-threatening intolerance which the state no longer controls – the Refuge City serves as an actual locus of individual freedom (IPW, 1995b: 6).[10] From the Refuge City as locus and as trope one can imagine democracy reborn – in cities and by cities around the world – possessing the twin features of global movement and local security: an image of transformation from *polis* to cosmos.

As Lopez elaborates (1995), Refuge Cities with pretensions to global responsibility model themselves as ideally open spaces, polythetic and multicultural spaces, without minorities or marginals. Citizenship is conceptualized not in inward-looking or isolationist terms but inclusively. It is envisaged that individuals in physical movement through space and in cognitive movement through their lives may all contract into civil and political rights and duties on the basis of choice and at will. The city becomes an assemblage of individual life-projects and trajectories. An exchange may then take place between the 'cultures', the perspectives, constructed by those who are citizens at one time and over time. A network of such cities – at the same time decentralized and coordinated – can amount to 'an archipelago of the imagination': a refutation of classificatory limits to migration, legal membership and sentimental belonging, and an effecting of voluntary community amid a world of movement. Just as the IPW publicizes at present the work of refugee artists and instigates readings and workshops, a network of Refuge Cities can hope to offer 'spaces of freedom for creation' (Soyinka, 1998: 1), both geographic and symbolic, by which the fields of operation of the censors and dogmatists might begin to be limited.

In the Network of Refuge Cities as envisaged by the International Parliament of Writers, in sum, legally constituted, social and physical 'free zones' are appraised in terms of the extents to which they are synonymous with 'free territories of the mind'. The Network, 'an arena for invention, a forum for inventors', intends an escape from the 'obsession with identity' (ethnic, cultural and linguistic) which threatens to render individuality 'speechless' (Salmon, 1993: 2, 1995: 4). A particular form of citizenship is here championed, one that sees beyond 'collective manifestations [of identity] based on coercive dogmas' to a recognition that the freedom to write and create individual worlds is the foundation of a vital, democratic society (IPW, 1999: 6). Here is a vision, in other words, which attempts to operationalize an idea of post-cultural communities as voluntaristic 'worlds of meaning in the minds of their members' (cf. Cohen, 1985: 82).

NARRATIONAL INDIVIDUALITY

Throughout this essay, I have sought to balance, to juxtapose, ideas of legal or procedural-cum-constitutional fixity against ideas of existential movement. Basic to an appreciation of individuals' rights to their own identities, I have argued, and the enshrinement this right (and its reciprocal duties and practices) in liberal-democratic laws and norms, should be a legal foregrounding of the concomitant right to movement. It is through movement that the individual accrues a sense of self and of world and continues to have these senses develop and change (cf. Rapport, 1997b: 64–79). This movement is both cognitive and physical, it is intentioned and it entails possible movement between perceptions, points of view, beliefs, values and meanings.

An existential politics should seek to ensure that this movement remains as untrammelled, geo-physically and conceptually, as possible. This privileging of movement has a dual logic. First, it is in individuals' interests to be as free to move – between polities, between voluntary associations and communities, between behavioural contracts – as they see fit, for such voluntary movement is both an instantiation of their creative construction of identity and the medium or means by which this creativity continues to fuel itself. Second, it is in the interests of liberal democracy that individuals be free to move and continue to practise movement because the more this takes place, and the more diverse identities which an individual thereby accrues, the less likely that an 'imperative', essential status – as member of this stereotypical collectivity or that – will be able to be imposed externally on the individual or will feel appropriate internally. The existence of classificatory identities and groups in society, of blocs of opposed interests and labels, becomes increasingly less likely the more multiple, diverse and ongoing are individuals' affiliations, relations and interactions within that milieu. Were liberal-democratic societies configured primarily in terms of movement and multiplicity – educationally, legally, bureaucratically, recreationally – then there would be both less desire for, and possibility of, groupism. Classificatory 'identity thinking' would be far harder to accomplish or maintain, and what groups there were would be shifting and fragmentary. The groups (from states to ethnicities to religious congregations to local communities) would be ambiguous and contingent entities, by their very nature oxymoronic: singular-named institutions which, it was known, admitted and expected, contained contingent multiplicities.

Finally, the identities which individuals accrue and exhibit in this setting can be described as narrational ones. Individuals are known not only by their choices of voluntary community affiliation – although these may serve as useful, temporary mailboxes and addresses for the purposes of tracking contractual responsibilities – but by their 'career', by the movement of their life-course in the way that they narrate it. We have heard Paul Ricoeur advocating a mutual hospitality regarding the life-narratives by which people come to compose and express their senses of self. By this means also, others can come to 'read' and appreciate individuals' life-trajectories, their life-project(s) and their works. For their narrational identity(ies) is something which every individual possesses: something which is ongoing, changing and never not in the process of being both told (to others and to themselves), read and lived (cf. Rapport,

1997b: 43–63).[11] At the same time that individuals' different life-narratives are particular in their constitution to themselves alone, being a shared phenomenon of human experience the narration of identity is something which extends the possibility of sympathy and empathy between individuals.

We have heard too Milan Kundera arguing that what he called the 'precious essence of the European spirit' – its 'respect for the individual, for his original thought, and for his right to an inviolable private life' – was being 'held safe ... inside the history of the novel, the wisdom of the novel' (1990: 165). The suggestion here is that the 'novel' that the individual, every individual, writes of their life – the story they compose, narrate, put into effect, live – can also be a political instrument: a means to organize a polity which both possesses legal-constitutional, univer-salizing norms *and* particularizing practices. For one recognizes that every individual is a 'novelist' and has a story to tell – *is*, indeed, the story they tell, the narrative they enact – and has rights to do and be so, and at the same time one accepts that every story and every telling might be, in the words of the poet, 'counter, original, spare, strange' (Gerald Manley Hopkins, cited in Quiller-Couch, 1961: 1011). Through narrative recognition and respect, in short, across a global archipelago of democratic cities, one can imagine a form of existential politics and liberal polity – as too of existential anthropology – in which the individual is known and accorded legal rights in a form which does not reduce that individuality to singular, fixed or classificatory universals.

NOTES TO PART II

1. Many of the participants in the political debate over civil society and the engendering of a 'constitutional faith' (Hugo Black), a '*Verfassungspatriotismus*' (Habermas), may also be said to hope for this (cf. Hann and Dunn, 1996).
2. This point bears spelling out. Gellner's understanding of 'liberalism', as with those of other commentators we shall meet (Karl Popper, John Gray, George Kateb, John Stuart Mill), does not equate with laissez-faire capitalism or any one, necessary economic system. The argument on behalf of Western, liberal democracy, therefore, should not be confused with advocating of a global market economy; Gellner is careful here to differentiate between individual liberty and 'the McWorld', and speaks of legal bulwarks to safeguard the former in the face of the latter. Moreover, as the examples of, say, Sweden, Britain and the United States attest, there are many ways in which this relationship between liberal democracy and economy can be conceived of. Critique of global capitalism, then, need not be seen to detract – as often is the case (e.g. Esteva and Prakash, 1998) – from a portrayal of liberalism as a politico-legal philosophy.
3. Besides in his novel, *Howards End*, Forster also makes use of the imagery of achieving proportion in essays such as 'What I Believe' (1939 in 1972), where he advocates tolerance, good temper and sympathy being amalgamated with faith if the former are to be stiffened sufficiently to withstand the advances of the many more 'militant creeds' likely to beset them.
4. Liberty, for instance, may throw up incompatible emphases on 'freedom from' versus 'freedom to'; while liberty *per se* may turn out to be incommensurable with equality or fraternity.
5. Hence, Bernard Williams: '[T]he anthropologist's heresy – cultural relativism – [is] possibly the most absurd view to have been advanced even in moral philosophy' (1993: 20).
6. I would differentiate cultural 'connoisseurs' (Ingold, 1976: 246–7) from Rorty's notion of anthropologists acting as 'connoisseurs of diversity' precisely because of the absence of the word 'culture' from the latter phrasing; I would argue that diversity properly belongs to individual actors not to hypostatized groupings they might purport to speak for.

    A fine example of this latter (illusory, self-promoting, Romantic) connoisseurship is provided by Esteva and Prakash (1998), two Western-educated intellectuals and academics who produce a diatribe against the ideology of individualistic human rights on behalf of traditional communitarianism. Human rights represents the invasion of local, indigenous, non-modern communities by a universal secular religion, they declare. It amounts to an abuse of power, both by the nation-state against the locale and by the West (in the form of a global economy) against the Rest, with tragically deleterious consequences. There is, for instance, a breaking up of local life and relations defined by custom, community and the commons; for human rights is incommensurable with cultural ideals or virtues as central to traditional life as notions of communal or cosmic solidarity. Furthermore, disembedded, post-traditional 'individuals' soon learn that the state and its promises cannot be relied upon, and that a new-fangled education does not give on to security of health, salary or pension. Hence, these individuals who have abandoned their communities for the cities – for menial jobs below their expectations and qualifications, for poverty and charity – disregarding the wisdom and skills of traditional elders (or modern intellectual elites) now proceed to 'plague' the world with 'endless needs', their desires having become their rights. Thus is 'the richness of tradition' transformed into 'a burden': 'wisdom into backwardness; awareness of self-limitation into apathy or lack of initiative' (Esteva and Prakash, 1998: 122).

Looking backwards from this flawed, progressive ambience, Esteva and Prakash recall a happy time when cultures as communities of faith practised social realities based on common backgrounds and shared horizons of intelligibility. Exercising equally traditional ways of dealing with outsiders, based on hospitality and tolerance, these cultural communities further effected 'a rich multiplicity of moral languages, concepts and discourses' (1998: 16).

The underlying reality, they conclude, is that we continue to live in a 'pluriverse' – in a world of diverse, irreducible and mutually incommensurable cultures – such that one group's torture, or slavery, or ritual injury, or lynching, or rape is not another's; what is 'torture' from one perspective is 'private ownership', or 'residing alone in hospital', or 'being singled out in a classroom', or 'being unable to nurse a child in public', from another. Any talk of 'the good life', in sum, can only take place within an ethnos, a hexis, a cultural context.

7. '[The] history of anthropology may thus be viewed as a continuing (and complex) dialectic between the universalism of "anthropos" and the diversitarianism of "ethnos"' (Stocking, 1992: 361).

8. Cf. Popper (1980: 176): ideologies of 'tribalism', of a form of closure which arrests openness in favour of a coercive totalism and rigid conventionality, exist where the 'strain' of 'civilization', of rational attempts at human improvement and the nurturance of the individual, is too great. Like Freud (*Civilization and Its Discontents*), Popper sees the desire to abdicate one's individual freedom and in this way to escape the responsibility of having to make choices and decisions and of living with the consequences, as representing a victory for the 'infantile' side of human nature.

9. Multiculturalism, as Barber puts it (1996: 135) is the rule rather than the exception within the world's nation-states, where less than 10 per cent are ethnically homogeneous and in only 50 per cent does one ethnic group comprise 75 per cent or more of the population.

10. The possible setting up of an IPW Assembly in the Arab world was the topic of a seminar among Arab intellectuals, held at Caen in 1998. Exposing politics and religion to the 'risk' of literature, it was argued, should not be denied in the name of Islamic spirituality (IPW, 1999: 6).

11. Cf. MacIntyre (1984): 'We all live out narratives in our lives and ... we understand our own lives in terms of the narrative that we live out.'

REFERENCES TO PART II

American Anthropological Association (1947) 'Executive Board Statement on Human Rights Submitted to the Commission on Human Rights, United Nations', *American Anthropologist* 49 (4): 539–43.

Amin, S. (1989) *L'Eurocentrisme.* Paris: Anthropos.

Anderson, B. (1991) *Imagined Communities.* London: Verso.

Appadurai, A. (1991) 'Global Ethnoscapes: Notes and Queries for a Transnational Anthropology', in R. Fox (ed.) *Recapturing Anthropology.* Sante Fe: School of American Research Press.

Asad, T. (1990) 'Ethnography, Literature and Politics: Some Readings and Uses of Salman Rushdie's *The Satanic Verses*', *Cultural Anthropology* 5: 239–69.

Ashley, K. (1990) 'Introduction', in K. Ashley (ed.) *Victor Turner and the Construction of Cultural Criticism: Between Literature and Anthropology.* Bloomington: Indiana University Press.

Augé, M. (1995) *Non-places: Introduction to an Anthropology of Supermodernity.* London: Verso.

Austin-Smith, B. (1990) 'Into the Heart of Irony', *Canadian Dimension* 27 (7): 51–2.

Ayer, A. (1968) 'Can There Be a Private Language?', in G. Pitcher (ed.) *Wittgenstein.* London: Macmillan.

Barber, B. (1996) 'Multiculturalism between Individuality and Community: Chasm or Bridge?' in A. Sarat and D. Villa (eds) *Liberal Modernism and Democratic Individuality: George Kateb and the Practice of Politics.* Princeton, NJ: Princeton University Press.

Barth, F. (ed.) (1969) *Ethnic Groups and Boundaries.* Boston: Little Brown.

—— (1992) 'Towards a Greater Naturalism in Conceptualising Societies', in A. Kuper (ed.) *Conceptualising Society.* London: Routledge.

Bateson, G. (1958) 'Language and Psychotherapy', *Psychiatry* 21: 96–100.

—— (1972) *Steps to an Ecology of Mind.* London: Paladin.

Bauman, Z. (1998) 'Postmodern Religion?', in P. Heelas (ed.) *Religion, Modernity and Postmodernity.* Oxford: Blackwell.

Berger, J. (1994) *A Telling Eye: The Work of John Berger* BBC 2, 30 July.

Berger, P. (1970) 'Identity as a Problem in the Sociology of Knowledge', in J. Curtis and J. Petras (eds) *The Sociology of Knowledge.* London: Duckworth.

Berlin, I. (1990) *The Crooked Timber of Humanity: Chapters in the History of Ideas.* London: Murray.

Bockhorn, E. and O. Bockhorn (1999) 'Who Benefits from "Ethnicity"', in B. Baskar and B. Brumen (eds) *Mediterranean Ethnological Summer School, vol. III.* Ljubljana: Institut za multikulturne raziskave.

Bourdieu, P. (1984) *Distinction.* London: Routledge & Kegan Paul.

—— (1995) 'In Interview', *Litteratures* autumn: 6.

Boulware-Miller, K. (1985) 'Female Circumcision: Challenges to the Practice as a Human Rights Violation', *Harvard Women's Law Journal* 8: 155–77.

Bradbury, M. (1994) *Dangerous Pilgrimages: Trans-Atlantic Mythologies and the Novel*. London: Secker & Warburg.

Brodsky, J. (1988) 'The Politics of Poetry', *The Sunday Times* 10 January.

Burridge, K. (1979) *Someone, No One. An Essay on Individuality*. Princeton: Princeton University Press.

Clay, J. (1988) 'Anthropologists and Human Rights – Activists by Default?', in T. Downing and G. Kushner (eds) *Human Rights and Anthropology*. Cambridge, MA: Cultural Survival.

Cohen, A.P. (1985) *The Symbolic Construction of Community*. London: Routledge.

—— (1994) *Self-Consciousness: An Alternative Anthropology of Identity*. London: Routledge.

—— (1996) 'Personal Nationalism: A Scottish View of some Rites, Rights and Wrongs', *American Ethnologist* 23 (4): 802–15.

Cohen A.P. and N.J. Rapport (1995) 'Introduction: Consciousness in Anthropology', in A.P. Cohen and N.J. Rapport (eds) *Questions of Consciousness*. London: Routledge.

Crawford, J. (ed.) (1988) *The Rights of Peoples*. Oxford: Clarendon.

Culler, J. (1981) *The Pursuit of Signs: Semiotics, Literature, Deconstruction*. Ithaca, NY: Cornell University Press.

Derrida, J. (1998) 'Reaction', *Correspondence of the International Parliament of Writers* 4 (spring): 1.

Devereux, G. (1978) *Ethnopsychoanalysis*. Berkeley: University of California Press.

Douglas, J. and J. Johnson (eds) (1977) *Existential Sociology*. Cambridge: Cambridge University Press.

Downing, T. and G. Kushner (eds) (1988) *Human Rights and Anthropology*. Cambridge, MA: Cultural Survival.

Doyal, L. and I. Gough (1991) *A Theory of Human Need*. Basingstoke: Macmillan.

Durkheim, E. (1973) *Moral Education*. New York: Free.

Edelman, G. (1989) *The Remembered Present. A Biological Theory of Consciousness*. New York: Basic Books.

Emerson, R.W. (1981) *The Portable Emerson*, ed. C. Bode. Harmondsworth: Penguin.

Esteva, G. and M.S. Prakash (1998) *Grassroots Post-Modernism: Remaking the Soil of Cultures*. London: Zed.

Falk, R. (1980) 'Theoretical Foundations of Human Rights', in P. Newberg (ed.) *The Politics of Human Rights*. New York: New York University Press.

Fernandez, J. (1995) 'Amazing Grace: Meaning Deficit, Displacement and New Consciousness in Expressive Interaction', in A.P. Cohen and N.J. Rapport (eds) *Questions of Consciousness*. London: Routledge.

Forster, E.M. (1950) *Howards End*. Harmondsworth: Penguin.

—— (1972) *Two Cheers for Democracy*. Harmondsworth: Penguin.

Geertz, C. (1957) 'Ethos, Worldview and the Analysis of Sacred Symbols', *The Antioch Review* 17 (4): 126–41.

—— (1973) *The Interpretation of Cultures*. New York: Basic Books.

—— (1983) *Local Knowledge*. New York: Basic Books.

Gellner, E. (1993) *Postmodernism, Reason and Religion*. London: Routledge.

—— (1995a) 'Anything Goes: The Carnival of Cheap Relativism which Threatens to Swamp the Coming *Fin de Millenaire*', *Times Literary Supplement* 4811: 6–8.

—— (1995b) *Anthropology and Politics. Revolutions in the Sacred Grove*. Oxford: Blackwell.

Giddens, A. (1990) *The Consequences of Modernity*. Stanford, CA: Stanford University Press.

Gilad, L. (1996) 'Cultural Collision and Human Rights', in W. Giles, H. Moussa and P. Van Esterik (eds) *Development and Diaspora: Gender and the Refugee Experience*. Dundas, ON: Artemis.

Goffman, E. (1972) *Encounters*. London: Penguin.

—— (1978) *The Presentation of Self in Everyday Life*. Harmondsworth: Penguin.

Goody, J. (1977) *The Domestication of the Savage Mind*. Cambridge: Cambridge University Press.

Gray, J. (1989) *Liberalisms: Essays in Political Philosophy*. London: Routledge.

—— (1995) *Enlightenment's Wake: Politics and Culture at the Close of the Modern Age*. London: Routledge.

—— (1996) 'What Liberalism Cannot Do', *New Statesman* 20 September: 18–20.

—— (1997) 'The Tragic View', *Times Literary Supplement* 4930: 8.

—— (1998) 'The Trusting Self: Is Moral Agency on the Wane?', *Times Literary Supplement* 4956: 5–6.

—— (2000) 'The light of other minds', *Times Literary Supplement* 5054: 12–13.

Greaves, T. (1998) 'AAA Proposes Declaration on Human Rights', *Anthropology Newsletter* September: 9.

Handler, R. and D. Segal (1990) *Jane Austen and the Fiction of Culture: An Essay on the Narration of Social Realities*. Tucson: University of Arizona Press.

Hann, C. and E. Dunn, (eds) (1996) *Civil Society*. London: Routledge.

Hannerz, U. (1992) 'The Global Ecumene as a Network of Networks', in A. Kuper (ed.) *Conceptualising Society*. London: Routledge.

Herzfeld, M. (1993) *The Social Production of Indifference. Exploring the Symbolic Roots of Western Bureaucracy*. Oxford: Berg.

Hinton, A. (1998) 'Why Did the Nazis Kill? Anthropology, Genocide and the Goldhagen Controversy', *Anthropology Today* 14 (5): 9–15.

Hutcheon, L. (1994) *Irony's Edge*. London: Routledge.

Ingold, T. (1976) *The Skolt Lapps Today*. Cambridge: Cambridge University Press.

—— (1986) *The Appropriation of Nature*. Manchester: Manchester University Press.

International Parliament of Writers (1994) *Litteratures* October/November.

—— (1995a) *Litteratures* autumn.

—— (1995b) *The Charter of Cities of Asylum*. Strasbourg: IPW.

—— (1999) *The Correspondence* 5.

—— (2001) *Autodafe* 1, June.

Jackson, M. (1989) *Paths toward a Clearing. Radical Empiricism and Ethnographic Inquiry*. Bloomington: Indiana University Press.

—— (ed.) (1996) *Things as They Are: New Directions in Phenomenological Anthropology*. Bloomington: Indiana University Press.

—— (1998) *Minima Ethnographica: Intersubjectivity and the Anthropological Project*. Chicago: University of Chicago Press.

Kateb, G. (1968) 'Remarks on the Procedures of Constitutional Democracy', *Nomos* 10: 215–37.

—— (1981) 'The Moral Distinctiveness of Representative Democracy', *Ethics* 91: 357–74.

—— (1984a) 'Democratic Individuality and the Claim of Politics', *Political Theory* 12 (3): 331–60.

—— (1984b) *Hannah Arendt*. Totowa: Rowman & Allanheld.

—— (1991) 'Democratic Individuality and the Meaning of Rights', in N. Rosenblum (ed.) *Liberalism and the Moral Life*. Cambridge, MA: Harvard University Press.

—— (1995) *Emerson and Self-Reliance*. Thousand Oaks: Sage.

Kidwai, A. (1996) 'Comment on Prina Werbner's Article', *Current Anthropology* 37 (Suppl.): S74–5.

Kotarba, J. and A. Fontana (eds) (1984) *The Existential Self in Society*. Chicago: University of Chicago Press.

Kundera, M. (1990) *The Art of the Novel*. London: Faber.

—— (1995) 'The Enigma of Old Booby Traps', *Guardian* 16 September.

Laing, R.D. (1968) *The Politics of Experience*. Harmondsworth: Penguin.

Lévi-Strauss, C. (1975) *The Raw and the Cooked*. New York: Harper Colophon.

Lopez, F.M. (1995) 'The Cities of the Asylum Charter', *Litteratures* autumn: 5.

Lyotard, J.-F. (1986) *The Post-Modern Condition: A Report on Knowledge*. Manchester: Manchester University Press.

Macfarlane, A. (1992) 'On Individualism', *Proceedings of the British Academy* 82: 171–99.

MacIntyre, A. (1984) *After Virtue*. Notre Dame, IN: University of Notre Dame Press.

—— (1988) *Whose Justice? Whose Rationality?* Notre Dame, IN: University of Notre Dame Press.

Madood, T. (1989) 'Religious Anger and Minority Rights', *Political Quarterly* 60 (July): 280–4.

—— (1990) 'British Asian Muslims and the Rushdie Affair', *Political Quarterly* 61 (April–June): 143–60.

Marcus, G. and M. Fischer (1986) *Anthropology as Cultural Critique: An Experimental Moment in the Human Sciences*. Chicago: University of Chicago Press.

Martin, G. (1983) 'The Bridge and the River, or the Ironies of Communication', *Poetics Today* 4 (3): 415–35.

May, R. (1958) 'The Origins and Significance of the Existential Movement in Psychology', in R. May, E. Angel and H. Ellenberger (eds) *Existence*. New York: Basic Books.

Messer, E. (1993) 'Anthropology and Human Rights', *Annual Review of Anthropology* 22: 221–49.

Mill, J.S. (1972) *Utilitarianism, On Liberty, and Considerations on Representative Government*. London: Dent.

Moskovitz, M. (1968) *The Politics of Human Rights*. Dordrecht: Kluwer.

Nietzsche, F. (1994) *Human, All Too Human*. Harmondsworth: Penguin.

Oppenheimer: (1989) *The Birth of the Modern Mind: Self, Consciousness and the Invention of the Sonnet*. New York: Oxford University Press.

Ortega y Gasset, J. (1956) *The Dehumanization of Art and Other Writings on Art and Culture*. New York: Doubleday.

Phillips, D. (1993) *Looking Backward: A Critical Appraisal of Communitarian Thought*. Princeton, NJ: Princeton University Press.

Popper, K. (1980) *The Open Society and its Enemies*. London: Routledge.

Prott, L. (1988) 'Cultural Rights as Peoples' Rights in International Law', in J. Crawford (ed.) *The Rights of Peoples*. Oxford: Clarendon.

Psathas, G. (1973) 'Introduction', in G. Psathas (ed.) *Phenomenological Sociology*. New York: Wiley.

Quiller-Couch, A. (ed.) (1961) *The Oxford Book of English Verse 1250–1918*. Oxford: Oxford University Press.

Rabinow, P. (1977) *Reflections on Fieldwork in Morocco*. Berkeley: University of California Press.

Rapport, N.J. (1993) *Diverse World-Views in an English Village*. Edinburgh: Edinburgh University Press.

—— (1994) 'Trauma and Ego-Syntonic Response: The Holocaust and the "New-foundland Young Yids", 1985', in S. Heald and A. Duluz (eds) *Anthropology and Psychoanalysis*. London, Routledge.

—— (1997a) 'The "Contrarieties" of Israel: An Essay on the Cognitive Importance and the Creative Promise of Both/And', *Journal of the Royal Anthropological Institute* 3 (4): 653–72.

—— (1997b) *Transcendent Individual: Towards a Literary and Liberal Anthropology*. London: Routledge.

—— (2001) 'Random Mind: Towards an Appreciation of Openness in Individual, Society and Anthropology', *Australian Journal of Anthropology* 12 (2): 190–220.

—— (n.d.) 'Mutual Guesting in the Post-National City: From "The Wandering Jew" to the Ironic Cosmopolitan', paper presented at the Dubrovnik Forum conference on 'Grounding Multiculturalism', Dubrovnik, Croatia, September 2000.

Rapport, N.J. and A. Dawson (eds) (1998) *Migrants of Identity: Perceptions of Home in a World of Movement*. Oxford: Berg.

Raz, J. (1990) *The Morality of Freedom*. Oxford: Oxford University Press.

Ricoeur, P. (1996) *Paul Ricoeur: The Hermeneutics of Action*, ed. R. Kearney. London: Sage.

Rorty, R. (1986) 'On Ethnocentrism: A Reply to Clifford Geertz', *Michigan Quarterly Review* 25 (winter).

—— (1992) *Contingency, Irony, Solidarity*. Cambridge: Cambridge University Press.

—— (1997) 'Progress, Intellectual and Moral', public lecture, Centre for Philosophy and Public Affairs, University of St Andrews, 30 April.

Rushdie, S. (1988) *The Satanic Verses*. London: Penguin.

—— (1991) 'Imaginary Homelands', *Granta*: 9–21.

—— (1994) 'A Declaration of Independence', *Litteratures*, October/November: 2.

—— (1997) 'Open Letter', *International Parliament of Writers*, June.

Ruthven, M. (1990) *A Satanic Affair*. London: Chatto and Windus.

Salmon, C. (1993) 'No to Speechlessness', *Litteratures*, November: 2

—— (1995) 'Within the Asylum Cities', *Litteratures*, Autumn: 3–4.

Sartre, J.-P. (1972) *The Psychology of Imagination*. New York: Citadel.

—— (1997) *Existentialism and Humanism*. London: Methuen.

Seligman, A. (1997) *The Problem of Trust*. Princeton, NJ: Princeton University Press.

Shklar, J. (1984) *Ordinary Vices*. Cambridge MA: Harvard University Press.

Shweder, R. (1991) *Thinking through Cultures*. Cambridge, MA: Harvard University Press.

Simmel, G. (1971) 'Social Forms and Inner Needs', in *On Individuality and Social Forms*, ed. D. Levine. Chicago: University of Chicago Press.

Soyinka, W. (1998) 'Letter from the President', *Correspondence of the International Parliament of Writers* 4 (spring): 1.

Stocking, G. (1992) *The Ethnographer's Magic and Other Essays in the History of Anthropology*. Madison: University of Wisconsin Press.

Taylor, C. (1992) *Multiculturalism and 'The Politics of Recognition'*. Princeton, NJ: Princeton University Press.

Trilling, L. (1951) *E.M. Forster*. London: Hogarth.

Vargas Llosa, M. (1998) *The Notebooks of Don Rigoberto*. London: Faber.

Wagner, R. (1991) 'Poetics and the Recentering of Anthropology', in I. Brady (ed.) *Anthropological Poetics*. Savage, MD: Rowman-Littlefield.

Washburn, W. (1998) *Against the Anthropological Grain*. New Brunswick: Transaction.

Weiner, J. (1991) *The Empty Place*. Bloomington: Indiana University Press.

Weissbrodt, W. (1988) 'Human Rights: An Historical Perspective', in P. Davies (ed.) *Human Rights*. London: Routledge.

Weldon, F. (1989) *Sacred Cows*. London: Chatto & Windus.

Werbner: (1996) 'Allegories of Sacred Imperfection: Magic, Hermeneutics, and the Passion in *The Satanic Verses*', *Current Anthropology* 37 (Suppl.): S55–S86.

Whitehead, A. (1925) *Science and the Modern World*. New York: Macmillan.

Williams, B. (1993) *Morality*. Cambridge: Cambridge University Press.

Wilson, R. (1997) 'Human Rights, Culture and Context: An Introduction', in R. Wilson (ed.) *Human Rights, Culture and Context: Anthropological Perspectives*. London: Pluto.

Wolfram, S. (1988) '"Human Rights": Commentary', in T. Downing and G. Kushner (eds) *Human Rights and Anthropology*. Cambridge, MA: Cultural Survival.

Part III

DIALOGUE: MOVEMENT, IDENTITY AND COLLECTIVITY
Vered Amit and Nigel Rapport

CONTENTS

12 VERED AMIT RESPONDS TO NIGEL RAPPORT

In Part II, Nigel Rapport provides us with an impassioned and articulate vision that is thoroughly humanist. He argues for an existential politics that can reach beyond the brutal and banal contrivances of categorical identities to individual consciousness, agency and responsibility. Making an analogy with the capacity of scientific knowledge to reach beyond any one culture and transform the universal human condition, Rapport, citing Ernest Gellner, posits the possibility of a moral arrangement which could also achieve globalism. Arguing for the possibilities offered by liberal democratic and human rights discourses, Rapport offers a vision in which it is the dignity and transcendent distinctiveness of the individual that constitutes the most fundamental and universal truth, the 'anthropological concrete'. Any notion of community, of society or culture that posits such collectives as prior to or superseding the individual is fundamentally illusory. It is individual human beings who make culture (or not), social groups (or not) and social relationships (or not). Communities and cultures do not determine individuals. Of course Rapport recognizes that persons render their identities within a social context but he wants us to privilege the agency of individuals acting sceptically upon that environment. And he believes that this capacity for scepticism or irony is universal, ensuring that everywhere individuals 'have some appreciation of the malleability and the mutability of social rules and realities, and the contingency and ambiguity of cultural truths' (p. 97, this volume). An anthropology made in this vision would treat cultures or societies ironically rather than literally and would not reduce individuals to their membership in such collectivities.

I agree, but I think this is also only the beginning of what we can demand of anthropology. The next step is surely to work through the implications of this contingent sociality. If we accept the importance of not confusing classificatory identities with actual flesh-and-blood rela-tionships – the slogans versus the conversations of sociality – if we accept that the construction of social collectivities is never merely a matter of habitual practice, if we accept that social groups are the outcomes of

161

myriad individual choices, interactions, conflicts and agreements, and if we accept that communities are only one of many possible forms and forums for social engagement, then we have set ourselves the challenge of exploring and portraying an extraordinarily complicated range of processes. How do we investigate, represent and theorize these processes without reducing anthropology either to biography or to an uncritical legitimation of what Rapport calls 'group think'?

If anthropologists are likely to have many differing responses to the philosophical views expounded by Nigel Rapport, I think most would nonetheless agree that our tools of investigation, analysis and representation are woefully inadequate when pressed up against the social and cultural mazes we are trying to weave our way through. So, we take conceptual short-cuts. We refer to 'the Caymanians', or 'youths' or 'Canadians', throwing in frequent qualifiers such as 'most', 'many', 'sometimes'. If nothing else, anthropologists are surely the masters of the qualified statement. Against the assurances of the statistical percentages offered by some other social sciences, we offer the hesitations and doubts of 'perhaps', 'maybe', 'seems that', trying sometimes rather woefully to mediate our unavoidably crude insights. I suspect that the 'cultures' and 'communities' we attribute to the people amongst whom we have conducted our research are often less a matter of our own personal convictions than of conceptual convenience.

In this respect, we are in good and abundant company. As Nigel Rapport has so cogently illustrated in an earlier work (1987), the popular discursive idioms of everyday life gloss over the differences and incomprehensions of its speakers. If the apparent commonality they impart is just a veneer of agreement, it nonetheless allows people to have conversations with one another and, in the process, perhaps explore some elements of their more profound disagreements and convergences. Social conventions are not existential truths but they are, nonetheless, crucial vehicles for social interaction. So, our daily efforts at muddling through the infinite complexities of the mundane are mirrored in our awkward efforts as analysts to offer insights into this bewildering mixture.

The obvious danger in all this is that we will become prisoners of our conceptual conveniences. Concepts such as *culture, community* and *society* are not problematic if they are simply treated as useful heuristic tools to think with, not so much answers as repositories of questions we should be considering. But when we begin to take them literally, or, even worse, when we begin to treat them as imperatives in their own right, then our conceptual shortcuts can be converted, as Rapport has aptly illustrated, into the underpinnings of some very dubious political philosophies. Less dramatically but equally important for us as researchers, we miss important developments around us. We end up unable to acknowledge relationships, forms and processes that do not fit our analytical conventions even when our own personal and ethnographic experiences point us elsewhere. I have therefore argued that anthropologists have not been very successful in engaging with new paradigms of movement or in acknowledging theoretically forms of social belonging that are not encompassed by long-standing notions of community.

These issues are hardly new. The concerns with which our book seeks to engage have been, in one form or another, the subject of repeated attention by anthropologists for, at the very least, the last half century. All too aware of the limitations of their analyses, anthropologists have repeatedly questioned and sought to re-work their limits of inquiry, theoretical concepts, representations, fieldwork ambits and contexts. If occasionally these efforts seemed more faddish than fundamental, and if we have sometimes over-indulged a ghoulish propensity to 'eat' our elders, I think it could still reasonably be argued that our efforts have yielded, on the whole, more sophisticated analytical frameworks and a much wider scope of ethnographic investigation. But in the midst of our most recent efforts at ethnographic innovation, adapting our methodologies to take account of movement, transnational connections and global agents, there appear to have been some disappointing retreats to fairly simple readings of our old conceptual standbys.

In part, this occasional retreat to fairly loose invocations of categorical distinctions as if they were groups rather than attributions, to treating culture as synonymous with identity rather than process may simply reflect the investigative scale of our latest ventures. Trying to locate our subject matter in moving, rapidly changing, transnational or even global contexts poses especially difficult challenges for our analytical frameworks. There is a temptation, therefore, to empty our concepts in order to stretch them over this new scale of complexity. But this tendency may also reflect the political contexts in which many of us have operated over the last decade. Culture, we have been told, has escaped the academy and has been conscripted in the last decade's explosion of identity politics.

I freely profess that I have never been able to understand how socio-economic inequality and oppression was supposed to be relieved by public recognition of essentialized categorical differences (Taylor, 1992). But I can understand the particular susceptibility of anthropologists to these political discourses. Very often, these revolved around the kinds of poor and subordinate groups that have been the usual focus of anthropological inquiry. They invoked relativist ideals and celebrations of cultural difference that had a familiar ring from our own earlier disciplinary discourses. Indeed, some anthropologists argued that we should now take our lead from more critical culturalists (Turner, 1993).

It is tempting to invoke categories of difference as frames around diffuse and ambiguously articulated relationships, and to justify that contrivance as an account of ideas of culture or community already 'out there', beyond the academy. Analytical shortfalls become happily reconstrued as recognition of new forms of social imagination, social movements and identities. I have therefore given prominence to a critique of recent intellectual celebrations of cultural imagination. At first glance, it may appear that Nigel Rapport and I hold very different perspectives on this matter, since he emphasizes the role of imagination in constituting the reference groups with which individuals identify themselves. But Rapport's conception of the role of the imagination is of a very different order than many of the depictions that worry me. For Rapport, imagination is fundamentally the work of individual cognition. It is the individual who is the interpretive agent and the imaginer of his/her consociate groups. Individual interpretations can coincide and be shared empathically but the impetus for social contextualization and classification is always the world-view(s) of the individual agent. In contrast, the imagined communities of national and post-national communities with which, following Benedict Anderson (1983), a host of cultural theorists have been concerned, are conceived as the work of the collective. Hence Arjun Appadurai's emphasis that 'I am speaking of the imagination now as a property of the collectives, and not merely as a faculty of the gifted individual ...' (1996: 8). For Nigel Rapport, globalization bespeaks possibilities for expanding an ethos of cosmopolitanism that would allow people to escape ascriptive associations. Ironically, however, it is precisely these ascribed ethnic and religious constituencies which all too often are being identified by cultural theorists – and wrongly so in my view – with new forms of cosmopolitanism. Thus Rapport and I are approaching cosmopolitanism from different vantage-points but neither of us would be likely to identify it with the development of yet new ascriptive identities, however far flung or post-national.

I am sympathetic to Nigel Rapport's hope for the truly empowering possibilities of global processes that might legally privilege the rights of individuals to choose their own identities and associations. As I described in Chapter 2 ('Embracing Disjunction') many of the travellers I have encountered through my fieldwork were indeed perceiving movement as an opportunity for longer- and shorter-term escapes from associations, roles and contexts that they had come to find unsatisfying or even stifling. The anthropological tendency to interpret these movements as part of the effort to extend existing collectivities across borders ignores the emphasis on disjunction that frames a very different paradigm of movement, not for all contemporary travellers but I think for many. But at the same time, I worry that the intellectual excitement about the possibilities of contemporary forms of transnational mobility which animates a gamut of rather different theoretical perspectives sometimes glosses over the costs of movement. As Thomas Wilson and Hastings Donnan have pointed out (1998: 2), we do not live in a world of open borders. A variety of rights and entitlements are determined in terms of national distinctions, and people who have sought the adventure of movement can be dismayed to find that the terms of their incorporation into new localities impose new limitations in place of the ones they were trying to escape. And it may be one thing to voluntarily seek new experiences and social relationships through movement. It is quite another thing to be required to move between places, jobs and institutions as if one were a socially unencumbered economic agent. The current capitalist market rhetoric of flexibility asks us to treat our occupational roles and choices as if they were independent of our other involvements and relationships, of consociations and personal intimacies that may be the stuff of our laboriously constructed sense of belonging and connection.

In our consideration of this sense of belonging, Nigel Rapport and I differ somewhat in our respective emphases. Rapport views voluntary communities as an ideal to be aspired to but regards community in practice as more often being imposed on individuals, chaining them to collective affiliations they are not free to reject. I think this is one version of community. It is unfortunate that over the last four decades, anthropologists have tended to privilege an ethnicized paradigm in which community is treated first and foremost as an ascribed identity, one that may well be devoid of social content even while it is symbolically marked in terms of oppositions between insiders and outsiders. If this is community, then it is certainly true that it is more likely to be oppressive and limiting than respectful of individual agency and autonomy. But it is extremely unfortunate that this has become a dominant scholarly interpretation of sociality. I have argued that some of the most common avenues for forming a sense of fellowship, of belonging and social connection are realized through modest daily practices that are often not strongly marked by symbolic categorical identities. These are people and relationships known loosely as friends, neighbours, workmates, companions in a variety of leisure, parenting, schooling, political activities. Many of these associations are partial and limited in time and space to particular places and activities. Some are extended into personal relationships that transcend the original circumstances of their formation. These are precisely the kinds of voluntary forms of sociality that Rapport calls for. For many people they already exist. But it is precisely these forms of connection that the ethos of flexibility asks people to treat as dispensable and that the emphasis on an ethnicized version of community in recent scholarly discourses ignores. Ironically, a neocapitalist emphasis on economic disembedding and an intellectual emphasis on community as resistance to these capitalist pressures may have more in common than their protagonists ever intended. And Nigel Rapport's emphasis on the individual's right to imagine and form communities as s/he chooses and my emphasis on the recognition of the efforts of individuals to do just that have more in common than may at first be apparent.

13 NIGEL RAPPORT RESPONDS TO VERED AMIT

How is 'culture', that abstract explanatory notion of causation and control by which anthropologists have put so much store – that 'set of control mechanisms ... for the governing of behaviour ... by whose agency the breadth and indeterminateness of [man's] inherent capacities are reduced to the narrowness and specificity of his actual accomplishments' (Geertz, 1973: 44–5) – to be properly 'seen' or made concrete? In Part I of the book Vered Amit begins by arguing that, as with 'place', portrayals of 'community' and 'collectivity' no longer convince as metaphors. And yet, while having finally given up on the fixity of locale as a necessary medium of cultural process (Olwig and Hastrup, 1996), anthropologists have been loath similarly to admit to serious critique their prejudices concerning the 'cultural' nature of collective life. To the contrary, indeed, the concept of 'community' has been employed all the more focally (and vocally) as means to invoke and re-instate traditional ideas of social life. In ethnic, occupational, political, religious, national, transnational and diasporic *communities*, people are assumed, as ever, to partake of common narratives and discourses by which their identities are 'enculturated' – caused and controlled – and their intrinsic capacities narrowed, specified and governed.

The result, according to Amit, is a missed opportunity to come to terms anthropologically with the inherent flux and fragmentariness of social life. By way of all manner of seeming 'translocal communities', Amit explains, there has been a reconstitution in anthropological theory and practice of an entrenched institutionalism, manifesting itself in a variety of integrated and bounded fields of sociocultural relations, which she would see as largely fictitious. Here, in empirical circumstances even less likely to prove amenable to convincing conceptualizations of this kind, is a re-instatement of traditional anthropological conceptions of 'identities' as essentially collective, given and maintained by sociocultural wholes: means and manifestation of a collectivity creating and controlling its member parts – whether individual or 'dividual'.

This has had (unfortunate) political consequences too, Amit advises. The anthropological insistence on integrated cultural communities has resonated closely with a movement of 'identity politics' seeking to further the aims and interests of certain lobby-groups which conceive of their membership (and others') in essentialized terms. A continuing 'communitarian' treatment of culture has played into the hands of those who would claim social identity to be a matter of collective, categorial absolutes: one is Muslim, say, essentially and inexorably, as distinct from being Christian or Jewish; or Black as distinct from being White or Brown; or feminine as distinct from masculine; or heterosexual as distinct from homosexual; or cosmopolitan as distinct from landed; or an incomer as distinct from a local or indigene; or a liberal as distinct from a conservative or radical. Anthropological thinking has aligned itself, that is, with those who would make political capital out of a conception of categorial identities as ontologically prior to others, a natural given of the human social condition. (In a revisiting of Durkheimian nostra, anthropology must then itself categorize those who would resist such collective identification – resist a collective underpinning of their senses of self and other, their personal narratives of interpretation and expression – as misguided or deluded regarding their 'true' nature as social beings.)

To counteract these tendencies, Amit focuses in her section of the book on epistemological and social disaggregation, on deliberate and routine disjunction. Her empirical 'fields of investigation' are those actors-in-situations where social relations clearly bespeak less homogeneity and conformity, fewer instantiations of purported *collective conscience* (or *habitus*, or ideological hegemony, or consciously-cum-unconsciously instituted social structure) than an aggregation of 'diffuse and parallel life-narratives' – the personal networks of consociated but not collectivized individuals. It is the case for many people that a sense of 'home', of comfort and belonging, is attached less to clear-cut collectivities than to ambiguous and diffuse sets of relations: to personal networks, and the familiar formulae of often casual interactions (Amit, 1998).

More precisely, Vered Amit calls for a more subtle and differentiated appreciation of social experience. She shows how invocations of 'community', whether made by anthropologists, 'community leaders' or policy makers, more often signify an expression of desire than an instantiation or a consequence of community as an aspect of social structure. Communities do not exist simply because people say they do or wish them to, for between such invocations and the actualities of social organization lie the considerable logistical difficulties of opportunity, persuasion, structuration and ideology.

No social relationship rests on mere categorial identification alone, Amit elaborates; a social group is not a category. Nor is a social group a network (albeit that in their creation and maintenance, networks similarly call for the actualities of opportunity and effort, contact and reciprocity). But slipping unscrupulously in their analyses between personal 'network', cultural 'category' and social 'group', anthropologists have been guilty of underplaying the discrete social experiences which these three represent.

In particular, such slippage has distorted accounts of contemporary experience of (global) mobility and of social fragmentation; following earlier critiques of anthropological practice such as that of Fredrik Barth (1969), Amit would unpack the lazy disciplinary (both functionalist and structuralist) conflation of place, people and community, its fetish for fixity, its reliance on the 'imperative status'. What is fundamentally at issue here, moreover, Amit asserts, is the need to problematize the relationship between culture, identity and collectivity. For this reason she would also critique other notions that anthropologists have recently employed in their pursuit of identity and its presumed collective manifestations. The so-called 'imagined community' (Anderson, 1983), for instance, is a misprision of the realities of community life and the sharing it actually entails, of the distance between the imagined and the social-structural (for what is imagined cannot be intrinsically collective). So-called 'communities of sentiment' (Appadurai, 1996), likewise, misconstrue the nature of connection between people which is brought on by the spread of institutional forms such as mass media. The 'ego-syntonism' (Devereux, 1978) whereby people come together in social groups, milieux or movements occurs not on the basis of them 'imagining or feeling things together' (Appadurai, 1996), but by virtue of their finding in the same social practice means for a gratification of a diversity of desires and needs. Members of a social group, movement or milieu come to exchange cultural forms whose very ambiguity facilitates the marching in step of those who, willy-nilly, imagine and feel very differently – certainly imagine and feel separately and distinctly. In this way, too, views of culture as a so-called 'distribution' (Goodenough, 1976; Schwartz, 1978) – of ideas, practices and products as cultural artefacts distributed across social situations and actors – are based on questionable assumptions that addition, or some other integrating procedure, must translate such distribution into cultural wholes. A notion of cultural holism needs to be replaced with a 'processual view of culture', as something in the making, existing in its use, whereby social milieux are neither internally coherent (and prone to addition) nor clearly bounded. Inasmuch as community exists it is a matter of an ongoing negotiating of commonality, working through division and disagreement, risking divergence as much as sharing, and likely to mobilize fracture and severance as much as belonging.

In sum, according to Amit, anthropology continues theoretically to privilege the collective over and against the personal and individual, and in so doing to make a number of erroneous analytical conflations: group and category; institutional community, imagined community and network; identity and collective identity. These confusions can be traced back ultimately to a (Durkheim-inspired) nineteenth-century, disciplinary division of labour (between the study of society and the study of psyche), to a participant-observatory methodology which hypothesized bounded and integrated groups, and to the developing of a holistic ethos of analysis (cf. Rapport and Overing, 2000: 249–57). The 'trouble with "community"', as conventionally deployed, is that the concept has furnished an arena within which these prejudices might continue to flourish; the radical agenda of this book has been explicitly to call these into question. It is an attempt to lay the groundwork for an anthropology which goes beyond the ontological priority of collectivity.

Vered Amit's section of the book and my own are underwritten, then, by a number of common understandings. These include the recognition that there is little that is intrinsically coherent or consistent about social life, and that what coherency and consistency there is emerges out of the ongoing, conscious and deliberate efforts of perceiving and interpreting individuals. A focus on moments of interaction is key, and an appreciation of the fragility of social connections to which the work of interaction may give rise; the coherence and consistency that does prevail largely resides in individuals' sense-making, in their cognitions and recognitions. Even in this regard, however, individuals continue to exercise that scepticism (Amit) or irony (Rapport) whereby they make themselves inconsistent and contradictory vis-à-vis their own world-views. In accounting for individual perceptions and interpretations, moreover, one need have no resort to determinism, structural, social or cultural; for, *contra* the likes of Bourdieu, Gramsci and Foucault, the embodied routines of life (*habituses*) are never so unconscious, the ideologies of hierarchy never so hegemonic, and the epistemic parameters of discourse never so imprisoning that the personal, private and doubting exchanges which individuals continuously have with (and within) themselves become merely formulaic, conventional or circumscribed. One thus retains a humanistic respect for an individual agency and consciousness which remains self-directing.

But, if the sense-making of individuals is not determined, what of its contextualization and its orientation? Here there are differences of sympathy between Amit and me. For Amit, individuals' interpretations may be seen as intrinsically socially orientated, both in their origination and in their implementation. For me, it is to be averred that individual interpretations are by nature personal and private; in their origination they owe more to individual imagination than to social context, and in their implementation they may abut against the features of social milieux (social structures and the interpretations of others) but are animated by their own logic and intention, fulfilling the purpose of individual world-views (Rapport, 1993).

Amit explains that, in her view, social context is fundamental. In their everyday, invisible acts of sense-making, individuals are reacting to and reinterpreting social structures which they do not control; they subtly transform and hence 'resist' them. One must never underestimate the constraints, physical and ideological, with which individuals wrestle, moreover, for this would be to risk underestimating their very achievements: the individual efforts towards making sense and coping in amoral and chaotic, social, political and economic contexts. To be humanistic in one's portrayal, Amit adjures, is to do equal representational justice both to social structures and to individual manoeuvrings: 'the true wonder of individual agency and consciousness is the way in which ordinary people cope with, react to, rework, rethink and silently resist formidable obstacles and structures that are not necessarily of their own making' (personal communication, 23 July 1996). Sense-making, in short, involves an ongoing dialectic between external context and internal consciousness; the former – the social 'obstacles and structures' – provides the impetus for the latter, for the attempts at manoeuvrings and control that individuals effect.

I would wish to formulate this slightly differently, and to question the extent to which individual sense-making should be portrayed as, in essence, social and reactive. Individuals' world-views and interpretations are essentially independent and autonomous, I would say, arising within the personal sensorium or phenomenology of the self and then 'externalized' by individuals in acts of world-making (Rapport, 1999). In their everyday, invisible acts of sense-making, in essence, individuals act rather than react, and interpret rather than reinterpret. This is not to downplay or deny the obstacles and structures individuals face, or the 'nihilistic violence' (Rapport, 2000) to which they might be subject. Rather it is to say that the constraints with which individuals deal – natural as well as social, physical and ideological – depend for their character and their effect on the manners in which they are construed and approached. There is a dialectic between individual and environment, but this relationship is individually 'energized' (Bateson, 1972: 126), and while there may be features of the world with which individuals cannot help but engage, they do so in (if not always on) their own terms. An 'internal nervous mechanism' (Humphrey, 1983: 47) is responsible, in short, for determining individual behaviour, and, while responsive to and engaged with, external milieux, nonetheless it 'operates in many ways autonomously' (collating information, drawing up plans, effecting decisions).

There is thus a sense in which individuals can be said to be who they are independent of the seeming contexts in which they act, inasmuch as it is they who make sense of the world's forms and who animate its structures by imbuing them with meaning. Individuals may be accorded respect independent of the external obstacles they might be said to have overcome, furthermore, for as agential makers of sensible worlds they are ends in themselves.

Another way of saying this is that a personal sense of context – context as 'personalization' – is ontologically prior to others (Rapport, 1999). That is, rather than something inherent to an interactional setting, I would urge an appreciation of context as initially particular to individuals, and likely to be private rather than commonly shared. Context is something which individuals bring to their interactions with others and deploy in their actions and interpretations, and concerns the ways in which individuals imbue culturo-symbolic forms with meaning, making sense of interactions on the basis of their prior world-views. By way of world-views, individuals significantly determine the lineaments, meaning and identity of particular settings – the 'contexts' of action – the links between settings, and the behaviours to be anticipated in each.

Furthermore, individuals may inhabit any number of different such contexts, at one time and over time, and the same context may pertain in any number of externally different settings (while, by the same token, the 'same' moment of interaction can be made cognitively significant in any number of different ways). This is not to say that there will not be regularity or consistency between contextual definition and external setting, but that the decision over this relation remains an internal one, not forced upon individuals by supposed structural immanencies of a situation, or by partners in an interaction.

This does not preclude the possibility of contextualization and meaning becoming shared, nonetheless. If interactions represent situations where individual contexts are deployed and expressed, then there is the possibility of individuals learning to share at least a sense of what it might be 'like' in the context of one another's worlds (cf. Fernandez, 1992). Through negotiation, through empathy and through chance, it is possible for the contextual constructions of different individuals (as with the same individual at different times) to overlap. Context begins as an individual classification, originating in individual processes of interpretation and externalization, but inasmuch as interactions between individuals give on to levels of social organization of more inclusive (if less meaningful, less meaning-rich) kinds, one might identify different levels of context, of greater and lesser simplicity and ambiguity, in which the primary contexts of greater or lesser numbers of individuals coincide (Rapport, 1994).

If contextualization is first and foremost a private process, a domain of significance of personal provenance, then there is a sense in which this holds true for social relationships too; they also originate in individual processes of perception, interpretation and externalization, and remain there, in significant ways, in their functioning. Inasmuch as individuals are who they are independent of the external settings in which they might be seen to be acting, their relations with those settings, social and other, are in important part characterized by the intention and the imagination of their individual construers. Thus, while it may be impossible to conceive of individual identities outwith social contexts – without the worlds individuals construe and routinely inhabit being peopled by significant and generalized others – it is necessary to recognize the interpreted nature of these others.

Another way of saying this is that the paradigmatic relationship between individual and world is originally an 'imagined', perceived and interpreted, one. The individual imagines himself or herself in relationship with neighbours Sid and Doris, friends Rachel and Uri, and with all manner of categorial others – 'parents' and 'spouses', 'kinsmen', 'tax-inspectors', 'strangers' and 'adversaries' – and orients him- or herself and acts towards these in precisely the same way as he or she does towards 'Friedrich Nietzsche', say, or 'Ekakura, Comanche brave', or 'God', or 'deceased stepmother'. It may not always be quite so easy to negotiate relations and anticipate reactions with 'living' interlocutors as with 'non-living' (although one's imagination will have its own random effusions [Rapport, 2001]), but in principle the relationships operate in the same way. This is not to say that individuals live in purely imagined (solipsistic) worlds, that their imaginations do not abut against the imaginations of others, not to mention the bruteness of certain materialities, social as well as natural (totalitarianism, say, as well as mortality). But it is to aver that perception, interpretation, the initiative for interpretation, and an experiential history of interpretation, remain individual properties. As a consequence, those in my reference group, my 'society', those with whom I engage in 'community' and cultural practices (Sid and Doris, Nietzsche and Ekakura), are first and foremost the consociates of my imagination; in order to understand the characteristics of social relations, and their course, it is to individual interpretation that anthropologists must initially look.

Finally, this understanding of context and relationship gives rise to a particular approach to the question of belonging. For Amit the crucial issue is how individuals might achieve social connections which answer to their needs – whether in the form of personal networks, casual acquaintanceship or membership of community groups – and be assured the right to do so. What I would emphasize is the need for individuals to be assured of the right to escape such membership and connectivity as externally designated and imposed, and to enjoy the freedom to experience – possibly to negotiate sharing – their worlds of imaginative construction. Here is an underlying commitment to human rights shared by Amit and me: to the rights which accord to individuals as independent and properly sovereign agents vis-à-vis the social groups to which they may lend their allegiances; our sympathies differ, however, regarding how individuals might be seen paradigmatically to exercise those rights. For Amit, then, processes of globalization by and large multiply the obstacles people face, threatening them with invisibility: their right to move imperilled by retrenchments of boundary-making bodies, their right to belong imperilled by delimitings of access to stable relations and 'home' spaces (cf. Amit, 1998). On my view, globalization more bespeaks a liberating expansion in the ethos of cosmopolitanism (cf. Rapport, n.d.). Through global processes, people might be assisted legally to overcome forms of association based on ascription, on the purported givenness of categories which prescribe essential identities to some and proscribe them from others.

This is why the Salman Rushdie affair received so prominent a place in my exposition. For here was the case of an individual whose right to imagination, to self-expression, to movement, indeed to his very existence, was challenged by the leader and members of a community whose rhetoric traded in categorial ascriptions as cultural absolutes, and which, in practice, translated into involuntariness and coercion not only regarding the (supposedly apostatic) Rushdie but also others. The logic of cultural principles and community norms, however, should never be seen to 'trump' human rights: no one, anywhere, should be punished for apostasy or blasphemy (Barry, 2000). To return to a formulation with which I initiated my section of the book, nothing in the 'theatre of culture' *tout court* ought to be accorded such respect if it gets in the way of ongoing individual (and hence 'cultural') creativity. Only the domain of scientific fact should be approached as 'sacrosanct' in this way – as possessing possible characteristics of objective truth – and individuals should be free to reinvent cultural truths, to leave and form communities, irrespective of the conventional senses of (merely) cultural propriety to which they might happen to do 'violence' (Rapport, 1999). (To paraphrase Voltaire's Enlightenment credo, individuals' rights to creative self-expression ought to be defended even to the extent that one feels violated by the [cultural] forms that eventuate.)

The reaction to the Rushdie affair in the West, however, according to Larry Siedentop (2000), demonstrates the moral confusion existing there under the impact of multiculturalism; it has made, he says, the West into an ineffective defender of its own liberal values. (Brian Barry concurs: to avoid making such judgements for fear of being 'culturally imperialistic' is cant [2000].) Maybe in the wake of the fundamentalist-inspired terrorism of 11 September 2001, this will change. Certainly I would like my work in this book to be part of such a revision:

[T]he restoration of religion to the sphere of the personal – its depoliticisation – is the nettle all ... societies must grasp. ... If terrorism is to be defeated, the world ... must take on board the secularist-humanist principles on which the modern is based. ... (Rushdie, 2001: 12)

A liberal morality might globally be promulgated in which the theatre of culture is constituted as a second-order construction, epiphenomenal on the creativity of individuals (and upon the science of consciousness which details the nature of the latter). This relationship would be enshrined in laws which protected the rights (and facilitated a deepening scientific appreciation of the capacities) of individuals always to partake of that theatre, to rewrite its roles and conventions, to 'improve upon' its dramas. The only thing individuals would not be free to 'reinvent' would be the legal underpinnings of their freedom; the procedures which enshrined individual rights and freedoms would be beyond their freedom to deny.

Echoing Milan Kundera (1990), Siedentop describes a liberal political morality as not only Western but specifically European: 'invoking conscience and choice against involuntary forms of association and subordination can plausibly be described as the genius of European civilization' (2000: 202). And yet one does not need (or want) this to be exclusivist in practice. Working towards a global liberal morality ought to be a global project; there is no ethical reason why, like human rights, 'postmodern bourgeois liberalism' (Rorty, 1992) cannot be exported in the hope of it becoming 'a universal ideology' (Weissbrodt, 1988). I would agree with Siedentop, however, that there are radical choices to be made. Either one assents to basic human rights, he says, to some version of natural law, or one does not: there is no middle ground (2000: 205). Quite so. Likewise, either one conceives of the morality of a secular ethics, legal in constitution, global in reach, which seeks a foundational separation of culture from science and church from state – or one does not.

REFERENCES TO PART III

Amit, V. (1998) 'Risky Hiatuses and the Limits of Social Imagination: Expatriacy in the Cayman Islands', in N. Rapport and A. Dawson (eds) *Migrants of Identity: Perceptions of Home in a World of Movement.* Oxford: Berg.

Anderson, B. (1983) *Imagined Communities.* London: Verso.

Appadurai, A. (1996) *Modernity at Large: Cultural Dimensions of Globalization.* Minneapolis: University of Minnesota Press.

Barry, B. (2000) *Culture and Equality: An Egalitarian Critique of Multiculturalism.* Cambridge: Polity.

Barth, F. (ed.) (1969) *Ethnic Groups and Boundaries.* Boston, MA: Little, Brown.

Bateson, G. (1972) *Steps to an Ecology of Mind.* London: Paladin.

Devereux, G. (1978) *Ethnopsychoanalysis.* Berkeley: University of California Press.

Fernandez, J. (1992) 'What It Is Like to be a Banzie: On Sharing the Experience of an Equatorial Microcosm', in J. Gort, H. Vroom, R. Fernhout and A. Wessels (eds) *On Sharing Religious Experience.* Amsterdam: Rodopi.

Geertz, C. (1973) *The Interpretation of Cultures.* New York: Basic Books.

Goodenough, W. (1976) 'Multiculturalism as the Normal Human Experience', *Anthropology and Education Quarterly* 7 (4): 4–6.

Humphrey, N. (1983) *Consciousness Regained.* Oxford: Oxford University Press.

Kundera, M. (1990) *The Art of the Novel.* London: Faber.

Olwig, K.F. and K. Hastrup (eds) (1996) *Siting Culture.* London: Routledge.

Rapport, N. (1987) *Talking Violence: An Anthropological Interpretation of Conversation in the City.* St John's, NFLD: Institute of Social and Economic Research, Memorial University of Newfoundland.

—— (1993) *Diverse World-Views in an English Village.* Edinburgh: Edinburgh University Press.

—— (1994) '"Busted for Hash": Common Catchwords and Individual Identities in a Canadian City', in V. Amit-Talai and H. Lustiger-Thaler (eds) *Urban Lives: Fragmentation and Resistance.* Toronto: McClelland & Stewart.

—— (1999) 'Context as an Act of Personal Externalization: Gregory Bateson and the Harvey Family in the English Village of Wanet', in R. Dilley (ed.) *The Problem of Context.* Oxford: Berghahn.

—— (2000) '"Criminals by Instinct": On the "*Tragedy*" of Social Structure and the "*Violence*" of Individual Creativity', in G. Aijmer and J. Abbink (eds) *Meanings of Violence: A Cross-Cultural Perspective.* Oxford: Berg.

—— (2001) 'Random Mind: Towards an Appreciation of Openness in Individual, Society and Anthropology', *The Australian Journal of Anthropology* 12 (2): 190–220.

—— (n.d.) 'Mutual Guesting in the Post-National City: From "The Wandering Jew" to the Ironic Cosmopolitan', paper presented at the Dubrovnik Forum conference on 'Grounding Multiculturalism', Dubrovnik, Croatia, September 2000.

Rapport, N. and J. Overing (2000) 'Methodological Holism and Individualism', in *Social and Cultural Anthropology: The Key Concepts.* London and New York: Routledge.

Rorty, R. (1992) *Contingency, Irony, Solidarity*. Cambridge: Cambridge University Press.

Rushdie, S. (2001) 'Islam versus Islamism: A War that Presents us all with a Crisis of Faith', *Guardian Saturday Review* 3 November: 12.

Schwartz, T. (1978) 'Where is the Culture? Personality as the Distributive Locus of Culture', in G. Spindler (ed.) *The Making of Psychological Anthropology*. Berkeley: University of California Press.

Siedentop, L. (2000) *Democracy in Europe*. Harmondsworth: Penguin.

Taylor, C. (1992) *Multiculturalism and the Politics of Recognition*, edited and with an Introduction by Amy Gutman. Princeton, NJ: Princeton University Press.

Turner, T. (1993) 'Anthropology and Multiculturalism: What is Anthropology that Multiculturalists Should Be Mindful of It?' *Cultural Anthropology* 8 (4): 411–29.

Weissbrodt, W. (1988) 'Human Rights: An Historical Perspective', in P. Davies (ed.) *Human Rights*. London: Routledge.

Wilson, T.M. and H. Donnan (1998) 'Nation, State and Identity at International Borders', in T.M. Wilson and H. Donnan (eds) *Border Identities: Nation and State at International Frontiers*. Cambridge: Cambridge University Press.

INDEX